EFFECTIVE COMMUNICATION Made Simple

The Made Simple series
has been created
primarily for self-education
but can equally well
be used as
an aid to group study.
However complex the subject,
the reader is taken
step by step,
clearly and methodically,
through the course. Each volume
has been prepared by experts,
taking account of
modern educational
requirements, to
ensure the most
effective way of
acquiring knowledge.

Accounting	Human Anatomy
Acting and Stagecraft	Human Biology
Additional Mathematics	Italian
Administration in Business	Journalism
Advertising	Latin
Anthropology	Law
Applied Economics	Management
Applied Mathematics	Marketing
Applied Mechanics	Mathematics
Art Appreciation	Metalwork
Art of Speaking	Modern Biology
Art of Writing	Modern Electronics
Biology	Modern European History
Book-keeping	Modern Mathematics
British Constitution	Modern World Affairs
Business and Administrative	Money and Banking
Organisation	Music
Business Calculations	New Mathematics
Business Economics	Office Administration
Business Statistics and Accounting	Office Practice
Calculus	Organic Chemistry
Chemistry	Personnel Management
Childcare	Philosophy
Commerce	Photography
Company Law	Physical Geography
Company Practice	Physics
Computer Programming	Practical Typewriting
Computers and Microprocessors	Psychiatry
Cookery	Psychology
Cost and Management Accounting	Public Relations
Data Processing	Public Sector Economics
Economic History	Rapid Reading
Economic and Social Geography	Religious Studies
Economics	Russian
Effective Communication	Salesmanship
Electricity	Secretarial Practice
Electronic Computers	Social Services
Electronics	Sociology
English	Spanish
English Literature	Statistics
Financial Management	Teeline Shorthand
French	Twentieth-Century British
Geology	History
German	Typing
Housing, Tenancy and Planning	Woodwork
Law	

EFFECTIVE COMMUNICATION
Made Simple

E. C. Eyre, MEd, ACIS

Made Simple Books
HEINEMANN   London

Printed and bound in Great Britain
by Richard Clay (The Chaucer Press) Ltd.,
Bungay, Suffolk
for the publishers William Heinemann Ltd.,
10 Upper Grosvenor Street, London W1X 9PA

First edition, May 1979
Revised reprint, October 1983

British Library Cataloguing in Publication Data

Eyre, E. C.
    Effective communication made simple.—
    (Made simple books, ISSN 0265-0541)
    1. Communication in management
    I. Title   II. Series
    651.7   HF5718

ISBN 0-434-98589-9

My aim in writing this work was to provide within the covers of one volume a study of the very many aspects of communication.

In doing this I was guided by the syllabuses of the various professional bodies that have a paper on this subject in their examinations, and particularly by the model teaching guidelines set by the Business Education Council. This book is, therefore, offered as a text both to those who wish to prepare for one of the many examinations in this subject and to those who have a personal interest in any aspect of it. I believe that it will be particularly valuable for those who intend to take the BEC courses. In addition, those who seek membership of those bodies that do not have a specific examination in communication, such as the Society of Company and Commercial Accountants, but expect their members to have the ability to communicate effectively, will find this volume valuable. I must also add that where the masculine form has been used in the text this has been done only for reasons of clarity and ease of reading: in all cases the feminine may be substituted.

So far as possible, I have endeavoured to make every chapter self-sufficient so that each can be perused without reference to others. This has meant a small amount of repetition but I hope this will be excused in view of the convenience afforded to those who wish only to dip into the parts that interest them.

My acknowledgements and thanks are due to the following professional bodies who kindly gave permission for the reproduction of questions from their past examination papers, identified by the initials following their names:

The Institute of Administrative Management   (InstAM)
The Institute of Chartered Secretaries and Administrators   (ICSA)
The Chartered Institute of Transport   (CIT)
The Association of International Accountants   (AIA)

I must also extend my grateful thanks to The Transport Tutorial Association who allowed me to draw on material I used in the communication course I wrote for them to cover the examination of the Chartered Institute of Transport.

Equally, I appreciate the permission given me by *The Times* to reproduce the two extracts in Chapter 18 and by *The Guardian* for allowing me to use the piece by Kevin Page in question 3 in the same chapter.

Finally, I must thank colleagues at Ealing College of Higher Education for helpful advice, and in particular Mrs Irene Hirst and Alan Harvey, as well as my son Colin, who kindly read and constructively criticised various parts of my manuscript.

E. C. EYRE

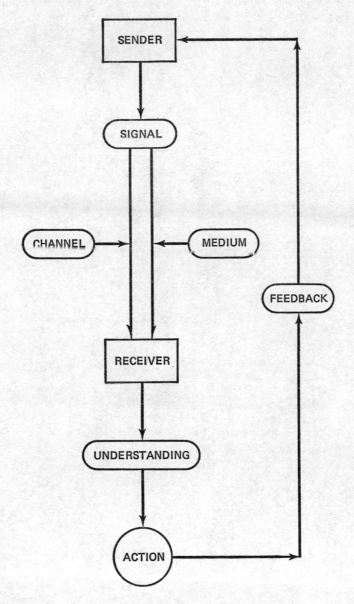

The cycle of effective communication.

Contents

To my wife, Irene,
without whose encouragement this book
would not have been completed.

1

INTRODUCTION TO EFFECTIVE COMMUNICATION

Communication is, and always has been, an important feature of life. Never, however, has effective communication been more important than it is in the modern world. As the world has shrunk so rapidly through the introduction of ever faster methods of transport, and as understanding has become more difficult because of the sheer rate of technological growth, so the need for understandable communication has increased.

A Definition

What do we mean, then, when we talk about effective communication? Somehow, dictionary definitions, such as 'giving a share of' or 'to reveal', do not reach the heart of the matter. Communication is not just the giving of information; it is the giving of understandable information and receiving and understanding the message.

Thus we can see that to communicate effectively there must be two parties: the transmitter and the receiver. In addition, there must be a common understanding. Thus we can define communication as the 'transferring of a thought or a message to another party so that it can be understood and acted upon'. The means of transfer are immaterial to this definition.

Just how important effective communication is can be seen in the amount of industrial unrest that is evident today. Managements in some organisations seem incapable of communicating successfully with the work force; some of the reasons for this will be explored later in this book.

The failure to communicate effectively, however, also afflicts people and groups quite outside the industrial world. This is very noticeable in what is commonly termed 'the generation gap'. The speed of social change in our society has brought with it the diminution of understanding between the various age groups, and the constant barrage of words and ideas by the broadcasting media has tended to widen the gap in understanding.

The Meeting of Minds

The meeting of minds across the gap often just does not take place. Yet a meeting of minds is essential to understanding. A simple analogy is that of radio broadcasting. A transmitter sending signals on 247 metres will not be picked up by a radio receiver tuned to 1 500 metres. Similarly, an older person brought up in a more leisurely world, where technology as we know it today scarcely existed, finds it difficult, if not impossible, to understand and come to terms with the manners and language of modern youth.

So the two participants in any communication, for it to be effective, must have both understanding and a similar language. To take an extreme example, how well would an Englishman having only English communicate with a Pole having only Polish? Some semblance of understanding may flow by the use of gestures or thumb-nail sketches, but how effective would real communication be? Unless the one could be sure, by the other's reactions, that understanding had taken place doubt would remain. Therefore, we can say that an understandable response is necessary for communication to be effective. In many cases performance will indicate that comprehension has been positive, but such indication is possible only in cases of person-to-person contact, either by face-to-face contact, or by telephone.

Where the performance will be delayed, as in the case of a written communication, then the purveyor of the communication will not know whether or not he has been understood. Lack of reaction will cause the communication flow to stop, and will cause uncertainty in the mind of the sender. Suppose you are invited to a limited meeting, and the invitation is by letter. Unless you send a reply by some means the organiser of the meeting will not know whether he should hold your seat for you, or whether he can invite someone else in your place.

Meanings of Words

In effect, communication, except in very simple situations, involves actions, reactions and interactions, depending on the flow of information, questions, answers and queries passing to and fro between the participants: and all the while there must be understanding. One of the most frequent causes of misunderstanding is that involved in the meanings of words.

Let us take a simple case as an example. We all know what the word 'capital' means—or do we? To an accountant it means the money value of the proprietor's stake in a business, and even here the word may be qualified by distinguishing between working capital, capital employed and so on. To the geographer the same word indicates the town where the seat of government of a country can be found. An architect will use the word 'capital' to signify the top of a column, and to some it is the word employed to state the opinion of the worth of a night out or of an idea.

Unfortunately, matters are made more complicated by the use of everyday words by specialists in many areas to describe specific conditions found within their work: particularly is this noticeable in the business world. Thus, computer people talk about 'dumping'. To the world at large this indicates that whatever is dumped is disposed of and is of no further practical use. The computer world, however, uses this word to mean to save for re-use. Thus, the contents of a computer's main store may be 'dumped' to magnetic tape—not to be destroyed but to be filed to await retrieval. Similarly, a practitioner in operational research uses what he calls 'models' but these are not three-dimensional replicas of full-size articles, but are mathematical equations that he uses in his problems.

Unless such people are communicating with those of their own profession, therefore, it is highly likely that they will be misunderstood: their minds will not be meeting the minds of those they are endeavouring to communicate with, and worse, some receivers will not like to display their ignorance and so will not seek elucidation. Thus misunderstanding occurs.

So it will be obvious that unless there is a meeting of minds and the use of a common language understood by both parties, no effective communication can possibly take place. The terms of our definition will not be met: understanding will not take place and thus action will not take place either, or at best will not be what the communicator intended.

Factors affecting Effective Communication

Often our efforts to communicate are quite successful, but at other times we fail dismally. Many factors are at work that have a bearing on our success or failure, some of which we can control and some of which are outside our command. The chief of these factors we will now examine:

1. The recipient of our communication must be able to **understand our language**, particularly if we are using technical jargon. Language embraces mother tongues, dialects, as well as technical usage, and it also includes the written as well as the spoken word, gestures and illustrations.

2. We must communicate at the **appropriate time**, both by the clock and by opportunity. A telephone call will not normally be welcome at 5 o'clock in the morning. Neither will a communication be effectively

considered if the recipient is rushing off to catch a train for which he is already late.

3. The **medium** used to carry the communication must be appropriate to the circumstances. One would not, for example, use a postcard for the conveyance of confidential information.

4. **Attitude** is important, and there must be mutual trust between the sender and the receiver. Mistrust, prejudice or acrimony between the parties can result in communication being ineffective and either un-intentionally or deliberately misunderstood.

5. **Willingness** by the parties to communicate is essential. 'There are none so deaf as those who will not hear.'

Careful attention to these points can make a great deal of difference to the effectiveness of our communications.

Communicating without Words

The means we use to communicate are many. The most primitive, perhaps, are gesture and physical attitude: a nod of the head, thumbs up, a smile can convey agreement—even enthusiastic agreement. The physical gestures and actions on the football pitch after the scoring of a goal need no words. A wink, a motion of the head, or the crooking of a finger can convey an invitation. Displeasure or anger can be signified by a shaken fist or a scowl.

Vocal methods of communication can also be simple or very advanced, or at any level in between. The first cry of a baby when it is born communicates to those around that it is alive and it uses this form of communication to indicate its wants and needs until it has some command of language. An irascible person may indicate favour or ill-favour by a grunt; and we all know the purport of a 'wolf whistle'.

Verbal Communication

Speech can be used very simply or may be employed with a high degree of skill. Verbal communication between friends or business colleagues will normally be fairly unsophisticated, using everyday vocabulary and construction. However, at the other end of the scale the orator or the debater will use language very skilfully. He will very carefully choose the words to use and the construction of phrases and sentences, in order to obtain the greatest effect. Great orators, such as Winston Churchill, employed all these devices to make telling speeches just as a great conductor uses the instrumentalists in his orchestra to create effective music. Thus, not only is speech used to great effect, but also facial expression, stance and gesture. All are employed to increase the impression and to sway the listener to the speaker's point of view, or to create the attitude and emotion in the audience that the orator requires.

Thus, face-to-face verbal communication is enhanced by the use of physical activities such as shaking a fist, thumping the table, smiling and many other physical gestures.

Verbal communication has been greatly extended by **modern technology**: we can now telephone to most parts of the world and carry on two-way communication with people tens, hundreds and even thousands of miles away: two-way communication has even been used between the earth and temporary inhabitants of the moon by means of highly advanced radio and television links. The great drawback with verbal communication through the telephone is, of course, that only the voice can be used, and any form of gesture to reinforce our communication is impossible at the moment. Videophones, as they are called—that is, telephones that can carry visual as well as verbal communications—have been developed but are not so far available to the public at large. Such a development, of course, would greatly increase the effectiveness of the telephone.

Radio and television have also greatly extended our range of verbal communication. Both are, by their very nature, principally information giving methods. Attempts to promote audience participation, and thus provide a two-way process, are being made increasingly by both media by the employment of 'phone-in' programmes, and as the difficulties of this type of programme are gradually learnt and corrected so these programmes should become effective channels of true communication. Within business and education closed-circuit television, often with a two-way facility, and two-way radio links, are increasingly being employed.

Interference and Distractions

All forms of communication can suffer from interference of one kind or another. Background noise may impinge on face-to-face conversation, and may also interfere when the telephone or the radio is being used. One or other of the parties may not be willing to participate freely and such an attitude will certainly influence clear understanding and prevent the true meeting of minds.

In the case of written communication, which embraces letters, invoices, reports, orders and the like, a delayed feedback is inevitable, and if the delay is prolonged then attitudes unfavourable to effective participation may arise. Communication over telex and teleprinter networks does not, necessarily, suffer from this drawback and is increasingly being used in business for this reason and for the reason that the telephone is not always conducive to accuracy.

Where the written word is used, slovenly English construction and misuse of words can reduce the authority of the communication, and the physical appearance of the message may give a good or bad impression, so affecting the attitude of the receiver.

Lastly, full attention to any form of communication may not be given by one or other of the parties because of some extraneous distraction. Very often a high level of noise may do this, or another nearby conversation. Commonly, domestic problems may cause one of the communicators to be less attentive than he might be, so causing the communication being carried on not to have his full concentration.

The matters mentioned in this short introductory chapter will be dealt with more fully later on: meanwhile you might wish to test your comprehension by answering the questions set out below.

Questions

1. What do you understand when it is said that effective communication requires the meeting of minds?

2. Explain what factors are important for there to be meaningful communication between two parties.

3. In almost all business organisations there exist barriers to good communications. Name and briefly describe any three known to you.

(AIA, Foundation Part A)

4. What is meant by the two-way nature of communication? Imagine you have to explain the regulations governing hours and pay to a newcomer about to work for you. Give details of how you would apply the principles of two-way communication to this situation.   (CIT, Intermediate)

5. Although speaking and writing are undoubtedly the main means of communication, they are not the only ones. Explain.

(AIA, Foundation Part A)

2

THE IMPORTANCE OF COMMUNICATION

Effective Communication is Essential

It is sometimes not realised how completely all activities, enterprise, and social and business intercourse are **dependent on effective communication**. Because we all breathe we all think that we breathe efficiently. Similarly, because we all communicate after a fashion we all think that we communicate effectively. Any teacher of physical education or singing will draw our attention to our faulty breathing: and just as we can be taught to breathe more efficiently so we can learn to communicate more effectively.

It is only of recent years that it has been realised how important understandable communication is to good industrial relations. In fact, many authoritics consider that it is a lack of effective communication between management and the shop floor that is the root cause of most of our industrial unrest. Unless an individual or a group of individuals can make known to others instructions, orders, wants, opinions, feelings, and so on, then these ideas, instructions, feelings, will remain locked in the mind of the intending communicator and no action can be taken upon them.

Whatever form the communication takes, it must be clearly understandable to the receiver: and the first requisite to this must be a **clear objective** in the mind of the originator of the communication. Indecision about the purpose of the communication will result in an indecisive message or instruction, and in the mind of the receiver this can mean only partial understanding of the transmitter's intentions. **Clear understanding** is, therefore, very much dependent on **clear thought** conveyed by precise expression. Clear understanding is impossible if the communicator's own thoughts are blurred or woolly.

As an aid to clear thinking and to a recognition of a precise objective, writing down a communication, even if it has to be given verbally ultimately, is very helpful to the communicator in sorting out his thoughts.

Nevertheless, even though the initiator of a communication has taken great pains to give a clear and precise message, this will not fulfil its function effectively unless the recipient of the communication is **willing to understand**. There is a maxim 'telling is not teaching'. Equally,

7

telling is not communicating. Broadcasting is not communicating if the receivers are switched off; and talking or writing are not communicating if the receiver's mind is not open to understand and react to the communication. To show that he is a willing participant the receiver must make some **response** or give some **feedback** to the originator.

In Chapter 1 we took a brief look at some of the main factors that interfere with common understanding between the communicators and inhibit cooperation. A great deal can, however, be done by the originator of a communication to solicit the ability and willingness of the other party to proper understanding. So let us enlarge on these factors.

Language

It has already been stressed that it is essential to use language that is understandable to those whom we address, and you are well aware that most words in English have more than one meaning—sometimes several meanings. In addition, many groups of people who habitually use common words in a special way in their technical or professional environments will almost automatically put this interpretation on them. Equally, it must be remembered that different social groups have also developed their own vocabularies using common words to denote something quite different. Thus, in certain circles favoured by the young we have the word 'bread' used to mean money.

Further, despite the fact that English is very rich in the ways that thought can be expressed, some groups have a very limited number of words at their command. It is also equally true that most of us employ a much smaller vocabulary in speaking and writing that we actually understand.

Seeking to impress, or trying to look superior, some communicators use long or unusual words, usually derived from Latin or Greek, instead of the more commonly used ones. An exaggerated example of this practice is:

'A slight inclination of the cranium is as adequate as a spasmodic movement of the optic to an equine quadruped devoid of its visionary capacity.' This, of course, merely means: 'A nod is as good as a wink to a blind horse.'

Another practice to avoid is the use of Latin tags or phrases in ordinary communications. Again, this practice is often used to seek to impress, but can also lead to misunderstanding in any but the circles in which they are habitually used. Phrases such as *quid pro quo* and *inter alia* mean little to many people and should be avoided.

So far as language is concerned, therefore, effective communication can take place only when words and phrases comprehensible fully by all are employed. Failure to observe this rule will have the result that the required meeting of minds will not take place: there will be a breakdown in communication, perhaps not realised by everyone at the time. Only when the expected actions flowing from the communication fail to take place, or to fulfil their objective, will this failure be realised.

American usage of the English language also has its pitfalls, but these are discussed later in this book.

Timing

The effectiveness of our communication may be reduced if our timing is not right. In the theatre it is often said that good timing is of the essence in comedy: it is no less important in normal communication.

First, we must consider the **time of day**. Our attempts at communication must be made at the appropriate hour of the day. Very few of us welcome a string of requests, or enquiries on matters of high importance, the minute we arrive at our office—sometimes even before we have taken off our coat. If we occupy a managerial position our staff will feel the same. The phrase 'let me get in' springs to mind. Similarly, a staff meeting called for last thing on a Friday afternoon is not conducive to effective consideration by its members unless the matters to be discussed are of very great personal concern. As the meeting wears on some of the group will become restless and will be taking surreptitious glances at their watches. Certainly their attention will be divided between the matters being discussed and the probability that they will miss their trains. In such a situation full concentration will not be given to the objectives of the meeting. Further, in an effort to draw the meeting to an early close, questions that might have been asked and discussed may not be put by members of the group, and the outcome of the meeting may well be less than was planned or expected. Worse, there would be a real risk of misapprehension and misunderstanding because of this divided attention.

Second, the **time of convenience** is important. In other words, we should not endeavour to communicate with another person if he is preoccupied with other matters: we will receive less than proper attention. For instance, if the company secretary is concentrating on arranging the agenda for a particularly important board meeting he is not likely to pay much attention to a request for authority to buy a new typewriter. The request could quite well wait for a more propitious moment.

The Medium

How often are conditions created that lead to a lack of expected response or to a less than perfect understanding by a disregard of the medium of communication and the method used? In all cases the medium of the communication and the method must be appropriate to the case in hand. Generally speaking, great care is required in this direction. Most people are very sensitive about how certain subjects are approached, and to ignore their sensitivity will often result in faulty communication: especially is this so with matters on a personal level.

Matters of a routine nature, such as the opening and closing times of the canteen, may well be appropriately conveyed by a notice on a notice-board. At other times a discreet personal word is called for—for instance, where a member of staff has started habitually to arrive late in the morning. A bald statement on a notice-board about lateness would be most inappropriate.

A more complicated situation, such as an alteration in working conditions, requires even more care in the choice of medium and method. Personal consultations with representatives of those affected is imperative to prevent misunderstanding and to gain the cooperation of those concerned. A memorandum inserted in everyone's pay packet would be less than appropriate.

Attitudes

The attitudes of both the sender and the receiver of a communication are among the most decisive features in attaining really effective understanding. It is a fact that, although we humans pride ourselves on being rational beings who can act from sound, unemotional reasons, on the whole very few people are absolutely rational in their thinking or in their actions. Emotion colours their reactions to most stimuli, and emotion is the basis for attitude. This is quite clearly seen in the actions of investors on the Stock Exchange: the emotions of optimism and pessimism play a large part in whether a holder of shares keeps them or tries to sell them. A rumour, not fact, can trigger off a movement of share prices up or down. It is here that the rational, cool-minded, investor can score.

Accordingly, **the attitude of the communicator can colour the emotion, and thus the attitude, of the receiver.** If the sender is arrogant then his communication may be gracelessly received: if submissive, then received condescendingly. In either case the result of this attempt at communication may be less effective than desired. Any of the emotions, and the attitudes consequently struck, by the sender will set up reactions in the mind of the receiver which will directly influence the way the communication is received and understood. Hence a faulty attitude in the mind of the transmitter may result in only a partial response on the part of the receiver, or no response at all.

Similarly, perhaps even more certainly, the **attitude of the recipient is**

important if a communication is to be a success. For example, if workers are mistrustful of their employers, for whatever reason, then however hard the management tries to communicate effectively with them, resentment and doubt will colour the workers' reactions adversely and cause such communication to be less than effective. In cases where mistrust is great the communication may even have the reverse effect from that intended. On the other hand, enthusiasm or eagerness to please may lead an employee to go far beyond the intention of the communicator.

In order to increase his effectiveness, therefore, anyone who seeks to communicate with understanding must be able to control his attitude to suit the case in point, and be able to judge with fair accuracy the attitude of mind of his correspondent, and to make allowances for it.

The ultimate in attitude of the target of a communication is, of course, an **unwillingness to communicate**—a refusal to participate at all. This attitude is usually the result of complete mistrust or animosity, however it arose. Sometimes it may be due to previous unfortunate experiences with the communicator; often it arises out of prejudice born of social or workaday contact with others who have a like mind.

Once it has developed, there is very little that can be done to remedy the situation. It must be prevented from forming in the first place, and the communicator's honesty and integrity must be made obvious from the beginning. Much of the prejudice which is obvious in many works today has been brought about partly by management having been insincere in the past and partly by attitudes engendered by some of the work force. Unfortunately, there seems no way to overcome this attitude.

Logic in Communication

We have just observed that it is a human failing to think irrationally and because of this to act in the same way, such behaviour being brought about by such emotions as suspicion, mistrust, animosity, or, on the other hand, by overzealousness and enthusiasm. It is this irrationality that gives rise to illogical thinking. Thus a communicator, recognising this fact, should use all the logic at his command to make his points clear, and to have them understood and accepted.

Here the word logic is used in its everyday meaning, which we may define as 'the art of reasoning and drawing inferences from that reasoning without the intervention of emotion'. It involves the impassive marshalling of thoughts and facts to present a clear, unambiguous case that can result in a sound conclusion.

We have already seen the necessity for clear thought, and this is very necessary to aid logical argument. Only by the use of logic can a communicator present a demonstrably sensible and acceptable case. This, in turn, means that he must have examined very carefully his objectives and have arranged them in a continuously progressive manner.

This also entails using words effectively and unemotionally. Many words and phrases have taken on connotations that evoke an emotional response, and this sort of language should be avoided if we are to present a logical case. The words 'profit', 'planner', and 'landlord' have taken on emotive overtones which the words themselves do not have. To use these and similar words and phrases in certain circumstances and to certain members of the public will bring about an emotional response that may be undesirable to our message. Similarly, the use of euphemisms can also evoke responses which may be undesirable. On the other hand, euphemisms carefully used may create the atmosphere that will aid our effect: this point belongs more to the area of psychology, however, than to the area of logic. So far as logic is concerned, unemotive language in partnership with clear thought and objectives is what is needed whenever and however we seek to communicate effectively.

Psychology in Communication

If the use of logic and a careful employment of words were all there is to effective communication, then the communicator's task would not be very difficult in the majority of cases. However, **most people are not completely rational**; they are motivated by illogical thoughts and by prejudices which can inhibit clear understanding. Hence, some attention must be paid to the psychological aspects of communication.

Most modern psychologists have stopped defining their science as the study of the mind, and have replaced it with the phrase 'the study of human behaviour'. Thus it is concerned with human emotion and its effect on behaviour, and so far as we are concerned this means on communication and understanding.

From childhood onwards we all become amateur psychologists by observation; we observe the reactions of others to our behaviour and to what we say and how we say it. Thus we know from experience the kind of reaction that may be expected from various stimuli given a knowledge of the circumstances surrounding our communication and of the character and attitude of the other party.

For example, if we are angry and speak in a wrathful manner to an equal, we can expect a similar response: equally, if we address a subordinate in a like manner it may well be that we shall engender resentment and grudging obedience. On the other hand, complimentary remarks can bring about positive cooperation in most situations. Thus, a skilled communicator can simulate an emotional state or an attitude in order to evoke a desired response in the recipient. In the past many political leaders in every country have used this device to further their causes, and the more tyrannical have been past-masters of this technique. So today, a number of our politicians and trade union leaders employ the same device.

We also know from experience that we can cultivate an attitude both in ourselves and in others by the way we act, how we use words, the form of our communication and its timing. If, therefore, we aim to communicate effectively we must learn the skill to project a suitable image and to recognise in the other party his attitudes to us and our ideas. Recognition of his attitudes in this way will enable us to frame our communications in such a way as to convince him that we should have a fair hearing.

Many circumstances affect the mood and attitude of the receiver of a communication at the time he receives it, besides the way in which it is delivered. In the working environment it may be boredom, anxiety about the job, mistrust of the management, domestic worries. In other environments it may also be domestic problems, health worries, money difficulties. Such negative circumstances will undoubtedly produce a non-receptive attitude. On the other hand, an optimistic outlook may engender an atmosphere of zeal, responsiveness and a positive will to cooperate with the communicator.

A communicator need not be a professional psychologist; but he must be sensitive to his opposite numbers and be prepared to take into account attitudes and the kind of responses he is likely to promote. In doing this he can adjust his language and timing so as to produce the most positive result. Besides being logical, the communicator must take into account the various human emotional factors likely to interfere with understanding and reception in the mind of the correspondent.

Subjectivity

So far in this chapter we have been stressing that the communicator should be objective: only by being objective will he be able to apply the suggestions set out for achieving the response he desires. However, there are times when the communicator will achieve his goal by being, at least to some extent, subjective. Subjectivity enters into communication when a communicator is enthusiastic—either actually or in simulation—about his subject. Perhaps the best example of this is in selling. A sales representative's attitude must be of complete confidence in the superiority of the product he is offering. He must necessarily be subjective in his opinion of his wares so that he may generate within himself the enthusiasm with which to infect his potential customer.

Hence, the positive advantages of his product are eagerly presented, but the disadvantages are conveniently forgotten. Many sales training courses have as a major element the engendering of this subjective attitude and enthusiasm in the sales force as a means of customer persuasion.

Objectivity

As to when a communicator should be objective and when he should be subjective very often concerns the recipient of the communication—that is, is the other party likely to be swayed by factual, clinical argument, or is he more likely to be persuaded by an appeal to his emotions? The first would certainly require a high degree of objectivity whilst the latter would probably be better dealt with using a large measure of subjectivity. Very often objectivity demands an impersonal style of presentation so that it is obvious that no personal prejudice enters into the communication. On the other hand, a subjective appeal often needs a more personal touch. However, neither need be entirely impersonal or personal. Provided the arguments are clearly and logically put, and any opinions expressed are based on soundly argued facts, then objectivity does not demand a totally impersonal style. In fact, if the communication were directed to a shop-floor work force it is highly likely that a fairly personal style would have the better response.

Questions

1. Describe and explain three of the factors that affect understanding in communication.

2. In what ways do logic and psychology influence the effectiveness of communication?

3. Discuss objectivity and subjectivity as qualities of communication. In what circumstances would you prefer one to the other? Does objectivity necessarily imply an impersonal style of writing?   (CIT, Intermediate)

4. 'The attitudes of both sender and receiver of a communication are among the most decisive features in attaining really effective understanding'. Comment on this statement.   (AIA, Foundation Part A)

5. In what ways is business dependent on effective communication? To what principles would you adhere in order to ensure effective communication?
(CIT, Intermediate)

3

PERCEPTION AND UNDERSTANDING

Perception and Experience

Consideration of perception as it relates to communication flows naturally out of the consideration of psychology, because involvement in any communication is tempered by our own psychological attitudes. It has been said that to perceive it is necessary to have understanding, and to understand it is necessary to have had previous experience or knowledge. A clear perception of the purport of a communication is vitally necessary for that communication to be effective to the receiver, and so must be within the limits of his understanding.

In fact, **perception** can be looked upon as a **coding system** that allows the mind to retrieve data stored in memory, and to process it with newly acquired data to produce an understandable image. Freud once said that we forget nothing that we have experienced; but we sometimes lack the necessary ability to recall that fragment of memory, until some association with it triggers off the recall. In this way, data coming out of a communication can effect the retrieval of an associated experience that the new data can be processed with, to provide an understandable message. If there is no associated, pre-stored experience then the brain will endeavour to provide some sort of image in the light of the incomplete information.

Perception can take place through all five senses, sometimes singly and sometimes with two or more together. This effect is clearly seen in the act of a ventriloquist. The brain expects the mouth to move when someone is speaking: during such an act, the dummy's mouth moves whilst the performer's lips remain still, so the brain infers that the words are coming from the dummy. Similarly, when we see television or a motion picture we 'see' the words coming from the mouths of the actors, when, in fact, the sound may be issuing from the side of the screen or from below it.

In the same way, the retinas of our eyes are stimulated only by the three primary colours, but our brain processes the proportions of these three primaries signalled to it by the eyes and converts these signals into a myriad of different colours. In other words, the brain will make an image of whatever is presented to it, referring to past memories for guidance. Thus, a blind person who has previously been able to see will be able to imagine colours when told about them: on the other hand, because of the lack of previous experience, a person blind from birth cannot.

Nevertheless, though experience or knowledge is lacking, the mind will endeavour to decode all messages it receives, and so **incomplete** stored **knowledge** may lead to **misconceptions** when applied to new data. In order to overcome this, often in our communications we make use of analogies to make our meaning clear; in other words, we try to promote understanding in the recipient by comparing the new information with that which we are practically certain he already knows. Hence, we may say something is 'hard as iron' or 'clear as crystal' and thus by association aid his comprehension.

Faulty Perception

Should there be no relevant stored knowledge then the brain will do its best to interpret the new sensation, and will then probably produce a wrong perception—the message will not be understood in its proper form. A simple example may be drawn from English and American language usage. Without previous knowledge an Englishman may well be forgiven for believing that an American is talking about suspenders when he uses that word in a sentence: however, he is talking about what the Englishman terms braces. The relevant code in the Englishman's mind does not interpret the American's meaning correctly because the English code for devices for keeping trousers up is braces.

Similarly, the brain will endeavour to transcribe separate bits of information as a whole message if they are in close proximity. This is a device well beloved by the advertiser and the propagandist, and well understood by them. A visual example is, perhaps, the easiest. In Fig. 1 are shown three separate angled lines, with no apparent connection. Arrange them as shown in Fig. 2, and though they are not joined—in fact, they remain as they were with only their positions and proximity changed—the mind will interpret a combined image of the letter 'E'.

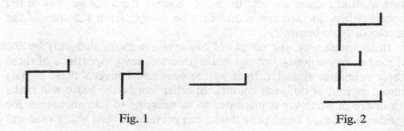

Fig. 1   Fig. 2

Almost everyone is familiar with the optical illusion of the line drawing of the vase that might be two profiles. If drawn as in Fig. 3, there is little doubt that the drawing depicts a vase, though at the back of the mind is the doubt as to whether it might be two facing profiles. Drawn in free association with its surroundings, this sketch is only slightly ambiguous.

However, if the drawing is enclosed in a frame (Fig. 4) ambiguity becomes very pronounced—and this is the way it is usually shown.

Fig. 3   Fig. 4

All the examples of optical illusions, and very common they are, result from faulty perception often because of the lack of points of reference. It must be remembered, however, that such faulty perception can result from any communication if information is given out of context or without suitable supporting data. Isolated words and phrases, or pictures and words in certain juxtaposition, either innocently or deliberately, can cause inferences to be drawn that are not directly stated. A photograph, innocuous in itself, has frequently brought a libel action from the person photographed simply because of an unfortunate (and often unintended) association with an item of news in a newspaper or journal.

Ambiguity

Ambiguity is also a hazard because of peculiarities in the English language. One of these hazards is the fact that a word may be pronounced differently in speech to give it different meanings, but may be spelt the same in all cases. A simple example might be:

'You read the *Financial Times*.'

Out of context, and written, it could mean that the *Financial Times* is being read or has been read. Only in context would the correct meaning be made clear.

Mental Retrieval

Clear perception, and therefore understanding, depends to a very large extent on our ability to retrieve the data stored in the mind and to bring it to consciousness. Mostly the retrieval is unconscious and instantaneous, and is stimulated by the communication that has been received and recognised. It must be remembered, however, that in many cases this ideal of situations is not achieved, particularly if the relevant experience was some time previously, or other experiences have been acquired since. Such a situation obtains, for instance, when a student is studying several subjects at a time: knowledge obtained from the first lecture in the term becomes overlaid with subject matter from subsequent lectures on a variety of topics. To communicate effectively in these circumstances, each lecturer will, ideally, revise very briefly at the beginning of each lecture what had been covered in the previous one.

Other devices for recall are, of course, the mnemonic, the jingle (well-used by advertisers), word associations and even the knot in the handkerchief.

We can understand only through perceiving messages in our brains. It is, therefore, very necessary to remember the traps for the unwary in the way the brain works to make perception possible. Remembering these, and applying our knowledge, we can make our communication more effective.

Questions

1. Explain the connection between experience and perception, and discuss how this affects understanding in communication.

2. Explain how the mind is misled by optical illusions.

3. In the light of this chapter, discuss ambiguity in perception.

4. What aids can be employed where there may be difficulty in recalling past experiences that are relevant to a present communication?

5. How is a person's perception influenced by previous experience? How would your knowledge of the nature of perception influence the way you introduced a new procedure to a long-serving foreman in your employment?

(CIT, Intermediate)

4

ATTITUDE AND MOTIVATION

Prejudiced Experience

In the previous chapter we looked at the role played by perception in communication, and we examined the need for previous experience or knowledge. It follows that lack of either in the receiver of a communication will inhibit his understanding and will thus form a barrier to proper perception. The matter is further complicated by the fact that some of our experiences may be such that we have formed a prejudice in the matter being communicated. In such a case our understanding of the transmitter's message may be unduly influenced by this prejudice, favourably or unfavourably. Two examples will illustrate this.

If a motorist is in the market for a new car, he may visit several showrooms and the various salesmen will endeavour to communicate to him the excellence of the products they offer. Should the motorist have had a previous unfortunate experience with one make of car, perhaps early rusting, this will probably have prejudiced his opinion of that make. Hence, the customer's perception of the dealer's persuasive arguments will be adversely coloured by this prejudiced opinion, whatever steps the manufacturers have since taken to remedy this fault.

Similarly, if a worker has been commended by his employer for some good work, and perhaps been given some merit award, adverse criticism of the firm by a fellow worker, however justified, will be unfavourably received.

People's own experiences and prejudices are formed through their social environment, by their educational background, and by their political and other affiliations. Sometimes prejudice runs so deep a person is incapable of understanding another's point of view: often he is not willing to try.

Personal Involvement

The amount of personal involvement in a communication has a great deal of influence on its effectiveness. In other words, to use an American phrase, communicators must identify with the subject. The nearer to their hearts the subject matter the more closely will they be personally involved. In these circumstances awareness will be at its highest. There is no doubt of the involvement of both parties in a wage claim: here communication is at its most effective as a means of conveying thoughts and ideas, schemes and counter-schemes. However, on both sides built-in prejudices and attitudes will hamper perfect understanding, and may result in deadlock.

In fact, it is in such situations that the results of self-centred involvement become most evident. In most discussions, negotiations and other forms of communication, flexibility and tolerance on both sides can result in an amicable agreement: both can display some appreciation of the other party's position. When involvement is completely self-centred, however, such tolerance is unlikely and the longer the communication goes on the more hardened become the attitudes of each party. Any solution, possibly imposed from outside, is reacted to with acrimony.

Such inflexibility is often the result of **previous conditioning**, as mentioned at the beginning of this chapter. People see what they expect to see and hear what they expect to hear, or, perhaps, what they want to see and hear. The well-worn tale about the pessimist and the optimist illustrates this very clearly. A glass containing water to the half-way mark will be described as half empty by the first and half full by the second.

This story also shows the extent to which emotions as well as rational thought colour our perception: the optimist wanted and expected to be pleased, whereas the pessimist had the disposition to be fault-finding and grudging. It also underlines how a communication is perceived and understood in terms of the receiver's experiences and prejudices. The **information** regarding the water in the glass was the same for both parties: the **interpretations** were quite different.

Motivation

Closely allied to experience, emotion and prejudice as factors affecting effective communication is motivation. This can be unconscious as well as conscious, and can affect both the receiver and the transmitter of a communication.

The principal objective of the initiator of a communication is to have his message received, properly understood and appropriately acted upon, and this can be said to be his prime motive, with the content having equal priority. Nevertheless, by various means the communicator may have **secondary motives**, both actively realised and also unrecognised. For example, letters and memoranda can be couched in terms that not only convey the message intended, but also convey an impression of importance, cleverness or other image of the sender.

Often this takes the form of long words or fashionable jargon. Sales letters are frequently typed on high-quality paper, using an electric typewriter with a distinguished typeface, not only to inform the receiver of the sender's goods, but also to convey the impression of the high quality of the goods or services offered. This secondary motivation on the part of the sales letter writer will be, for the most part, only unconsciously absorbed by the customer.

Memoranda are frequently sent from department to department, not only with the motive to convey information but also to act as a defence mechanism in case the message is ignored, or acted upon incorrectly. Some companies have a rule that copies of all outgoing correspondence must be sent to the appropriate departmental manager. In many cases where this rule applies, the writers of the letters, perhaps quite unconsciously, level the tone, language and arrangement of content as much to the departmental manager as to the outside correspondent, perhaps to impress, or to justify a decision.

Sometimes the ostensible prime motive is really only the secondary one. Thus, the acknowledgement of an order to a customer may appear to confirm its receipt by the supplier. However, it also puts responsibility on the customer for the correct interpretation of the order by the supplier and, in addition, often imposes conditions of sale which override the conditions set out on the customer's order form. Unless the customer notifies his dissatisfaction with the contents of the acknowledgement then this is the effective document.

The receiver of a communication will respond according to the factors that motivate him generally in the context of the communication and his past experience of the sender. Where goodwill has been built up between the parties the motivation of the receiver which helps to determine his response will be different from where this is not the case. For example, a supplier who has a high regard for a customer will be motivated to accede to a request for temporarily extended credit, whereas unhappy financial experience with this buyer would motivate the supplier to refuse such a request.

Where the communication is on a management/staff basis, the interpretation of communications will be very much affected by the motivation, conscious or unconscious, of the receiver. Where good staff relations exist, workers will consider themselves part of the company and will be motivated to receive and interpret company communications at their face value. On the other hand, if relations have not been good, suspicion or discontent may motivate workers to put incorrect interpretations on such communications, and they will look for—and find—all sorts of hidden meanings that were very far from management's mind (this is often referred to as 'reading between the lines'). This state of affairs is particularly apparent where workers are subject to the influence of groups whose intentions are always to embarrass the employer.

In the final analysis, individual motivation is determined by personal attitude, and as has been seen previously, this is engendered by many factors, such as experience, social influence and other causes.

Group Attitude and Motivation

Where people are members of a group, the group attitude and motivation may be, and very often are, different from those of the individuals who make up the group. The attitude of a group is often not established when the group is formed: its members are drawn together by common interest and each individual member will have his own particular attitude to the subject of this common interest. However, every group throws up its leaders, people who are of strong personality and generally of persuasive tongue. This may not happen immediately, but is virtually inevitable within a short period of time. Thus we find that in due course the group strikes an attitude which is more likely to be the attitude the leaders desire than the sum of the personal attitudes of the individual members. Those who have a strong objection to the attitude that has evolved will leave the group whilst those with less dedication will continue to be members but will cease to try to make their voices heard and will cease to take an active part in the business of the group.

Thus, the group attitude will be established and this will have a significant effect on communications to and from the group in the same way as personal attitudes have, except that the strength of the group will magnify the effect.

Similarly, group motivation is generated by the **sinking of individual motivations**, brought about by skilled oratory and the effective persuasion of the group leaders. Such motivation can be less rational and more easily managed by the group leaders than individual motivation free of such influence, and by the same token, **outside influence** will have much **less effect** on the group. In effect, group motivation can make the group much more adamant in its objectives and much less flexible than would be the case with individual members of the group. Psychologists have long pointed out that there is such a phenomenon as the mob mind which can act impetuously, irrationally and at the whim of the mob leaders, and that it behaves in a quite different way from the individual minds that make it up.

Improving Motivation

When trying to communicate in these circumstances, and in circumstances where prejudice may affect understanding, some guidelines such as those set out below may help to improve the situation:

1. When initiating a communication try to visualise the recipient's educational and social background: how will he react to your communication?

2. Ensure that the language—words and phrases—you use are within his range of understanding, and avoid emotive statements or words with unfortunate connotations.

3. If you are aware of the existence of any prejudice, specific attitude or adverse motivation in the mind of your correspondent, try to construct your communication so that it has the least possible chance of being distorted by these conditions.

4. If possible, endeavour to ensure an early response or feedback from your correspondent so that you know whether your communication has had the effect you sought

Whilst all four guidelines are important to consider, that in number three is probably the most significant when communicating with a group. It is very probable that the group leaders have reinforced the already-held prejudices of the individual members of the group, and in addition have induced others which the individuals had not previously held. Further, it must be remembered that it takes a brave man to deviate from the main stream of the group of which he is a member.

Inflexibility of Group Motivation

Where the communication is originated by a group, a similar rigidity of outlook and inflexibility of purpose may be observed. Numbers give the feeling of strength, and the motivation of the group will lead to a style and approach in the communication that may cause the recipient to react adversely. This may be readily observed in the case of trade unions, particularly those with a great deal of industrial strength. Alterations in conditions of employment for members, whether for higher wages, better holiday entitlements or an improved working environment, or for any other purpose, are never 'asked for' or 'requested' but are always 'demanded', reinforced by an overt or tacit threat of the withdrawal of their labour. The reaction of some managements is to threaten closure of factories, or to dismiss the workers concerned. Both sides, because of the working of the mob mind, strike attitudes which can be nothing but damaging, both for the workers and for the employers.

On the other hand, when the group motivation is for a socially desirable objective, the mere fact of the group strength may be very persuasive indeed in influencing the receiver of the communication. Some demonstrations illustrate this.

To sum up, group motivation leads to similar reactions as personal motivation, but is almost certainly intensified because of group strength. It will be less rational and more rigid; more easily guided by the group leaders. The opposite party to the communication will have far less influence on it.

Questions

1. How does the motivation of the recipient of a communication influence his understanding of that communication?

2. Is there any difference in the way attitudes and motivation work in communication with individuals and with groups? If so, what are the effects?

3. What are the major conflicts which prevent the reaching of an agreement in a bargaining or negotiating situation? How may one attempt to resolve each of them? (InstAM, Dip. Part I)

4. There are, unfortunately, various barriers to effective communication. Two of these are background and attitude. Describe what is meant by these terms in the context of good communication (AIA, Foundation Part A)

5

FACTS, OPINIONS AND THEIR PRESENTATION

So far we have examined the factors of perception, attitude and motivation and have discussed the effect these have on the effectiveness of communication. In this chapter we shall have a look at facts and opinions and also at the way prejudice can influence the presentation of both.

Fact or Opinion?

Facts, one supposes, cannot be denied; they are there and that is that. In a concrete sense, this must be so. If there are fifteen people at a bus stop this cannot be disputed; they are there and can be counted: this is a concrete fact. If the time-table states that the bus will arrive at 11 am and it does so, likewise this is a fact: if it arrives at 11.05 am it is late. This, also, is a fact. However, if the bus is due officially at approximately 11 am, and actually arrives at 11.05 am, is the bus late? This would be a matter of opinion, and would hinge on the interpretation put upon the word 'approximately'. The opinion would be qualified by the amount of tolerance one would allow within the term 'approximately', or even how precisely one construed punctuality. In regard to the case of punctuality, of course, opinion would differ according to whether the interpretation is by the one who is arriving or the one who is waiting!

The use of **facts** in communication **gives authority to statements and arguments**, and makes them more worthy of consideration by open-minded people. Hence, facts, particularly when supported by evidence of reliable sources, are very important in making our communications effective and more acceptable. They must be presented as facts which are within the context of the communication, and must be clearly and unambiguously stated. Further, they must reinforce the logic of the communication so that they aid the formation of sensible conclusions, or create the response that is desired.

Opinion is also very important in the furtherance of the effectiveness of our communication, but we must be careful to distinguish opinion from fact, because fact is irrefutable but opinion is open to challenge. Hence, it is most important to be sure which is which. This entails developing a questioning attitude to information that purports to be fact, and if it is significant in the communication in which it is going to be used to have it checked. Further, the omission of a known fact can be detrimental to the acceptance of a communication, thus the correct use of all relevant facts is very important.

Honest Opinion and Prejudiced Opinion

There are two sorts of opinion—honest opinion and prejudiced opinion—and it is just as important to be able to distinguish between these as it is to be able to distinguish between fact and opinion. Honest opinion can be defined as that which is formed from all the information available and is thought through logically and rationally. Prejudiced opinion, on the other hand, is that which is influenced by emotional factors, often quite unconnected with the factors concerned. For example, most nations have a national prejudice that can colour their opinions, and it takes a very rationally minded person to ignore this. During war-time this irrationality is at its highest. For instance, 'their bombers hit civilian targets but ours hit only military objectives'. Again, sex prejudice very readily colours opinions. Do you consider women drivers are less good than men? This very much depends on whether you are a woman or a man. In the political arena prejudiced presentation of facts can so distort them as to make them appear to be the opposite to what they are.

Opinions Used as Facts

Statements put out by reputed experts are frequently treated as facts, especially if put into print, and are often accepted without question. Herein lies a danger. A great many of the assertions taken as facts, by whatever source they are made, are frequently not facts at all but merely opinions, albeit honest opinions, of experts in their fields. Such statements must be very carefully examined. If it is found that they are opinions and not hard facts, the supporting evidence for these opinions must be carefully checked before such statements are used in support of any communication in which they are to be cited. Failure to do this can so often result in embarrassing misunderstandings causing bad relations between communicators, or a lack of total trust. The acceptance of rumour is even more dangerous, as this is often prejudiced opinion based on other biased opinion, and it is usually impossible to trace either the source of the so-called facts or the origin of the rumour.

Opinions taken as facts appear in countless communications inside and outside business. Most business reports contain opinions that are acted upon with confidence just as though they were facts. For example, computer A may be installed in preference to computer B on the recommendation of a computer consultant. His report will certainly set out the facts that he has gathered during his survey of the company's requirements and systems, but his final selection of a machine will depend on his opinion of what is most suitable.

Statistics, again, **are often referred** to and used **as though they were facts.** Figures of past performance, population numbers to date or numbers of units produced in the past can, of course, be quite factual, though it must be remembered that many such statistics are based on samples, and not on a complete survey. It is when statistics are used to forecast trends that the real danger occurs. Any such figures are projections which incorporate estimates or adjustments (both of which are opinions) made by the statistician. A prominent case in point is that of political opinion polls. Much faith is put in these reports by many people, almost as if the projections were actually facts. That they are the honest opinions of the compilers is not doubted, but they are so often proved totally wrong by subsequent events that they do significantly emphasise the necessity to guard against the use of opinion as though it were fact.

How Facts Can be Twisted

There is a saying 'there are lies, damned lies and statistics'. This is very harsh but, as has been shown, contains an element of truth. The misuse of statistics is probably the most frequent practice in twisting facts to suit a case, but there are many other ways which must be guarded against. For instance, over-emphasis of one particular fact out of many, perhaps more important than this one, can distort a communication and make it unreliable or much less than the truth. This practice, of course, is rife in political propaganda, particularly in some countries.

Nearer home, however, such twisting of facts because of prejudice, or to serve less than honest ends, is also common, as is the same practice to allay public fears or to promote a point of view.

For example, a politically biased report of an affray between two rival factions may quote the number of casualties caused by the 'other side'. To put the opponents in a bad light each small scratch may be included in such figures, though the amount of injury might be totally insignificant. The fact has been twisted; it may be literally true, but practically incorrect.

The art of the half-truth is, of course, very well known, and here again fact is used to support a point, but only part of the fact is reported. It may be a fact, for example, that a tenant's colour television set has been taken away by the bailiff and sold to satisfy rent or rates arrears, and this may be the subject of a short article in a local newspaper, possibly to put the landlord in a bad light. What may not have been reported is that the tenant had had several requests made to him over a considerable period of time which he had completely ignored, and that, in fact, he had been treated by the landlord with patience and consideration.

Facts stated out of context can also be used to give a false picture. The fact that a company has made a considerable profit in money terms is often quoted as headline news, particularly when efforts are being made to help reduce inflation by keeping wages down and controlling prices. Such profit figures are facts drawn from the published accounts of the company concerned and on their own are facts out of context. The complete context includes the amount of capital utilised to earn the profits declared, and only the complete context can provide a fair picture. Thus, a profit of £20 million may be announced without qualification. This certainly does seem a tremendous figure, and those with an axe to grind may very well use this figure (which is a fact based on the accountancy rules used in making up the accounts) on its own to illustrate excessive profit-taking and, by implication, overpricing. However, put in context with a capital employed of £500 million, it will quickly be seen that the declared earnings represent a return of only 4 per cent on the capital employed, which is a very low figure. The use of facts in isolation is a frequent device employed to discredit an opposition and should be viewed with care. This device is also used to attract attention, and one should be wary of accepting statements in newspaper headlines without reading the complete text that follows.

Appropriate Presentation of Facts

The use of relevant and appropriate facts in a communication helps to give it authority and to make it more readily acceptable to the unprejudiced. The same thing is true about the honest, considered opinions of experts, so long as they are given as such. The use of opinion, however expert, can sometimes be treated as fact and in this respect great care must be taken in using statements of opinion. Over-emphasising opinion, and dressing it up as fact can often have the reverse effect from that intended, and may prejudice our communication in the eyes of the receiver. Not only will this result in a diminished chance of its being accepted, but may also prejudice our future communications.

In a similar way, it is important to assess the relevant importance of the facts that we intend to use in our communication, and to rate their significance to the subject matter we are putting forward. Some facts will carry more weight than others, and some will be too trivial to use at all. Further, the relative significance of our facts will depend upon the target of our communication and the response we wish to evoke. Any error in our emphasis may quite well defeat the object of our communication and thus lead to failure. In most cases it is the importance to the receiver of our communication that should determine how we present our facts, and our own prejudices and enthusiasms should be held in check in favour of his needs.

For example, in communicating information about a new duplicator he is trying to sell to a prospective buyer, a salesman may stress the ease of changing from one colour to another, or the very long runs that may be expected from a single master. However, the customer may be interested in only very short runs of one colour at any time, and his anxiety may be about image quality and clean working. The salesman's enthusiasm about colour change and long runs has caused him to put the emphasis on the wrong facts so far as the customer is concerned. Such an error could, also, have an even less desirable effect: it could lead the customer to assume that the facilities he requires of the machine are less than adequately provided, though this may not necessarily be so.

It must also be remembered that opinion and prejudice can distort facts both in the mind of the giver and in the mind of the receiver, sometimes to such an extent that the veracity of the fact is lost and it becomes merely an expression of opinion. Nevertheless, it must not be concluded that there is no value in communicating opinions, particularly if we can make use of the opinions of our correspondents to reinforce our communication.

Such harnessing of opinions is often used by the various protest groups and conservationists. In many cases where motorways and other developments have been planned such schemes have had to be severely modified, or even abandoned, because the protestors have harnessed their opinions to the natural reluctance of the population to change, and have defeated the planners even where clear economic facts have indicated the benefits to be derived from the scheme under discussion.

It is evident, therefore, that communication is most effective when it is based on facts where they are available, and where they are presented in a logical and clear manner, provided they are relevant to the objectives of the communication. Where precise facts are not available, then recourse may be quite properly made to honest and informed opinion, which must be presented as such. It must be remembered, however, that in seeking to communicate effectively due regard must be paid to the attitudes, motivation and prejudices, where they are known, of our correspondents, so that they have as little effect as possible on understanding.

Questions

1. Facts are irrefutable and are given in evidence before industrial tribunals, arbitration boards and other such bodies conducting inquiries. Why is it, then, that decisions reached at such inquiries are often questioned or rejected by one of the parties to the dispute and their protagonists?

2. In what ways can facts be presented so that they support the contentions of opposing views?

3. What are the dangers inherent in using opinion instead of fact to support a case? Would you associate these dangers with the use of statistics?

4. Discuss the differences between facts, opinions and conclusions. If you were presenting a case to a committee, state the principles you would need to observe in preparation and presentation of the case, concerning facts, opinions and conclusions. (CIT, Intermediate)

6

METHODS OF COMMUNICATION

The Three Main Methods of Communication

In the area of business and social communication with which we are concerned in this text there are three principal methods of communication that are employed. These are: (a) oral communication, including direct speech and the telephone; (b) written communication, including letters, invoices, forms; and (c) visual communication in which are included posters, charts, slides and similar means.

All three methods will be dealt with fully in subsequent chapters: for the moment it is necessary to look at the general aspects which should guide our selection of any particular one, because generally very little thought is given to this most important matter. Even where some consideration is given to the method itself there are numerous examples to show that the effects of the environment within which it is to be used have not been given sufficient attention.

Examples of Inappropriate Methods

The most obvious one, which we have all experienced, is the use of public address systems at railway stations to announce train destinations and departures. The first problem here is the acoustics of the railway station itself, which often render the announcements unintelligible; secondly, the general station noises often make the messages difficult to hear properly and, of course, it is not unknown for the station announcer to give his or her announcement at the exact moment that a train is moving in or out of the station, so making the message impossible to hear.

Another well-known example is the provision of telephones on factory floors where the noise of the machinery makes hearing very difficult: in the office the positioning of a telephone near a typist or an accounting machine has a very similar effect though often not so well appreciated. As a final example we can cite the provision of poor carbon copies of documents to be read in less than adequate lighting conditions (despite legislation on office lighting).

Again, some means of communication are more likely to give rise to errors than others. The most notorious in this respect is the telephone,

31

even where the line is clear and free from noise. Particular care has to be taken over numbers, such as five and nine, eleven and seven, and alphabetically over words containing the letters *f* and *s*, *m* and *n*, and so on. Where the line is a bad one, intelligent conversation is often impossible.

Practical Considerations

The practical ways in which we communicate take many forms, some oral—as in face-to-face conversations or over the telephone—some written, such as letters and telex messages, and some by illustration through the use of diagrams, graphs and transparencies. Which method to use should be the result of assessing the precise requirements of the communication and the attributes of the methods available. We can set out the first under eight factor headings.

1. Speed

Is it necessary that the communication reaches the receiver in the shortest possible time, or is some delay acceptable, and if so, how much? What effect will the delay of one hour, one day or one week have on the effectiveness of the communication? Is there a deadline that has to be met?

A radio link with an ambulance to pick up the victim of an accident is vital, and may save a life. A radio link with the television repair van is helpful in customer relations and the maintenance of goodwill, but is otherwise a questionable expense. The meeting of a delivery date for a tender to an architect will often justify the use of a personal messenger to deposit the tender at the architect's office at the right time on the right date: such considerations of speed very rarely concern the delivery of sales circulars.

2. Accuracy

This is an important ingredient in all forms of communication, but in many cases is of vital concern; names and addresses, dates and times, money amounts, and many other items need to be precisely communicated.

The problems encountered over the telephone have already been mentioned. Often essential parts of a telephone conversation have to be confirmed in writing so that there is no question of error. Unquestionably communication in clear, legible writing, typing or print is the most accurate, provided always that the language used is unambiguous and understandable. Face-to-face verbal communication can also be accurate, particularly because doubt can be clarified on the spot and both parties can check their understanding. Unfortunately, subsequent recall can be unreliable sometimes and written confirmation of the main substance of the conversation is often desirable.

The least accurate method of communication is probably that of conveying information verbally through a third party, and the position is aggravated if the message has to be passed through a number of mouths to the final recipient: often the message received is very different from the message initiated by the original sender.

3. Impression

All means of communication create some impression on the mind of the recipient, and we must be aware of the impression we wish to create when choosing the method. A company wishing to create the impression of quality and reliability may choose to use expensive note-paper with a sober, embossed heading, and the typing may be by an electric typewriter fitted with print-style type with proportional spacing. The impression of urgency may be generated if a communication is by telegram, even though a telephone call would, in fact, be quicker. The office junior would not seek an increase in salary by sliding a memorandum under the managing director's door!

4. Circumstances

Often circumstances themselves dictate the method of communication to be used. The purpose of the communication is one such factor: for example, an auditor's report must be in written form. The distance between the parties concerned and the means of communication at one point or the other will have a very great bearing on the problem. Whether both parties are at fixed locations, or whether one or both are moving about will also be important. For example, communication between the office of a taxi firm and its cab drivers may call for radio links.

5. Safety

How important is security to a particular communication? If safety is of paramount importance, then a special messenger may be called for, or we may use registered post if this is suitable. Where certainty of delivery is more important than the intrinsic value of the document, then recorded delivery may be adequate. Again, where the contents of a communication can be easily reconstructed safety is not quite so important, other factors apart, than if reconstruction would be difficult or impossible.

6. Confidence

This factor is often bound up with safety, and safety is frequently demanded solely on the grounds of the confidential nature of the communication. Much communication is private or secret and for the eye or the ear of the recipient only. In such cases a method must be chosen which will provide conditions of secrecy.

In normal business correspondence it is usually sufficient to mark the letter and the envelope 'Confidential', and it is wise to address the communication to a person by name. In very stringent cases, the letter may be delivered by hand by a trustworthy person instead of being entrusted to the ordinary mails. Certain methods, however, can never be taken as confidential: these include the telephone, telegrams, normally addressed letters and, of course, postcards.

7. Copy

Many communications require the retention of a copy for reference purposes or for record, others do not. The tendency to take a copy of everything whether this is necessary or not is wasteful and should be strongly resisted. Nevertheless, a high proportion of business communications do require copies to be kept, usually as a reminder of content or to re-establish fact. On rarer occasions a copy may be required as proof, or as legal evidence. Where an exact copy is needed then some form of written communication, such as typewriting, is required where a facsimile can be made at the same time as the original. Notes made of a verbal exchange may be unacceptable if the records made by the parties do not agree. Similarly, a tape recording of a verbal discussion will be suspect if doubt can be thrown on the identity of one or other of the voices on the record: further, tapes can be edited. Thus proof of authenticity is required if such recordings are to be admitted as legal evidence. Therefore, the type of use to which the copy is to be put will determine how it should be made.

8. Expense

Though our principal aim in communication is to be effective, and the foregoing seven factors properly applied will assist in this, we must not forget that all forms of communication cost money. It is important, therefore, that the question of expense must be assessed in choosing our methods, though this must be subordinate to the achievement of our principal goal. The cost of any form of communication includes more than the prime cost of the materials used, and these should be realised. Thus, the cost of communicating by letter entails not only the cost of the dictator's time and that of the typist, the paper, envelope and stamp, but also the value of the use of the typewriter, the rent of the space of the desk it occupies, the cost of lighting the typing space and of heating it, and also the various costs involved in filing copy letters and other administrative expenses. Consideration must also be given to the delay involved in receiving a response to our communication, which may be important or insignificant depending upon circumstances.

Criteria for the Choice of Method

On the practical level a great deal of thought is required about how our communications are transmitted quite apart from their content. The criteria for any particular instance will be found among the foregoing eight factors and the method should be selected that best meets these criteria. Thus, if the communication demands accuracy and absolute safety a written message delivered by hand might be preferred. If speed and accuracy over a long distance are the criteria then perhaps telex will be chosen. It cannot be overstressed, however, that effective communication demands clear thinking on the part of the originator. Clear thought, clearly expressed, is essential whatever method of transmission is used.

The Distinction between Written and Spoken Communication

To a large extent the form of communication employed determines the style and precision possible, and these differ very much as between the written and the spoken word. When we write a letter to someone he is not with us when he receives it and cannot, therefore, question us directly on any point. Consequently, when writing we should endeavour to be both precise and concise. A written message should never be longer than absolutely necessary; generally speaking people will concentrate on short written communications but are apt to skim over long ones. However, when we write we normally have the time to seek out the exact words we wish to use to convey our meaning, and to trim down the length of our sentences.

This cannot be said when we are speaking to people. Here our words come spontaneously and we do not have the time to seek out the precise ones to express ourselves, nor to examine the length of our phrases and sentences. Instead, we make ourselves clear by intonation and expression, and by answering questions that are generated during the discussion. Normally we can gauge by the other party's responses whether we are being properly understood. This does not imply in any way that we should be slovenly in our speech. What it means is that we may use a freer range of words and expressions when talking and yet still make our meaning clear.

Questions

1. In business we communicate by speech, letters, the telephone, telex. Give instances when each method would be appropriate and suggest two possible cases where you would use the telephone rather than write a letter, giving your reasons.

2. What are the main differences between oral and written communication? What are the most important practical implications of these differences for the professional administrator who wishes to communicate effectively within an organisation. (ICSA, Part I)

3. The telephone is a notoriously inaccurate method of communication. Bearing in mind the eight factors mentioned in this chapter why, then, is it so popular?

4. Before making any communication in business the need, mode, etc., should all be considered. Draw up a suitable checklist which could be issued to those whose duty it is to communicate frequently within business organisations. (AIA, Foundation Part A)

7

COMMUNICATION IN INDUSTRY AND COMMERCE

Different Organisations, Different Needs

At this point we shall make a start at examining the factors involved in creating an effective system of communication in an organisation. It is not possible, of course, to devise a communication system that will have universal application because no two business enterprises are the same. The needs of a large manufacturing organisation employing 20 000 workers spread over five factories are very different from those of the local departmental store employing 100 people all under one roof. Similarly, outside industry and commerce, the communication requirements of a charitable fund-raising organisation will differ from those of the local amateur dramatic society.

Nevertheless, there is a great deal of common ground, and what we shall do is to examine the general requirements, on which can be superimposed the particular requirements of individual organisations.

First it must be recognised that there are **two areas** in which communication has to take place: (*a*) with the **outside world**—that is, with customers, suppliers, government departments and so on; and (*b*) **internally,** with employees, managers and others. We shall start by examining the more difficult of the two: internal communication. Why

is this the more difficult of the two? Essentially because over the past decade or two there has been a change in attitude among workers to their employers. In the present industrial climate there has been a move away from the old idea that management could tell staff and workers what to do and expect unquestioning obedience. Nowadays it is more necessary to invite the cooperation of the work force.

The reasons for this are many, and include the growth in the strength of the trade unions, the increasing complexity of the large industrial enterprises in which personal relations between managers and workers are so very difficult to establish, and the changed attitude to discipline of modern society. It is probably true to say that present-day Jack feels as good as his master. He is not willing just to take orders but often demands to know how management instructions and decisions will affect his future, his earnings and his job prospects. The outcome of this change of worker attitude has been for management to appreciate the necessity to communicate with its work force in a real sense. In some parts of industry this has gone even further, and workers demand not only information and explanations about management decisions but seek participation in actual decision-making.

Management Objectives

In a purely economic sense, management in commerce and industry has one main objective: that is, to operate at a realistic level of profit for the benefit of the owners. Arising directly out of the attainment of this objective will be financial strength and provision for expansion as well as the replacement of assets as the need arises. Other necessary or desirable objectives are also the concern of management though they must be secondary to the principal objective of profitability. These include providing a first-class service to customers, paying fair wages to work-people commensurate with their skills and the demands of their jobs, the provision of good working conditions and other benefits such as pensions and sick pay, and establishing high worker morale and loyalty. Similarly, organisations not prompted by the profit motive, such as local authorities, charities and the like, have comparable objectives. Effective communication between workers and management has been found highly desirable to promote an acceptable work performance by staff, which is essential for the achievement of the objectives given.

Management Communication and the Worker

Thus the individual manager has a heavy duty nowadays to communicate clearly with his workers in such a manner that they can understand the facts he is trying to convey, and to be able to interpret them within the context of their everyday working environment. He will also have a duty to instruct his subordinates, both to carry out their normal, known duties, and also to instruct them in new skills. How he does the latter is of extreme importance, as future work efficiency will depend on the excellence of his communication. It has been said that telling is not teaching: this also applies to managers giving instructions. Instruction, therefore, particularly in respect of new kinds of work, requires a sensitive appreciation of how to pass on practical knowledge. Patience and tact are required, and the process might be summarised by the expression 'say, do, know'. In other words, a trainee should be told in detail what he is to do, he should be shown and then asked to try to emulate the task, and on the successful conclusion of these exercises he should know. During this operation, the manager or instructor would be well-advised not to give orders, but to invite cooperation, as he must when giving instructions to carry out day-to-day jobs already within the worker's duties.

Creation of Worker Attitudes

In the matter of all communication between manager and worker, but particularly in this matter of giving instructions, a cooperative attitude must be cultivated in the worker. Perhaps nowadays this is the manager's highest skill, without which he will find it hard to operate. No precise guidelines can be set down to develop a harmonious management/worker relationship: so much depends upon the past history of the company in regard to industrial relations, the backgrounds of the various sections of the work force, and the fundamental attitude of the managers at the top. However, in general terms it may be said that satisfactory relations cannot be established unless there is respect on both sides, and this best stands a chance of being created if management is seen to be open in its dealings, provides reasonable information about its policies and programmes, and is ready to listen to representatives of its work force. In this sort of atmosphere communication is more likely to be effective than if there is an air of hostility between the two sides and, possibly, a dictatorial attitude by management.

Perhaps one of the most common omissions by managers is that of not **expressing appreciation** for substantial worker effort. The idea that a good job is to be expected because that is what the worker is paid for is still very prevalent. A 'pat on the back', however, is likely to be repaid by a better attitude to the job, thus making the worker more ready to accept management communication.

Similarly, problems can be encountered when **reprimands** have to be given. More than ever good relations are essential if a worker's inefficiency has to be brought to his attention, or there is any other complaint about his conduct. At these times the manager is likely to be overcritical and the worker emotional, so communication between the two should be as calm and rational as possible. In this respect the manager is in control of the situation, or should be, and can initiate the tone of the interview. If industrial relations and morale are bad then this particular area of communication can be explosive. One thing is very important: all reprimands, however slight, should be given in private. It is also helpful to the situation if the manager remembers the amount of satisfactory work that has been done.

In the area of communication within an organisation, particularly between those managing and those managed, **human relations** are very important. How and when communication should take place depend a great deal on internal morale and attitude. Human relations, however, are a study in themselves and a book on communication can only draw attention to their place in the art of managing, which depends on effective communication.

Questions

1. 'I hear and forget; I see and remember; I do and understand.' Using this principle explain how you would (a) instruct a beginner in the use of a duplicator, (b) give an elementary lesson on fire precaution in the office of a group of learners.   (ICSA, Part I)

2. It can be said that communication is the means whereby industrial management is activated. Write a short essay on this theme, illustrating your answer with examples.   (CIT, Intermediate)

3. Explain why an individual's efficiency as a manager is directly proportionate to his or her skill as an effective communicator.
(InstAM, Dip. Part I)

4. What are the most important principles of communication which a professional administrator should bear in mind when giving instructions to a subordinate? What problems may occur if these principles are overlooked?
(ICSA, Part I)

5. Describe the problems contributing to the communication gap between management and employees.   (InstAM, Dip. Part I)

8

LINES OF INTERNAL COMMUNICATION

In any discussion of communication within an organisation, it is usual to emphasise the vertical flow from top to bottom. Indeed, when examining management objectives in Chapter 7 we did just that.

Vertical Communication

In the past, of course, it was true that communication was almost wholly downward, and this was the only line of communication consciously recognised by management. The board of directors or their top representatives made the decisions and these were passed down through the various strata of management and supervision to whatever level had to implement them. This was the traditional authoritarian approach to communication within an enterprise. It was considered that those who were managed had no right of question or information: orders were to be carried out, not to be questioned or explained.

However, as has been pointed out in a previous chapter, modern industrial relations demand more than a mere giving and blind acceptance of instructions and orders. Workers at all levels are now aware of the effects that management decisions may have on their livelihoods and working conditions, and they feel that they have the right to be heard before any significant decisions are implemented. Inevitably, most of the concern is with pay and working conditions, but there have been many cases where management intentions have been thwarted, at least for a time, by a determined work force, even to the extent of delaying the closure of a business. The modern concept of **two-way vertical communication** has, therefore, developed. Not only must an organisation now provide a channel for the downward flow of communication, it must also make formal provision for a flow upwards from the shop floor to the higher levels of management. In fact, if this upward flow is not provided for management may well be making decisions in a vacuum. It will then have great difficulty in persuading those lower down the management line to accept and act upon these decisions.

The two-way flow obtains not only through the organisation as a whole, but also within each individual department, with the result that there exists a main vertical channel, from chief representative to chief representative, and also as many **secondary channels** as there are depart-

41

ments. These secondary channels carry communication between different levels within departments, from ledger clerk to chief accountant, for example.

It remains true, of course, that the main vertical flow is downwards, because this is the way that instructions and directives have to be given. However, suggestions, comments and objections are now part of the accepted upwards flow.

The Communication Burden on Middle Management

As a result of this change in the concept of vertical communication an increased burden has fallen on middle management, including supervisors. Not only do the people in these positions have to receive,

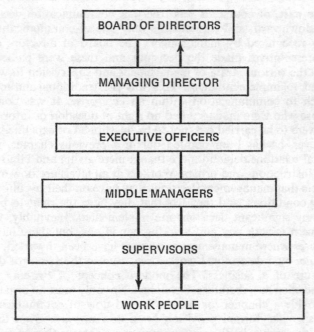

Fig. 5. A diagram of basic vertical communication.

interpret and pass on in an understandable fashion to their sub-ordinates down the line communications coming from the top, but they are also required to do the same thing with communications coming from the lower levels on the factory floor and in the office. If these communications are handled clumsily, without understanding, perhaps even reluctantly, the effect on those trying to communicate upwards could be very unfortunate. Worker attitude to the firm, and thus morale, can easily be damaged at this point. At this stratum of management there is usually personal contact between the manager or supervisor and those being supervised and this should give the opportunity to prevent misunderstandings.

However, there is a greater danger to good relations higher up the management scale. Inevitably the secondary lines of communication upwards merge at some senior manager's office, and at this level the person concerned very likely has not the advantage of personal contact with his middle manager's subordinates. In this case there is a greater danger that the communication, or the reaction to it, may be misunderstood and so cause a breach in worker/management relations. Added to this, of course, a senior manager, burdened with an ever increasing flow of communication, has little time to examine each suggestion, complaint or query in detail and he must rely heavily on the communication skill of his subordinate manager.

'Quasi-Vertical' Communication

There is a further complication in vertical communication in many industries nowadays. This is a channel which runs parallel to the one we have been discussing, and which has, or can have, considerable influence on the internal vertical channel. It might be called a 'quasi internal' vertical communication channel and is brought about by the existence in the organisation of trade unions, staff associations and professional bodies. These bodies are intimately concerned with the personal and professional aspects of the work of their members within the organisation. Trade unions and staff associations usually have, or take upon themselves, the right to speak for or negotiate on behalf of their members on all aspects of pay and working conditions, and often deal directly with the higher levels of management, by-passing the middle managers and supervisors. Similarly, professional societies lay down standards of practice and of ethics which are communicated to their members without recourse to management. In these circumstances, unlike those of true internal vertical communication, the upward flow carries as much weight of authority, or nearly so, as the downward flow, derived from the strength of numbers of the outside bodies.

It will be seen from what has been written that the **vertical lines** of communication in a large enterprise **can become very complicated** indeed, and make the operation most difficult unless due attention is paid to the problems arising from this complexity.

Horizontal Communication

In order that the day-to-day business of an organisation may proceed smoothly there must be effective and **unimpeded communication across departments** between persons at about the same level of authority. Thus, the production manager may have to communicate with the sales manager or with the purchasing manager, the sales manager with the transport manager, and so on. Similarly, interchanges will take place

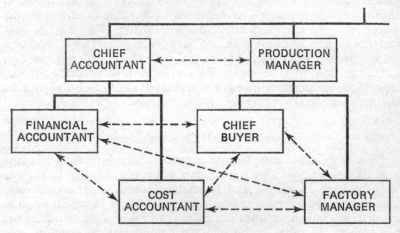

Fig. 6. Part of a line organisation chart showing horizontal communication. The second-rank managers have been shown at different levels for clarity of presentation.

between the bought ledger clerk and the purchasing clerk, a sales representative and a sales ledger clerk. This form of communication is termed 'horizontal communication', and forms a very important element in an organisation's communication system. Without it the day-to-day business of the concern could not carry on, and if it is inefficient the running of the organisation is impaired.

In the main, contact takes place through the internal telephone system or by memoranda, but frequently face-to-face consultation is preferred and may prove necessary.

Horizontal communication works best when morale is high and a cooperative attitude exists between departments. It is most difficult when there is a sense of competition between departments which generates suspicion, sometimes leading departments to work as watertight compartments. In such a situation great difficulties arise and at times horizontal communication can become blocked altogether if ill feeling exists between two different departments, particularly at supervisory level. **Communication is only a tool that helps an enterprise to function,** but when that tool is impaired then the enterprise functions less than efficiently, or ceases to function altogether. Good horizontal communication is, therefore, essential.

Difficulties in Vertical Communication

More often than not failures in internal communication occur in the vertical flow, especially upwards. First, there must, of course, be an adequate system for the conveying of instructions, directives, information, suggestions and grievances between management at all levels and the work force, ensuring that communications reach those they are intended to reach. Equally, some method of obtaining feedback, where required, must be provided. The practical methods that may be used will be discussed in Chapter 11. For the moment we will look at the generally experienced difficulties found in vertical communication.

Perhaps the most common difficulty encountered is that of **lengthy chains of command** between top management and operatives. This occurs where there is a multi-level management hierarchy and almost inevitably leads to ineffective communication. At each level through which a communication passes some distortion may occur so that the final message is sometimes quite different from the original. Particularly is this so if the transmission is verbal. A familiar example is the army story of the request for 'reinforcements' that became distorted to a request for 'three and fourpence'.

Another particular difficulty in vertical communication, particularly upwards, can be attributed to **geographical location.** Many organisations have branches and depots located considerable distances from decision-making centres, and this circumstance leads to delays and frustrations within the communication system. More especially is this so where one of the locations is constantly changing. Imagine the difficulty a long-distance lorry driver, perhaps on a Continental route, may have even in communicating with his immediate line manager.

We have already considered the effects of attitude on communication generally. Attitude also has a profound influence on the effectiveness of vertical communication. At any level of management an **authoritarian attitude** to those down the line will result in reluctant acceptance of communications and an unwillingness to cooperate fully, even though outright rejection of authority is unlikely. Equally, uncooperative attitudes may already exist at the lower levels leading to a grudging response to management's communications. Bad industrial relations in the past may have resulted in frustrated staff who have set up emotional barriers to the acceptance and understanding of management communications.

Similarly, **barriers** may be **set up by managers** at various levels, but particularly at middle management level, with the attitude that the manager sees no reason for his subordinates to be made aware of the company's affairs or objectives, even where these have an important influence on workers' jobs. In such a case the communication may come to a stop on a particular manager's desk. This lack of cooperation, of course, breeds resentment in the work force making normal communication either up or down much more difficult.

Equally, of course, at almost any level a **manager may be overburdened** with a very heavy work-load and this in itself may cause a slowing down of vertical communication flow, or even cause it to stop. Horizontal communication must go on to keep the business moving, but to a large measure vertical communication is not so urgent and pressure of other work leads to its neglect. Unfortunately, though the formal flow may have stopped at a particular level for whatever reason, nevertheless often it continues to descend by rumour or hearsay. When this happens, not only is the communication ineffective, it may be positively harmful because of distortion, the normal accompaniment of rumour.

In the main the difficulties discussed so far have related to communication flow downwards. However, difficulties also abound in the upward flow. Although it is widely accepted that an **upward flow** of communication from shop-floor level is highly desirable, provision for **such a flow is often lacking**. Where no such flow exists management is making decisions without proper knowledge of workers' attitudes and feelings. There is then the danger that such decisions may not be readily acceptable by those lower down the organisation.

Even where provision exists, however, difficulties still present themselves, and these are similar to those already discussed. Thus an **uncooperative attitude by a supervisor** or a manager through whose hands the communication must pass may lead to distortion or even stoppage. Higher up the management hierarchy there may be a lack of response which leads to the eventual discouragement of lower level employees even to attempt to communicate.

Previously **language** has been mentioned. In vertical communication upwards it is necessary for management to make itself familiar with the language of its subordinates; unwillingness to do this results in misunderstanding and unnecessary problems.

Difficulties in Horizontal Communication

The problems and difficulties arising in horizontal communication should be fewer than those in vertical communication, and should more easily be corrected.

A great deal depends upon the **attitudes prevailing between departments,** and particularly between departmental heads. There must be an atmosphere of complete cooperation throughout the organisation. If even only one department is uncooperative it can have a very real influence on the effectiveness of horizontal communication, and on the functional procedures which depend on efficient communication.

A great deal of publicity is given in the press about demarcation lines in inter-union disputes. Such **demarcation lines,** however, are also present between departments within an organisation and a determined attitude by a department about preserving these can result in difficulties. For example, a salesman may discuss a customer's account with that customer: however, the accounts department may take exception to this communication on the grounds that accounts matters are the exclusive province of their department. This could lead to the accounts department refusing to communicate to the sales staff any information regarding customers' accounts.

Again, so-called **'empire building'** can interfere with free horizontal communication. If a departmental head is anxious to see his department grow, and to assert its importance, then he may be reluctant to pass on certain departmental information to other departments when they need it. He may even require them to ask for it rather than provide it as normal information flow, thus slowing up inter-departmental communication.

As with vertical communication, horizontal communication can suffer from **distortion.** Here, because so much communication between departments is verbal, the danger is greater. Particularly is this so where most contact is by internal telephone: the danger is less where face-to-face discussion takes place.

Finally, the problem of **language** arises again, especially between a specialist department and a line department. A typical example, of course, is communication between the computer staff and the staff of a user department. The world of computers is bedevilled by jargon which ordinary line staff do not understand and this is a fruitful source for misunderstanding. Equally, the majority of computer staff are quite ignorant of the problems encountered by line staff in the running of the organisation, and this lack of understanding may result in computer systems or programs not altogether suited to the purpose for which they were supposed to be designed. Fundamentally, the problem is one of language.

Questions

1. It is widely accepted there are various causes of bad communication between people in large organisations. Discuss these and suggest ways in which they can be avoided.   (CIT, Intermediate)

2. Why, in your opinion, does upward communication in a firm often get blocked?   (AIA, Foundation Part A)

3. Describe some of the more common difficulties experienced in 'horizontal communication' within a business.

(AIA, Foundation Part A)

4. What are the main barriers to effective communication which occur in large business or government organisations? How can they be overcome?

(ICSA, Part I)

5. Compare and contrast three barriers to effective communication which may occur between management and staff. Also indicate how the barriers you describe may be overcome or minimised.   (InstAM, Cert.)

9

THE EFFECTS OF AUTHORITY AND RESPONSIBILITY

The Effect of Authority

The effects on communication of the holding of a position of authority or responsibility are often overlooked, though they can be very significant. The holding of a post carrying authority can easily lead a communicator to take the attitude that his word is law, and that his instructions and opinions should be accepted without question. We have already seen, however, that nowadays this is not necessarily the case. The recipients of a communication will question it, seek explanations, or even try to amend it with their own ideas. The authority held by the originator does not command automatic acceptance.

Nevertheless, authority does add weight to a communication, and the wise communicator in this position uses this to add force to his message whilst at the same time he takes into account the likely reaction that may result. He will probably find it necessary, therefore, to temper his authority with explanations in order that he may gain the response he requires.

The Effect of Responsibility

Whilst the holding of authority gives rise to considerations of acceptance, the holding of responsibility gives rise to considerations of consequence. The fact that the communicator will be held responsible for the outcome of his communication should make him use more caution than he would if he were not to be held accountable for the consequences of his communication. Perhaps the most public example of the way responsibility affects attitude can be seen in Parliament. The party in power talks and acts with much more caution than it did when in opposition: in the latter case it knew quite well it could not be held accountable for its ideas or its utterances. Responsibility usually, therefore, causes more care and consideration to be given to the possible consequences of words and actions than if there were no responsibility, and this in turn results in more restrained and carefully worded communications. The use and abuse of authority and of responsibility in communication have a considerable effect on staff receptiveness and hence on the effectiveness of communication within an organisation, particularly vertically downwards.

49

Staff Responsiveness

If, through clumsy use of authority or otherwise, management does not communicate with its staff effectively, then to a greater or lesser extent its success in effective management will be reduced. A good working relationship must be established between those managing and those managed, and this demands that the objectives and authority of management are acceptable and that it is seen to take its responsibilities in all matters seriously.

Generating Staff Cooperation

Positive steps are required from management to engender a receptive attitude in the work force: trust and cooperation must be created, and having been established must be nurtured in order to endure. The study of this area properly belongs to the world of industrial psychology and industrial sociology: nevertheless, its importance is such that it cannot be ignored in any discussion on communication, particularly communication within industry.

Workers are people, and people like to feel that they matter: therefore, staff must be made aware that management has concern for them and their welfare. This should start at the very beginning, when they are engaged. Many organisations have short **induction programmes** during which the newcomer is shown the workings of the establishment and has its objectives explained. In particular, it is important for the new employee to be made aware exactly how his or her job fits in with the scheme of things, and of its importance to the system as a whole. The new employee is made to feel important and responsible and is thus prepared to be cooperative and receptive to management's ideas.

Again, **workers** have a right **to know about general company policy**, projected changes in the company's objectives and activities, and how these will affect the jobs and career prospects of the workpeople. An open policy in these matters is one way of creating goodwill within the work force and a responsive attitude to management communication.

Participation is a third way in which to encourage a responsive worker attitude. They can, for instance, be involved in the decision-making process by being consulted about pertinent matters. In many organisations formal machinery is set up to provide the necessary apparatus for consultation, and **joint consultative committees** are becoming common within the larger enterprises. Often these committees are formed of representatives of management and of trade union shop stewards from the factory floor. The danger here lies in the fact that such committees can cut across the normal, formal, internal lines of communication, and in particular can by-pass middle managers and foremen. When this happens there is a possibility that the authority of these supervisory staff is undermined to some extent, which can lead to difficulties of staff discipline. In such cases, therefore, the line authority of middle managers and foremen must be clearly defined and universally recognised, and they must be kept fully informed of the activities of the joint consultative committee.

However, a formal committee is not essential for consultation, particularly in the medium and smaller concern. Managers at all levels can pursue an 'open door' policy where supervisors and workpeople have reasonably free access to them, and the work force should be encouraged to elect representatives to speak for them so that their voice can be heard. Properly used, consultation can result in more effective organisation, cooperation and coordination, and the feedback can be recycled in the process to improve performance. Thus we can think of consultation as leading to acceptable decisions out of which appropriate orders and actions can take place. The results of the decisions and actions can be re-introduced into the consultation system for modification in the light of experience, and all parties concerned have the feeling of true participation with the attendant improvement in management/staff attitudes.

Joint Consultative Committees

Before leaving this matter of consultation, a word about joint consultative committees will not be out of place. Such committees can be set up to cover a range of activities from simple grievances, when they are generally termed grievance committees, to full-scale joint consultative committees which can discuss a very wide range of topics of concern to everyone. Such committees provide a formal structure of communication between workers' representatives and management, and as such must have properly constructed terms of reference and formal constitutions. Who may serve on these committees is of paramount importance and must be properly agreed between all parties and written into the constitution. Similarly, the topics they may deal with must be properly understood and set down, as must the question of the amount of executive power they should have. At all times both the company and the workers must honour their obligations as to the conduct of the committees.

Joint consultative committees of any kind must not try to usurp the responsibilities and authority of management. They can, however, assist management in its decision-making problems, and can undoubtedly help to create a responsive and cooperative attitude in the workers. These committees must be properly constituted and their powers precisely defined. All employees must be made aware of them and of how to communicate with them. They must be supported actively by management: if it becomes apparent that management is paying only lip service to the committee then its relations with its workers can very soon turn sour, with all the consequences that can stem from that.

Suggestion Schemes

Another way in which worker involvement is encouraged is by the institution of suggestion schemes. These take many forms, a common one being the installation of suggestion boxes at various strategic points throughout the premises. Workers are expected to write their suggestions on paper and slip them into the boxes. Any idea that is relevant and could lead to some improvement in performance or productivity is required, and usually, if it is accepted, a prize is awarded according to the value of the suggestion. As with any scheme to encourage worker participation, management must take this seriously or it can backfire and cause a rift in relationships. The company must be seen to take an interest in the suggestions put forward, even where they are not adopted.

It will be obvious from what has been written that staff need to feel that the company has some concern for them. Most large employers these days, therefore, publish and circulate a **house magazine** or **staff paper**. This gives a great deal of information about the company, its progress, sales successes, and so on, but also contains items of personal interest to members of the work force, such as successes in sport by staff, promotions, engagements, marriages and similar matters. Such journals also give the opportunity to air views and make suggestions: not infrequently competitions are set which may produce useful ideas for the company's benefit.

A contented employee, satisfied with his job, is willing to respond to communications from higher up the line: he identifies himself with his firm. The employee who is not satisfied with his employment is less receptive, and he is less responsive to management communication. The proper handling of authority and the overt acceptance of responsibility go a long way to instilling confidence into the workers. However, the use of the methods of achieving staff cooperation discussed in this chapter are unlikely to be successful unless authority and responsibility on the part of management are seen to be properly used.

Questions

1. What is the relationship between (*a*) morale, (*b*) responsibility, and (*c*) authority in industrial organisations? What part has communication to play in promoting a high degree of industrial morale?   (CIT, Intermediate)

2. What are the usual aims and functions of a Joint Consultative Committee representing elected membership from management and employees? Suggest why such committees sometimes fail.

(AIA, Foundation Part A)

3. Your firm is thinking of introducing a suggestion scheme. Write a memorandum setting down how you think such a scheme might be organised and the basic requirements which should be observed by management to ensure its success. (ICSA, Part I)

4. There is a widespread acceptance of the need for a greater degree of involvement by all employees in the enterprises in which they work. The practice of 'participation' is based on the assumption that a community of interest between the employer and the employee will further the long-term prospects of the enterprise and those working in it.

(a) List five appropriate formal communication channels by which effective communication could be encouraged.

(b) Describe some of the main benefits that you consider will be achieved by increased employee participation inspired by recent legislation.

(InstAM, Dip. Part I)

5. What problems in communication can limit the effectiveness of an employee suggestion scheme? How can these problems be overcome?

(ICSA, Part I)

10

CONSIDERATIONS OF EXTERNAL COMMUNICATION

An organisation lives by communication with the outside world: with its customers, with its suppliers and with the various statutory bodies. An effective external communication system is, therefore, vital for the continued healthy existence of any enterprise. In this chapter, accordingly, we shall look at the various ways in which efficient external communication is achieved.

Written Methods

Most external communication is conducted in writing by one means or another, though the telephone, without a doubt, plays a very large part in business communication.

Letters

Letters play the major role in written external communication, either as original narration or to confirm something that has been discussed verbally. They have **two prime objectives**: first to provide a channel for communication and second to provide a permanent record of that communication. The latter objective gives an exact copy for future reference and also serves as confirmation of the communication should disagreement subsequently ensue. Such copies are, of course, admissible in court as evidence should disagreement go so far as litigation. Letters satisfy many of the factors mentioned in Chapter 6—namely, **accuracy, record, reasonable secrecy, reasonable safety**—and may be made to create any **impression** we wish to give. They are, however, fairly expensive; far more expensive than a telephone call. This is because they attract many costs that the telephone does not. Assuming that a letter is dictated, then there is the cost of the time of the person doing the dictation, and if the letter is being given to a shorthand writer, there is the cost of this person's time. Added to these are the cost of transcription on to the typewriter even where a dictating machine is used, the cost of typewriter depreciation and maintenance, the rent of the office space taken up by the typing desk and of lighting and heating this space, and other similar expenses, quite apart from paper and stamp. Various figures have been given by large undertakings as to the cost incurred per letter, and these range up to £5 each.

So using letters as a means of communication can be quite expensive, and a costing investigation by those who use letters a lot might prove a salutary exercise.

Methods of Sending Letters

So far as speed is concerned, normal first-class inland mail for letters takes between 12 to 36 hours, depending upon where the letter is posted and at what time of day. Unfortunately, present experience leads one to expect a less reliable service than in the past, and the sender can help to minimise delays by attention to one or two important points. First, the full name and address of the recipient, clearly set out, must appear on the envelope, and where the post code is available, this should be used. For some districts the Post Office has its own form of address, particularly for places near large towns, and these should be used where they are available. Often the county required in the Post Office address is different from the administrative county in which the address is situated. For example, Stoke Poges in Buckinghamshire has the Post Office address Stoke Poges, Slough, Berkshire. Use of the latter will assist early delivery. Again, when using first-class mail, it is wise to post not later than midday to make sure of next-day delivery, particularly if it is required that the letter arrive by the first post.

Second-class mail is, of course, available for letters that are not required to be delivered next day, and the delay here may be anything from three to five days. The cost of postage is, naturally, slightly lower than that of first-class mail, but if the letter is an individually dictated and typed one, the difference is trifling compared with the other costs of producing the letter. Circulars, invoices and similar documents are, of course, a different matter.

Where a speedier service than first-class post is needed, the Post Office has available a range of services to meet this need, and these include express letter service, special delivery, railway and railex letter services and even an airway letter service. Readers who require fast postal services are recommended to consult the *Post Office Guide* in which full details of the services offered and the charges entailed may be found.

Where a more secure service is required than that furnished by the ordinary mail, or where it is important to have proof of delivery, recourse can be made to one or other of registered post or recorded delivery; the first is really for things of intrinsic value and the Post Office will pay compensation where loss occurs up to the value declared when the item is posted, and the latter is principally to provide a record of posting and delivery, the maximum compensation being £18. Full particulars of these services are, of course, to be found in the *Post Office Guide*. One must not forget that, in addition to the services offered by the Post Office, many private companies also provide quick delivery services.

In fact, over the past two or three years the provision of these services by private firms has grown remarkably. Many, mostly small, organisations specialise in local deliveries and give a collection and delivery service often well within the hour. Such a service is invaluable in the cases of extremely urgent letters, contract documents and the like. Other, larger, undertakings offer a world-wide service for urgent letters and documents, again with the emphasis on speed of delivery. The Post Office does, of course, provide a guaranteed next-day delivery operated by courier, called Datapost, but cannot yet match the speed of the private firms.

Letters are such an important method of external communication that some consideration as to their construction will be given in Chapter 14.

Postcards

At one time, because of the fact that they attracted a cheaper postage rate than a sealed letter, postcards were in common use for such purposes as acknowledgements of orders, enquiries and letters, and for advices of the despatch of goods, sales representatives' intended calls and the like. Where preprinted cards were used providing spaces for the variable information such as dates, times and so on, they were quick and easy to use. Their popularity waned when second-class post was introduced, enabling a sender to use a sealed envelope for the same rate as a postcard. Nevertheless, they can prove beneficial to the recipient in cases where high volumes of incoming mail bearing information or requests are expected. In these cases the addressee is saved a great deal of labour and expense in opening envelopes. A typical example is that of requests to the BBC, where postcards are always asked for. The postcard, of course, lacks privacy.

Cables

Cables are widely used for rapid written communication abroad. However, the cost is now very substantial and more modern alternative methods are being increasingly used. In order to reduce the expense of cables, codes can be used which reduce the number of words that have to be transmitted, these forms of transmission being charged by the word. Many firms have cable addresses to reduce costs even further. There are standard codes, such as ABC, for cables and particulars of these may be obtained from the various cable companies, one of which is Cable and Wireless Limited.

Telex

The modern method of transmitting written communications, both inland and overseas, is telex, which is operated by British Telecom. A subscriber to the system is provided with a teleprinter, a machine rather like a typewriter, which can transmit and receive messages by electrical impulses carried over the British Telecom telex network. The system works rather like that of the conventional telephone. The sender dials the telex number of his correspondent, and when the connection is made he types out his message on his teleprinter keyboard and an identical typed copy is produced virtually simultaneously at both ends of the connection. The party called can respond in like manner. Thus, continuous communication can take place between both parties, but in typewritten form instead of in speech. Contact is just as swift as with the telephone, but the accuracy obtainable is that of the written word. Further, the telex service extends throughout the world so that it can be used to communicate with subscribers in Europe, Africa, America, Australasia and Asia. A telex directory is provided by British Telecom to all users, similar to the ordinary telephone directory. With the rapid growth in this form of communication it is no wonder that cable services are shrinking.

A further advantage of telex over the telephone and cables is that there is no need for anyone to be in attendance at the receiving end. The teleprinter will receive and type out messages quite automatically and the problem of stationery is taken care of by the simple means of having rolls of paper instead of single sheets as in a normal typewriter. Thus, where the receiving office is closed, perhaps because it is abroad and in a different time zone, communications will still be typed out ready for attention when the office reopens.

As with the telephone, telex is charged on a part rental and part time/distance basis—that is to say, the apparatus attracts a rental charge in the same manner as the subscriber's telephone and outgoing calls are charged on a time basis dependent on the distance involved. Nevertheless, it is estimated that telex costs considerably less than cables whilst providing the users with a faster and more efficient service: and, of course, unlike the older system, there is the facility of an immediate reply where this is necessary.

Teleprinting machines have a further, very great, advantage: they can be fitted with a **paper tape punch and reader**. Using this device, the teleprinter may be caused to punch a paper tape with the information being generated at either end of the line, and also it can read and transmit information coded on to punched paper tape. This facility has many uses, some of which are:

1. Where the information to be transmitted is complicated, and/or needs careful checking, then it can be advantageous to punch this into paper tape, with the machine 'off-line' (that is, not connected to the receiver) so that it can be checked before transmission, and any corrections made. Checking may be done from the typed sheet (this is termed 'hard copy') and so there is no need for formal verification of the tape itself. Further, transmission from punched paper tape is faster than from the keyboard.

2. In some organisations (the Automobile Association is one example) it is necessary to transmit an identical message to two or more receivers. Punched paper tape renders this task quick and easy.

3. Many electronic machines, from accounting machines to computers, can read and operate from punched paper tape. It is thus possible to transmit data via a teleprinter with a punch attachment and so capture it for further processing without any manual intervention, and without the need for mailing material or sending it by special messenger. Where the codes of the teleprinter and the processing unit are not compatible, a conversion machine is used. If input to the processing unit is by magnetic tape, then the teleprinter punched paper tape will be converted to this medium by a paper tape to magnetic tape converter.

Facsimile Telegraphy

However, the teleprinter can handle only matter that can be the subject of original typing on the machine. It cannot deal with matter already typed or printed, neither can it transmit or receive photographs, drawings or anything handwritten. To overcome this problem we have to resort to facsimile telegraphy. This operates in very much the same manner as telex so far as switching and connections are concerned, but the machines are capable of transmitting and receiving only images already in being, such as typewritten scripts, sketches and photographs. In fact, they are rather like photocopiers with telegraph line or radio links. At the sending station the document to be transmitted is fed into the sending machine where it is optically scanned. The variances of reflected light thus obtained are converted into electrical impulses that are transmitted to the receiver, where they are reconverted. The advantages in connection with the transmission of graphic material or photographs are obvious: there has to be no manual copying, and transmission and receipt are almost instantaneous. The operation of the machines requires little skill. Even typed or hand-written messages, however, can be transmitted by this method with advantage, rather than using the teleprinter where the document has to be retyped, for the simple reason that copy typing can lead to errors and thus has to be carefully checked whereas facsimile transmission does not require this operation and is, therefore, error-free.

Telewriting

Whilst facsimile telegraphy can provide fast and efficient trans-mission of images already in existence, many organisations require the rapid transmission of graphic material as it is being produced: sketches, architectural detail, handwritten information and even, perhaps, personal signatures. This need is met by telewriting. This system, of which Telenote and Electrowriting are two examples, uses a small machine at both the sending and receiving stations, each with a stylus attached. The sender writes or draws on the paper contained in the machine, using the special stylus, and the image is reproduced exactly by the receiving stylus attached to the complementary machine. Whilst a very large number of applications for this technique are internal systems where errors in internal telephone messages could be dangerous or embarrassing, such as in hospitals or police establishments, tele-writing can be used very successfully for external communication. As with facsimile telegraphy and telex, distance is no barrier to the use of this system and it is very valuable where accuracy and speed are essential and where the communication is not conducive to type-writing.

The Telephone

The final method of external communication to be looked at is the telephone. This has the advantage that it provides immediate contact, and because it is verbal it provides for easy formal and informal dis-cussion between the parties concerned. Queries and uncertainties can be clarified straightaway, and act on taken without delay. It does have, however, the grave fault of proneness to error, and it can also lead to a considerable waste of time. The telephone, therefore, is a means of communication that requires a great deal of thought and because of this we shall look at it in greater detail in Chapter 20.

Selection of Appropriate Methods

It is not possible to lay down specific rules for the selection of methods of communication, as this depends upon many factors which may differ from case to case. To a large extent, for instance, the trading habits and the special requirements of an industry or a particular business in that industry will dictate the probable methods from which to choose. Even within an organisation different departments may select different methods because of the special circumstances attending their function. Thus, communication between a tour operator and his associates on the Continent may be by telex, because of the need for speed with accuracy, and the necessity for a written record. A lawyer in the same organisation, however, would be more likely to use letter post because speed would probably not be of the essence, and a lawyer prefers to see original documents with original signatures. Where the legal department needs instant communication with sight of signatures, of course, facsimile telegraphy could be employed.

Still using tourism as an example, small travel agencies are unlikely to be equipped with telex machines, and so they make extensive use of the telephone because of the need to keep abreast of the changing situation with regard to booking vacancies. However, bookings are promptly followed up by confirmations by first-class mail. Here, in fact, is a case where the use of telewriting might be of great advantage thus obviating the need for postal confirmations.

In any event, due regard must be paid to the eight factors relative to effective communication set out in Chapter 6, when considering means of external communication. In this way the most efficient method for any particular circumstance is most likely to be selected.

Questions

1. An effective external communication system is vital for the existence of any enterprise. Elaborate on the principal factors that should be considered when choosing any method of external communication (such as letters, telex, telephone, etc.).   (AIA, Foundation Part A)

2. Account for the increasing popularity of facsimile transmission and outline likely effects this may have on the UK telex network. Briefly mention suitable applications for each of these systems.   (InstAM, Dip. Part I)

3. Your teleprinter has provision for punching and reading paper tape. Explain the uses to which this device can be put.

4. List the main forms of written communication used in business. Describe the main characteristics of each form.
What advice would you give to the administrator who wishes to make the most effective and appropriate use of these different forms?

(ICSA, Part I)

5. Draw up a memorandum to all heads of sections in your organisation outlining the relative merits of communicating by letter, telephone and telex and giving guidelines showing under what circumstances each method may be appropriate.   (CIT, Intermediate)

11

CONSIDERATIONS OF INTERNAL COMMUNICATION

Who May Use the System

The establishment of a formal external communication system, though requiring much thought and consideration, is usually a relatively less difficult task than the setting up of a formal internal system. Earlier we examined the way the effectiveness of communication is affected by worker and management attitudes, motivation, prejudices and other factors relating to the staff/management relationship, and these all have a tremendous influence on internal communication systems. Thus, when we design a formal internal system we have to consider not only what means and methods to use, but also who may use the system and with whom he may communicate direct. The lines of communication must be clear, precise and known.

For example, may the assistant sales manager approach the general manager direct, or must he go through his sales manager? May the transport manager communicate with the sales representatives personally, or must he use the services of the sales office hierarchy? Precise understanding on this point is even more significant where the communication of instructions and orders is concerned. For instance, should a sales representative be allowed to instruct a sales ledger clerk or a credit control clerk, a not uncommon occurrence when the salesman is endeavouring to extract an order from a client who is overrunning his credit terms? Should the senior bought ledger clerk be able to instruct a buyer as to whether he may continue to order from a certain supplier? It is not possible to set down rigid general rules on these matters; the criteria will be determined by the size of the business, the working relationships already established, and the organisation pattern.

The Organisation Pattern and the Communication Network

How a concern is organised has a decided bearing on the way lines of internal communication operate. If there is a tightly-knit line organisation in being then there will be very obvious communication channels laid down by the very nature of the organisation plan. The hierarchy from top to bottom and from bottom to top within each

61

department, and for the establishment as a whole, will be quite clear-cut and the vertical channels for communication will follow these. Horizontal channels will also be quite precise. Where, however, the organisational plan is more functional or is designed on the line and staff pattern, then formal lines of communication will not be so clearly defined, and the flow patterns must be formally laid down. If this is not done confusion is apt to follow when conflicting views or suggestions are made by line managers and by the functional officers. Hence, for example, it must be clearly understood whether the personnel officer may give firm instructions to a member of staff, or whether such orders must proceed through the worker's own line supervisor.

Methods of Internal Communication

The Internal Telephone

Probably the most frequently used mode of internal communication is the telephone: it is quick, access is instant and the effort to make the contact is at a minimum. However, two significant problems are posed when coming to a decision to use this method:

(1) would it be preferable to have an entirely separate installation, a simple intercom or a private automatic exchange (PAX), or should use be made of the main external telephone equipment and its extensions;

and (2) who should be equipped with a telephone?

The solution to (1) seems simple. We have British Telecom apparatus and extensions to all who need them. Almost certainly we have a private automatic branch exchange (PABX) so that all internal connections can be dialled without troubling the switchboard operator. Why, then, go to the expense of a separate installation? However, the real answer is not so simple. A most important consideration is the amount of external traffic passing through the main switchboard. If this is heavy then the desk instruments may be tied up constantly with external calls thus preventing their being available for internal communication. Similarly, if the internal traffic is heavy, outside callers may be subject to grave inconvenience because they cannot talk to an extension that is frequently engaged on internal business. In the circumstances where an external caller requires one internal extension to consult another internal extension (say a sales office consulting the works regarding an order whilst the client holds on) then the use of the main telephone installation can become very frustrating. True, modern equipment allows an external call to be held whilst another extension is rung, but in such cases the caller is quite unable to make contact while the hold condition persists and this can become most annoying, particularly if the inside conversation becomes a lengthy one.

It follows, therefore, that the **circumstances** of the traffic to be expected **dictate whether a separate internal telephone network** is required. If outside traffic is heavy but inter-office and consultation requirements are light, then it is highly likely that the main telephone system can be used for internal calls. If, on the other hand, internal traffic is heavy, whatever the external call rate, then a separate internal installation is probably called for.

Who shall have a telephone is often a very thorny question. This matter should be judged first on the expected volume of use of the extension in question, and second on the cost. Unfortunately, often cost is the first consideration with the result that a telephone is not provided where it should be. The outcome of such a policy is that staff have to leave their desks in order to use their colleagues' instruments. This waste of staff time is a hidden cost which may be many times that of the cost of an additional extension and of which management remains blissfully unaware.

There are very many varieties of internal telephone systems available, and most can be tailored precisely to the user's requirements.

Personal Contact

The telephone is, essentially, a verbal method of communication, and so is personal contact. The latter is frequently used for internal communication and can be extremely effective. For some purposes, such as appreciation or reprimand, it is preferable to any other method. However, in cases of day-to-day communication it can be very time-wasting and is possibly used as an excuse to stretch the legs or have a change of scene.

The Memorandum

The memorandum is a very usual method of internal communication, where the accuracy of the written word helps to avoid the errors that may occur with verbal methods. Secondly, where a copy is taken by the sender this serves as a record of the transmission of the communication as well as a ready reference for later use. Unfortunately, memoranda are often used, not for these two advantages, but rather as a defence in case the sender is accused either of not sending the message at all or of sending a different message. Bearing in mind the high cost of the typing operation, this is a very expensive defence. So important is the memorandum that more attention will be given to this in Chapter 14 where we shall discuss fully that other popular method of written communication, the letter.

Transmitting Paperwork

Once written, a memorandum has to be conveyed physically to the intended receiver. There are several methods of achieving this. The oldest and the most usual is the **office messenger**. Normally the messenger will have a route that he or she follows at stated times of the day, calling on offices and departments to deliver and pick up documents of all kinds, including memoranda. Usually the direction in which travel takes place is reversed at different times so that offices at the end of the route are not constantly at a disadvantage. Special memoranda, or those requiring urgent attention, are frequently conveyed outside of this arrangement by a special journey by the office junior.

In organisations where the incidence of internal mail is heavy various mechanical means of transmission can be used. Perhaps the best known is the **pneumatic tube**, frequently seen in department stores for the conveyance of accounts and cash from the sales counter to the accounts office. This method consists of tubes connecting the necessary departments through which cartridges containing the paperwork are propelled by compressed air. Modern installations allow of automatic switching so that the cartridges can be routed from any one point to any other point on the system without manual intervention. Each manufacturer has his own method of doing this. It is interesting to note that the transmission of express post in Paris is done by pneumatic tube, and very fast it is.

Two other methods for horizontal travel are the **conveyor belt** and the **vee belt**. The former can accommodate large, bulky documents as well as small items such as memoranda, and can be constructed to rise over obstacles to a certain extent. The vee belt is much faster, but can be used only with thin documents travelling mainly horizontally. In this case the papers are moved on edge. Both methods are able to negotiate bends and are designed for each individual situation.

Vertical physical conveyance, apart from pneumatic tubes, can be accomplished by **document lifts**. These are small lifts of a size to accommodate the paperwork to be moved. Again, installations vary in accordance with the needs of the organisation and the peculiarities of the premises concerned.

Communicating on Staff Matters

Meetings have an important part to play in internal communication, particularly where opinions need to be sought, doubts resolved, or where matters of great importance need to be examined. They are the normal procedure where policy matters and executive decisions are determined, but may be usefully employed at any level throughout the organisation, or between members of various levels. There should be formal rules laid down both as to who may attend and what procedures should be adopted. There are many kinds of meeting, and this subject will be fully discussed in Chapter 25.

One particular kind of meeting, however, should be examined whilst we are discussing methods of internal communication. This is the briefing group.

Briefing groups, also often known as briefing sessions, are growing in popularity in large business organisations, and are a means of bringing supervisors or managers together with their immediate subordinates in order to have discussions on various matters appertaining to the work in hand, or to some project that is proposed. In other words, the subordinates are 'briefed' by their supervisor rather in the same way as air crews are briefed in an air force.

The essence of the briefing group is that it consists of only the manager or supervisor and his immediate subordinates. It is, therefore, a tightly knit group, the members of which are well-known to each other, and would normally number somewhere between five and 25 people. Their shared experience and knowledge enable them to discuss problems in a useful and practical way, and their personal relationship helps them to put their points of view without embarrassment. The usual pattern of briefing sessions is that the supervisor or manager puts a proposition and he then invites comment from the group. In this way the members of his staff are kept aware of what projects management has in mind for the particular work force concerned, and the workers are enabled to ask questions and seek advice, and also to put their own points of view on the issue. The briefing group is a very important sounding board for propositions that affect the workers' job prospects, their pay and possibly their future career structure. Indeed, any proposals that will have repercussions on the workers' security of employment and on their job practices are matters of high concern for briefing sessions: many employers use them solely for this purpose.

The value of the briefing group is that it provides for the direct involvement of the workers in management decisions that affect them intimately. Being led by the workers' immediate supervisor, it invites close cooperation with him and at the same time emphasises his supervisory authority.

Conferences are also a popular method of exchanging views and opinions and of sounding out ideas. They are usually of much longer duration than meetings or briefing sessions, have a very much larger membership, and are normally held away from the premises of the organisation. The venue is frequently some beauty spot or holiday resort, and the proceedings are partly formal and partly informal. The opportunity is often taken on these occasions to present experts in some field or other, particularly in marketing, to give lectures relating to the organisation's business problems, and thus to bring outside ideas into the enterprise which otherwise might not be available. Only very large establishments are able to mount such conferences as a form of internal communication because of the expense and the inevitable disruption to routine that they cause. However, members of an organisation can often take part in conferences arranged by trade associations, professional bodies and the like, and though these do not rank as internal communication, much benefit may be derived from such attendances producing a fresh outlook and new ideas that may be injected into the internal deliberations of their organisation.

Some communication to staff needs no immediate response, or is by way of information or instructions only. In these cases notices and posters on **notice-boards** around the premises are often used. It is good to remember that notices are often only skimmed through, and sometimes not read at all. It is helpful, therefore, to make sure that such notices are as short as possible so that they can be read quickly, that they have pertinent, clear headings, and that their origin is stated. Further, they should be dated, and notice-boards should be constantly cleared of out-of-date announcements. The latter point is important: people soon become tired of consulting notice-boards that are cluttered up with old notices, making the locating of current notices difficult or time-consuming. Eventually such notice-boards cease to be inspected.

In cases where management seeks to obtain the cooperation of its workers in a specific matter, or feels it needs to explain certain of its actions, then the **insertion in wages packets of memoranda** is sometimes resorted to instead of putting up notices that may be ignored or incompletely read. In such circumstances the memoranda need to be very carefully worded and presented, and their acceptance may depend a great deal on the management/worker relationship that exists.

Regulations relating to conditions of employment need to be communicated to staff, and in some areas are required by law. This problem may be satisfactorily dealt with by the issue to each worker on engagement with a **staff handbook** which sets out all the relevant conditions, such as rates of pay, holiday entitlements, pensions rights, regulations regarding notice and so on. Usually these handbooks are bound, but some form of loose-leaf binding does make keeping the book up to date much easier.

In order to generate worker interest in their company, many employers publish a **staff journal or magazine**. These publications attempt to build loyalty and goodwill in the staff by providing interesting items of news about the organisation itself and about members of its work force. Thus, significant successes in the fields of sales, research, development and other areas are included, as are news items concerning members of staff such as weddings, engagements, retirements and successes in sport and other activities. Often competitions are run through these journals, usually concerned with improving performance in some part of the company. Staff magazines also often provide a platform for ideas and opinions from staff through a letters page and through encouraging staff to write articles for the paper.

It is interesting to note, probably because of the sheer size of many modern undertakings, that notice-boards, staff journals and other similar means of communicating with the work force are termed 'mass media' by some practitioners in communication.

Numerical Information

Much information passing internally through an organisation is numerical and it is necessary to communicate the purport of such

Revenue and Cost Statement: Tipper Hire 1976–1979

	1976	1977	1978	1979
Revenue	£136 905	£153 929	£188 011	£252 750
Wages Fuel Maintenance	75 028 11 813 2 537	89 278 16 932 3 848	113 821 19 116 4 013	141 540 22 747 5 055
Operating costs	89 378	110 058	136 950	169 342
Operating profit	47 527	43 871	51 061	83 408
Total admin. costs	36 351	36 173	46 296	55 605
Total cost	125 729	146 231	183 246	224 947
Net Profit	£11 176	£7 698	£4 765	£27 803

Fig. 7. A tabulation.

information to many sections of the concern. Unfortunately, it is a fact that very many people find it difficult, if not impossible, to draw conclusions from tables of figures: particularly is this so at the operating level. Consequently, ways have to be found to make comprehension easier, so that the work people who need to understand can do so. Graphic presentation is of great assistance here, and we will look at those most commonly used. Fig. 7 shows a tabulation of a revenue and cost statement, and as it stands this would be virtually incomprehensible to a very large number of workers.

The Pie Chart

The pie chart is, perhaps, the clearest way to represent figures from a tabulation such as the foregoing, where it is not required to show comparisons with other figures. It is simply a circle (the pie) divided into segments proportionate in size to the significance of the amounts they represent. Thus the 1979 column of the revenue and cost statement would be represented as in Fig. 8.

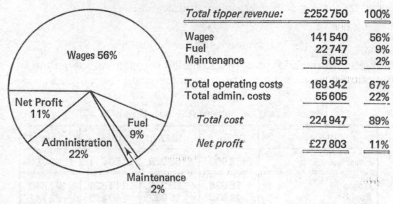

Total tipper revenue:	£252 750	100%
Wages	141 540	56%
Fuel	22 747	9%
Maintenance	5 055	2%
Total operating costs	169 342	67%
Total admin. costs	55 605	22%
Total cost	224 947	89%
Net profit	£27 803	11%

Fig. 8. A pie chart of the tipper revenue and cost statement for 1979.

Although not absolutely necessary in very many cases, a pie chart is often accompanied by a table which shows the figures used in the preparation of the chart. An example is given in Fig. 8. Sometimes, to give greater emphasis to the message, the pie is discarded for a representative sign, such as the £, which is split up into proportionate sections.

The Graph

The familiar graph is a useful way to present figure information. To the initiated it needs no interpretation at all: a falling line represents the lowering of amounts and a rising line the opposite. Those who understand graphs more fully may, if they wish, read off actual figures from the horizontal and vertical axes. Fig. 9 is a simple graph showing one factor only.

Fig. 10 shows a compound graph, and indicates how more than one type of associated information may be represented visually, the relationship between each type being shown most clearly. The information used relates to the revenue and cost statement shown in Fig. 7.

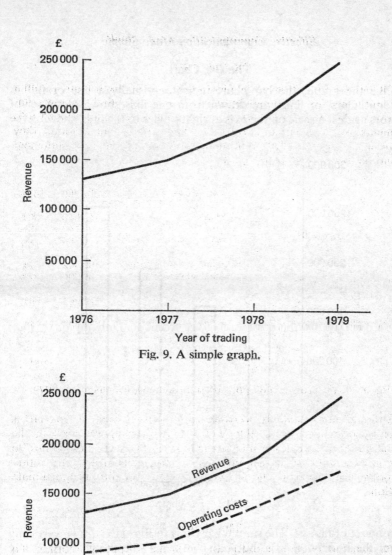

Fig. 9. A simple graph.

Fig. 10. A compound graph.

The Bar Chart

Like the graph, the bar chart indicates visually a rise or fall in amount. Bars, or lines, are drawn from one axis showing one set of factors against a scale on the axis at right-angles to the first, showing the

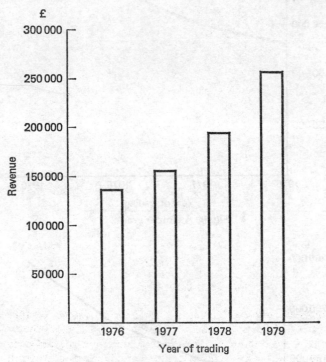

Fig. 11. A bar chart.

second set of factors. The simple bar chart in Fig. 11 is drawn vertically from the horizontal axis, but bar charts may be drawn horizontally from the vertical axis where this is more convenient.

Just as graphs may have a compound form, so may bar charts, when several related factors may be shown on the same chart—see, for example, Fig. 12.

The Pictogram

The presentation of figure information in this form lends itself to very easy understanding, where simple figures only are involved. A

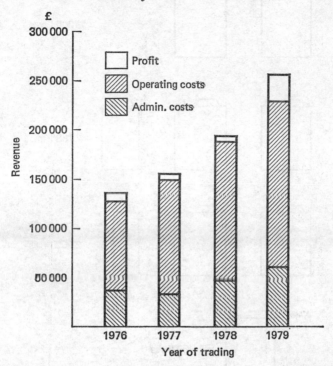

Fig. 12. A compound bar chart.

small, outline sketch of the item concerned is drawn to represent a fixed number of units. Totals of units are then indicated by drawing a number of the sketches in rows. Where the total quantity cannot be shown by a number of complete sketches because a fraction of the fixed number of units is required, then a proportion of the sketch is drawn for the incomplete fixed unit (say half the sketch for half the fixed quantity). Fig. 13 shows an example of one of these pictograms.

The Gantt Chart

Finally, mention must be made of the Gantt chart which, whilst not directly related to statistics, may be profitably used to indicate clearly expected performance and actual achieved performance over a period of time.

It is in the form of a bar chart drawn horizontally. On it is shown by a horizontal line the planned performance for a period, split up into manageable sections. As time progresses, actual performance is plotted

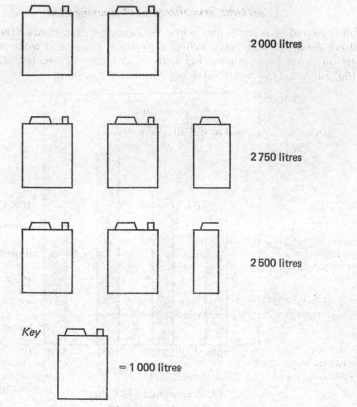

2 000 litres

2 750 litres

2 500 litres

Key = 1 000 litres

Fig. 13. A pictogram.

OUTPUT—SHOP B

	Jan.	Feb.	Mar.	Apr.	May
Monthly target (units)	400	400	400	400	400
Output achieved (units) %	300 (75%)	350 (87.5%)	400 (100%)	375 (93.75%)	450 (112.5%)

Key ----- Target

⊢———⊣ Achieved

Fig. 14. A Gantt chart.

on a second horizontal line below the expected performance bar. Thus it is easy to see how performance is running, and if and when remedial action should take place. This chart, a specimen of which is shown in Fig. 14, is easy to understand and simple to maintain.

Questions

1. Write notes on each of the following:

    Charts
    Diagrams
    Graphs
    Tables

as an aid to effective communication.   (ICSA, Part I)

2. What are the most important reasons for presenting information in a visual form in a talk or report?
Outline the relative advantages and disadvantages of the following forms of visual presentation; charts, diagrams, graphs and tables.

        (ICSA, Part I)

3. What points need to be borne in mind concerning notice boards to ensure they are an effective communications medium?

        (AIA, Foundation Part A)

4. 'Although inadequate communication may be a problem in many organisations, it is essential for management to impose some restriction on communications.' Suggest some areas in which such restriction may apply.

        (AIA, Foundation Part A)

5. What is the purpose of a company's house journal? Comment briefly on the usual contents of such a journal.   (AIA, Foundation Part A)

6. In many organisations the system of using briefing groups has been found useful. What are briefing groups and how do they operate? How can they assist the communication process in organisations?

        (InstAM, Dip. Part I)

12

STAFF LOCATION

Internal communication depends on the two parties being able to make contact, and so this chapter is devoted to the problem of staff location, which can sometimes present difficulties. If a person spends the best part of his day at his work station then there is no problem, but many members of staff at all levels have duties that cause them to move about either within the organisation's premises or away from it, and ways have to be devised to be able to locate them without undue delay.

Internal Telephones

We have already touched on internal telephone installations in Chapter 11 as a means of internal communication, but we can now look at them in a little more detail, concentrating on private installations. These vary from very small configurations linking only two or three extensions to very large ones involving hundreds of extensions, some connecting with other buildings many miles apart.

The smallest installations normally provide direct access from extension to extension by means of push-buttons on the instruments themselves and, generally speaking, these follow the design of the conventional hand telephone similar to those supplied by British Telecom. Larger installations of the same type of instrument provide dialling facilities, for which a small private automatic exchange unit is fitted, and thus many more extensions can be accommodated according to the capacity of the auto-switching unit. As these installations are fitted with the conventional handsets the receiver side of the conversation is secret, but it is necessary to hold the instrument in the hand to use it, thus restricting movement to some extent.

Other types of internal telephone are, therefore, available which consist of a small cabinet equipped with a loudspeaker and a built-in microphone which picks up speech from a short distance. With this type the user's hands are left free to handle papers and, further, other people around the instrument can take part in any conversation if this is necessary. If privacy is desired some designs allow the use of a handset, which automatically cuts out the loudspeaker.

One advantage claimed for some of the loudspeaker-type internal telephones is that several instruments can be connected together, and so discussions and 'meetings' can take place with several members of staff without their having to leave their desks. Such installations can be either key-operated or dial-operated, and a few provide both so that direct access can be made to much-used extensions by simply pressing the appropriate keys, whilst lesser-used extensions are dialled.

Again, some installations, termed 'executive' installations, have a master instrument that provides priority of connection so that, for example, the managing director can make direct contact with an extension even if that extension is already engaged on another call. The different facilities that are available on internal telephone systems are many and varied, and the exact requirements of any particular organisation can usually be accommodated by one supplier or another. The present trend appears to be towards the key-operated loudspeaker type, particularly at the upper management levels. However, in noisy situations preference will probably be given to the handset type which, to some extent, suppresses extraneous noise.

Teleprinter Installations

Where the rapid transmission of typewritten communications is required between depots and branches many miles apart, the teleprinter is often pressed into service. As with telex, the teletype machine is employed, but unlike telex, the machines are linked by direct lines and are not switchable in the same manner as the telex system of British Telecom. The apparatus itself may be rented from British Telecom or may be purchased or leased from the manufacturers, while the telegraph lines are usually rented from British Telecom. With the direct link, connection is permanent and messages can be passed merely by operating one of the machines, when the second machine will respond. Being very similar to typewriters, teleprinter machines pose few problems for the competent typist, and contact is instant.

Large organisations often have a need beyond the fixed links already described. In these cases, a central switching station is set up to which all the teleprinters are connected, and through which any machine can be connected to any other. This is still quicker and cheaper than using conventional telex.

By means of the direct-link teleprinter installation, therefore, staff at distant points can be located and accurate, typewritten messages passed to them with minimum delay. Directly linked telewriters could, of course, be used for the same purpose, as could facsimile telegraphy, but such installations are less common than teleprinter systems.

Public Address Systems

A common method of staff location is, of course, the public address system, in which loudspeakers are placed in strategic positions about the premises and announcements are made to locate members of staff wanted through a microphone and amplifier installed in the telephone office. All of us are familiar with those used at railway stations. Whilst effective in some factories and in yards, this method can cause disturbance with work in offices and other areas where concentration is required. Other methods have, therefore, been developed, and the following are the most popular.

Signal Lights

In this method units of a combination of colours or numbers, or a mixture of both, are located about the premises, linked to and operated from the telephone switchboard office. Each member of staff who may be wanted from time to time is allocated a code combination. When his attention is required, his particular code combination is flashed on all the units about the building and on seeing this he will call the telephone operator through the nearest telephone extension. This system is noiseless and effective when seen, but can, of course, be overlooked. To attract attention, therefore, some installations also have buzzers fixed to the units.

Personal Paging

Signal lights are nowadays fast giving way to the more modern method of personal paging, in which direct personal contact is provided by means of a small receiver carried in the pocket. There are three forms of personal paging, all operated from a central transmitter usually placed in the telephone switchboard office:

1. **Simple Paging**: This is the cheapest and the simplest of the systems. Each receiver is allocated a separate frequency, and when a member of staff is wanted, his frequency is activated to cause his instrument to 'bleep'. On hearing this signal he will go to the nearest telephone to contact the switchboard operator. This method is very quiet, and is much used in hospitals and similar areas where disturbance must be kept to the very minimum.

2. **One-way Speech**: In circumstances where the main requirement is to pass messages or instructions to staff, particularly where personnel is unlikely to be near a telephone, then one-way speech paging is useful. This has developed from the simple 'bleep' system, and permits speech

to be transmitted to the receiver, but does not provide means for the transmission of a reply. Of course, it can also be used as a direct substitute for simple paging at slightly greater expense.

3. **Two-way Speech:** This has taken personal paging a step further, and allows the receiver to reply in speech when called. This two-way communication is made through the central transmitter and, of course, obviates the need for the person paged to go to a fixed telephone. Costs are higher than for the other two methods, but convenience is much greater, and the pocket apparatus itself is very little larger than that employed in the simpler systems.

All these three methods of staff location are operated either by radio wave, short wave or VHF, or by induction loop. The induction loop is, in effect, an aerial wire that surrounds the area within which it is desired to operate the paging system, and is connected direct to the transmitter, there being no connection to the receivers. Its main advantage is that transmission is limited to the area defined by the loop and no interference can be caused beyond this: a certain amount of privacy is also assured. With the radio wave, no such limits can be defined, and this can be a very real advantage where an organisation's premises and staff are located over a widely dispersed area. There are Post Office regulations to be complied with when using both systems, but due to the wider possibility of interference with other radio transmissions these are more stringent for the short-wave and VHF installations.

Two-way Radio

The paging installations we have just discussed are all based on communication through a central transmitter—that is, all contact is to and from the central point. For some purposes, however, this does not meet the need, which may be for communication between two different points away from the main centre: one can think of many instances, such as the need for communication between various parts of a civil engineering project, or in a very large depot spanning many acres. This problem is solved by the use of two-way radio, once called 'walkie-talkie' radio. The transmitter/receiver units of this system are now pocket size and are carried by any member of staff who has the requirement of instant communication with other members of staff on the site. Each instrument has its own individual frequency to which callers can tune and so make contact with the required party. The range is fairly limited, the equipment being of relatively low power.

The Radio Telephone

Because of the restricted range of the system discussed above, it is of no use for locating staff operating away from the premises, people such as maintenance engineers, taxi drivers, ambulance personnel and the like. For such communication a more powerful installation is required, and this is provided by the radio telephone which is, in effect, a short-range broadcasting system. Outward communication from the central point can be selective so that individuals may be called, but often a blanket broadcast system is employed, and the required person or vehicle is named or otherwise identified so that other receivers will ignore the call. Inward calls and responses must all be to the central transmitting station, and there is no provision for contact between individual receivers.

These radio telephone systems are essentially private staff location installations and cannot be connected into the public telephone network. It is well to point out, however, that British Telecom does have a system of public radio telephones which can be installed in cars and other vehicles and which are, in fact, part of the general telephone system. From such telephones the users can receive calls and make them in the same way as may be done in the office. At the moment this provision is quite expensive, and is limited to a small number of areas, but there are plans in hand to extend this facility country-wide.

Questions

1. Describe the salient points of two types of staff location system, stating circumstances where their use can be justified.

(InstAM, Dip. Part I—adapted)

2. You have difficulty in communicating with staff who are dispersed over a large depot and who have cause to move about the depot in their work. Describe a suitable staff location system you could adopt, and give reasons for your choice.

3. Suggest reasons for the growth in the popularity of personal paging, and explain why, in your opinion, the older methods of staff location have declined.

13

INFORMAL METHODS OF COMMUNICATION

We tend to think of communication, particularly in business, as being dealt with solely through the formal channels provided, but we must recognise that a very great deal of communication is done informally. In fact, if the formal channels are weak or vague then informal communication can be very strong and may even, in some circumstances, take precedence over formal communication.

The 'Grape-Vine'

Within an organisation the informal lines of communication are usually termed the 'grape vine' or the 'jungle telegraph' and operate most strongly horizontally, both between members of the same department and between members at the same level in different departments. However, where vertical lines in the formal network are particularly weak, then the 'grape-vine' can be very active both downwards and upwards. Its great **danger**, both horizontally and vertically, is that it is most active in passing on **rumour** and **gossip** much of, if not most of, which consists of half-truth or complete falsehood often operating to the detriment of the organisation.

Further, as the information passes along the line it becomes more and more **distorted** and embellishments are often added at various points. Thus, even if the content of the communication starts by being substantially correct, it may be far from the truth by the time it has reached the end of the line. Obviously this method is an open invitation to the malicious and the malcontents to spread untrue rumours and falsehoods to the detriment of the organisation. It is a fact that the 'grape-vine' commonly **carries more bad news than good** and this can be very disturbing in some cases, especially where workers are worried about their job security for one reason or another. The arrival of a work study team, unannounced and unexpected, would be an example where unsubstantiated speculation of an adverse nature might circulate in the 'grape-vine' and cause anxiety within the work force. To circumvent this sort of situation, and to maintain satisfactory working relationships and high morale in an organisation, it is **essential** that **management keeps** its **employees fully informed** about all decisions likely to affect their job security and their career prospects. This is best done by establishing strong formal lines of communication, both vertically and horizontally, and by using them fully and promptly.

On the other hand, it is virtually impossible to keep staff fully informed at all times about all matters likely to affect them, especially where confidential negotiations are taking place. Such occasions will be accepted as inevitable and no ulterior motives suspected if trust and confidence have been built up in the staff. However, faith will be maintained in management only if information is imparted at the earliest opportunity so allowing rumour as little opportunity as possible to enter the 'grape-vine'.

Perhaps the greatest difficulty about rumour and gossip is the fact that it is practically **impossible** to **trace the source**, and thus prevent further communications of a similar character. It is most important, therefore, to do everything possible to make sure unauthorised and dubious statements do not circulate in the first place, by building up an effective and trusted formal communication network.

Using the 'Grape-Vine' to Advantage

Despite what has been said, however, the 'grape-vine' can have its uses and can be employed for the benefit of the organisation. Sometimes it would be injudicious to make a formal announcement about a possible course of action when the idea is only tentative, as this might lead to the assumption that a firm decision has actually been made: in such a case a hint dropped into the 'grape-vine' could quite well test staff reactions. An instance would be where management considers that it might be advantageous to move office. An official announcement that management is considering such a move might quite well cause the staff concerned to take up attitudes for or against, which they might find difficult to reverse later. However, an appropriate rumour fed into the 'grape-vine' would probably give management an opportunity to observe staff reactions and so help management with its ultimate decision without committing staff definitely at the outset. There are many such cases.

The Canteen Lunch

Other informal communication channels, both internal and external, are worth consideration before we close this chapter. Perhaps the most common one within an organisation is the canteen lunch. Very many of the larger organisations, and many of those not so large, have staff canteens where staff and workers take their meals. Almost invariably these lunches provide the opportunity for unofficial exchanges of ideas, complaints and suggestions. A great deal can be learnt by a sensitive manager or supervisor at these meals which can give clues to staff attitudes generally and to individual aspirations or grievances in particular. As a channel for informal communication they are first-class, and it must be remembered that they are often part of the 'grape-vine' system. Similarly, of course, the more deliberate **working lunch** is made a vehicle for informal communication, where suggestions and plans may be discussed without record or firm commitment. The Americans are particularly prone to hold 'working breakfasts' for this purpose.

Social Gatherings

Social gatherings are also used as instruments of informal communication deliberately or by chance. Thus, attendance at such functions as house parties, charity fêtes and the like may provide the opportunity to make contact with appropriate people for informal discussion on topics of interest. Sometimes the contact is pure chance, but often the particular meeting is engineered by appropriate action regarding invitations.

Membership of Social Organisations

Akin to this is the opportunity afforded by membership of specific organisations, professional or otherwise, or by invitation of such members. In the past membership of the local church was almost obligatory for the local businessman in order to further his business, where informal introductions and pertinent discussions took place. Nowadays membership of the golf club or similar society is more likely to provide the openings for informal communication and introductions. The clubhouse rather than the playing area is the place where discussion will take place, and in this respect the bar of the local public house may be likened to the clubhouse. However, usually in the public house communication will be incidental rather than deliberate, and the people concerned will probably be lower down the management ladder. Nevertheless, the astute observer will often glean a great deal of information unwittingly provided or purposely passed on. In addition, of course, this venue can also be used for the informal working lunch.

Other Channels

A channel of informal communication often overlooked is the **sales representative**. He is frequently the purveyor of much useful information by virtue of his admission into various organisations and his conversations with his customers and their staff, information that would probably not be obtainable from any other source. Again, he may be made the carrier of information we may wish to have disseminated but with which we do not wish to be officially associated. In fact, many face-to-face situations of this nature can be used as vehicles for informal communication and they can be very effective. **Rumour**, particularly, is apt to be spread and take effect by informal external contact, and rumour can be especially potent. A very clear illustration of this is the vulnerability of the Stock Exchange to rumour whether founded or unfounded.

Finally, we must not forget the '**secretary's ear**'. Whether internally, or in another organisation, if it is desired to get a point over to a manager where a formal communication would be difficult, especially at a personal level, a quiet word in the ear of the personal secretary to the manager concerned will almost always eventually find its way to the desired quarter.

Questions

1. What is meant by the distinction between formal and informal systems of communication within organisations?
What are the most important implications of this distinction for the administrator? (ICSA, Part I)

2. What is meant by the term 'the grapevine'? Explain the reasons for its existence in large organisations, the drawbacks of this form of communication and the best ways of forestalling them. (ICSA, Part I)

3. Set out your ideas as to the uses and disadvantages of informal methods of communication in business.

4. 'The formal communication network is often inadequate or too slow. In such cases the informal communication networks—often called the "grapevine"—spring into action to meet the needs of people.' Discuss.
(AIA, Foundation Part A)

14

LETTER WRITING

Functions of a Letter

The writing of a letter in business or other formal situations performs two functions: first to communicate ideas and information without personal contact and secondly to record that communication in permanent form. Further, the letter has two aspects, that of the recipient and that of the sender. To the recipient it is the means through which the sender conveys his communication and it is in such a form that the receiver may study its contents with deliberation. To the sender it provides the opportunity to keep a copy of his communication for future reference so that there shall be no misunderstanding of his communication when discussion arises in the future. In fact, it is unwise in all formal situations to fail to take copies of all correspondence particularly if the matters concerned are likely to entail the exchange of letters and documents over a period of time. Human memory is fallible: a complete file of correspondence both inwards and outwards is the only sure memory.

Points in Writing Effective Letters

To avoid possible misunderstandings and possible confusion, it is necessary that all letters are clear and concise, and to this end the letter writer should bear in mind the following points:

(1) Even before he starts to write his letter, or to dictate it, the writer should be quite **clear** what he **wants to convey**: this means giving careful thought to the subject matter of the letter and to being sure that there is an understanding of the matter. Woolly thoughts can give rise only to vague, indefinite communication which means that vague and imprecise information will be conveyed to the other party.

(2) Allied to the question of clarity of thought is the question of **lengths of sentences and paragraphs**. These should be kept short and to the point. Verbose sentences and long, rambling paragraphs frequently obscure the meaning of a communication. At best they may confuse; at worst the reader will tire of them and not read them fully.

(3) It is worth the trouble to **seek out the exact word** to use in any

particular case, and not to be content with the first one that comes to mind. In English we have a language that is very rich in synonyms, but only rarely will two words have precisely the same meaning: an example is 'beautiful' and 'lovely'. The word 'lovely' has a more all-embracing and calmer feeling than the word 'beautiful'. Hence, in letter writing the exact word should be chosen to convey the precise meaning required: if the writer's vocabulary is inadequate, then there are books that can help such as a good dictionary, a good dictionary of synonyms and antonyms or, for the more dedicated, Roget's *Thesaurus of English Words and Phrases.*

(4) **Ambiguity** in letter writing **must be avoided** at all costs: it causes mistakes and confusion, and in some cases can even lead to litigation. If the writer is clear in his mind precisely what he wants to say, as suggested in (1) above, this will help a great deal. In addition, the writer should try to put himself in the place of his correspondent and endeavour to imagine how the letter will be interpreted by the recipient. Are the contents clear and the wording precise? What foreknowledge of the subject matter has the correspondent? Punctuation and syntax, as well as correct word meanings, affect ambiguity and must have attention. For instance, compare 'However, we shall see' with 'However we shall see'. The former means 'Nevertheless, we shall see' and the latter 'By whatever means we shall see'.

(5) Understanding in letter writing is greatly assisted if the **ideas** are **expressed logically**; that is, the letter should flow from one point to the next in a logical progression. If the reader's mind has to keep going backwards and forwards in trying to assimilate the meaning of the letter then comprehension becomes difficult and misunderstanding results. Development in an orderly fashion is very important for any matter to be clearly presented.

(6) Verbiage is a bar to understanding, and this is now well appreciated by many letter writers. However, this has led to brevity bordering on discourtesy. Letters that are **concise** are easier to understand than long ones, and save much time both of the writer and of the reader. Nevertheless, they must never be concise to the point of abruptness which verges on rudeness. The common courtesies need to be remembered when letters are composed; failure to do this may give a bad impression and lose goodwill.

(7) A common pitfall for the letter writer is the use of **slang** expressions or slang words. True, it is good advice that the writer should visualise his correspondent and try to write as though he were speaking to him. This advice should not, however, be used as an excuse for using slang instead of using good English. To some correspondents the use of slang may appear distasteful and to others may give the impression that the writer is slovenly. At all times the rule should be 'formal English for

formal letters'. Similarly, **hackneyed expressions** are best avoided as far as possible. **Technical jargon** also poses a problem. When corresponding with others within a specific technical sphere then it can be taken that the use of technical jargon is permissible, but otherwise more formal language should be employed. Thus, computer people writing to computer people may give instructions to 'dump' a file: when writing to non-computer people they would preferably refer to the preservation of the contents of a computer file. A letter writer should, on the other hand, resist the temptation to use or coin odd or unfamiliar expressions so as to be different.

Making Letters Easy to Deal With

It is not the purpose of this book to teach the art of letter writing, nor to teach punctuation and associated subjects. There are many textbooks available to do this, including a very helpful volume in the Made Simple series, *English Made Simple*. The aim here is to provide an understanding of the principles involved in composing understandable and acceptable letters. To further this aim we should now examine three ways in which we can make our letters more easily dealt with by our correspondents:

The first of these concerns, in the main, our replies to letters received. Usually these will bear a **reference** of the sender, and this should always be stated on any reply. This enables the correspondent's mail department to route the reply quickly and correctly and so speed up the correspondence procedure. Omission of this small detail is likely to cause unnecessary delays in the system.

Secondly, if more than one topic has to be dealt with by letter to the same organisation, it is helpful to write a **separate letter for each topic**. In the event that separate departments will be dealing with the various matters, as will be most likely, again delays are reduced as each letter can be routed directly to the correct and appropriate section.

Thirdly, it also helps sorting at the receiver's end if letters bear a **heading** giving briefly the topic dealt with. This should be in addition to a reference, if known, and assists in determining the precise recipient who is competent to deal with the matter concerned.

It used to be thought wasteful to post letters to different departments in the same organisation in separate envelopes, and great pains were taken to assemble them all together so that one posting was made. The advent of the computer and the high salaries now paid to office staff have changed this attitude. It is now considered as cheap, if not cheaper, to post such letters separately. Whether one method or the other is employed depends upon individual circumstances, and each organisation will make up its own mind. The main consideration is the time that will be saved, and this is also an important consideration when replying to letters.

Saving Time in Letter Writing

There are several ways in which time can be saved in writing or answering letters and we will now examine some of those most used.

The Form Letter

The form letter is very common and has been employed for a very long time. It is, in fact, a pre-prepared letter of suitable standard wording in which variable information is added in spaces left for this

SENDER Send both blue AND yellow copies, RETAIN pink for file.	WRITE or TYPE - NO CARBON REQUIRED	RECIPIENT Reply on blue copy but retain this. Despatch YELLOW copy to sender.

TO

FROM

| Subject | Your Order Ref. | for |

MESSAGE   Date

We thank you for your order as above. As this is the first credit transaction which we have had the pleasure of doing with you we should be most grateful if you would let us have trade and/or banker's references for our accounts department. The reply section of this PING PONG memo set will enable you to do so with the least possible trouble.

Yours faithfully,

.SA9

PING PONG
BRADSHAW BRODIE LTD.   Signed ....

REPLY   Date

In reply to your request we would quote trade/banker's references as follows:
.... BANK LTD.
Address ....
....
....

Trade Suppliers:
Name ....
Address ....
....
Name ....
Address ....
....
....

Signed ....

Fig. 15. This is a specimen of a proprietary form letter, by courtesy of Bradshaw Brodie Limited of Halesowen, in their 'PING PONG' series. Normally, the name and address of the sender would be printed in the 'From' section.

purpose. It is used for acknowledging customers' orders, acknowledging receipt of letters and enquiries, quotations for standard items, covering letters accompanying sales brochures and in many other areas. The actual letter forms may be printed in ordinary printers' type, imitation typewriting characters or, sometimes, italics, or they may be produced on the office duplicator from stencil skins prepared by the office typist. Simple acknowledgments are frequently printed postcards on which the variable information is inserted by hand, whilst more important acknowledgments may be in ordinary letter format in facsimile typewriting as befits their importance. This latter method is very useful in the acknowledgment of customers' orders where it is sought to impose conditions of sale, as these can easily be printed in full on the back of the form letter.

The matching in of the variable information, such as date, name and address, figure amounts and so on, is not easy, as the typewritten matter is always noticeably different from the printed material. This problem, where it matters, can be overcome by the use of **automatic typewriters**. These machines employ a master of the static information from which they can type an almost unlimited number of copies. The master provides the facility of stopping where variable matter is to be inserted, and this is typed by hand on the same machine, so that an exact match is produced. When running on the automatic master their speed can be as much as 180 words per minute, without error, which outpaces the average typist by three times.

Selection from Pre-written Paragraphs

A second method of speeding up the production of correspondence is really an extension of the idea of the fixed form letter.

Here several paragraphs to cope with a variety of situations are composed and numbered. By simply telling their typists the code numbers of the paragraphs they wish to have included in their letters executives, who would otherwise have to spend time dictating, can easily and quickly dispose of their correspondence.

Whilst the manual use of this method is time-saving, the automatic method is very much faster indeed. In this case **automatic typewriters** have been extensively employed that have the facility to **select chosen paragraphs** from a large number stored on their masters. However, automatic typewriters are rapidly being superseded by **word processors**, which are faster and more flexible.

Word Processing

Whilst this is not a textbook on office machines, it is worth mentioning that, over the past decade or so, great strides have been made, and many innovations introduced, that have accelerated the output of typewritten matter even over the speeds achieved by the more conventional automatic typewriters which are operated by punched paper rolls or punched paper tape. These new methods are grouped under the heading of 'word processing' and the machines used are able to achieve speeds of between 200 and 500 words per minute, employing new typing techniques such as the 'daisy wheel' instead of the usual 'golf ball' of the normal automatic typewriter. Masters are recorded on magnetic material, such as magnetic tape, which enables the operators to edit the contents of the master without a great deal of difficulty. The more advanced word processing systems have magnetic storage devices for the permanent retention and reference of standard matter and some have even developed into mini-computers which are able to display the work on a visual display unit for checking before actual printing is done. Such systems are approaching the sphere of data processing, and their uses go far beyond ordinary letter writing into the realms of sales promotion correspondence, report writing, where much editing is required and thus many rewrites need to be done, conveyancing and, indeed, any area where first-quality, repeated work is necessary, and where a good deal of editing may be required.

Composition of Letters by the Secretary

Coming back to the simpler methods of speeding up correspondence, especially to save the time of high-salaried executives, one frequently used is to leave the secretary to compose the letter herself rather than the executive having to dictate it. This requires secretarial assistance of a high order as the letter is written entirely by the secretary from brief notes given to her, often verbally, by the executive. Provided the secretary is of sufficiently high calibre, this method is very effective.

The Simplified Letter

Another way to save actual typing time, and thus accelerate the letter writing process, is the use of the simplified letter. The purpose of this is to avoid unnecessary carriage movement on the typewriter, and thus such letters are devoid of paragraph indentations and every line, including the date and letter heading, is started at the left-hand margin. This idea is occasionally extended to the point where everything that does not further the sense of the letter is omitted; thus the salutation and the subscription do not appear. This style can become terse and may leave something to be desired visually, but it does save much typing time.

The 'Speedy Reply'

Finally, we have the method which avoids the typing of a reply at all. Kodak call this the 'speedy reply' method. Simply, where a very brief response only is needed—perhaps just three or four words—these are handwritten on the original letter and the letter then photocopied. One of the copies is returned to the sender of the original letter and the other is filed for reference. One could consider the request for an appointment. 'Yes, 3 pm, 8th October' could be written on the request, a photocopy made and despatched, and the reply has been dealt with speedily and effectively without the intervention of the typist.

Using Dictating Machines

Before leaving the question of correspondence and how to deal with it more quickly, we must take a brief look at the use of dictating machines. The arguments as to when to use shorthand and when the dictating machine, as to the manner in which dictating machines are employed, and as to whether a centralised dictating system should be installed, do not concern us here. What does concern us is that the dictating machine should be used as efficiently as possible, and the onus here is squarely on the person giving the dictation. The following short rules will not, therefore, be out of place:

1. **Know** what you want to say before beginning dictation, and plan the order in which points should be made. Short notes help.
2. Give all the necessary **instructions before beginning dictation proper,** such as number of copies required, special instructions regarding layout, and so on.
3. **Speak clearly** and distinctly and at a slightly slower pace than normal. Remember that the recording process distorts the voice to some extent and a little more precision is required in enunciation.
4. It is advantageous to **pitch the voice a little lower** than normal, and to avoid dropping the voice at the ends of sentences.
5. It is advisable to **spell names,** especially foreign and difficult ones, addresses and difficult or technical words.
6. Whether to indicate **punctuation** is a matter of personal preference. Consistency in this matter is, however, important to avoid confusion for the typist.
7. Remember to **stop recording whenever there is a break,** however small, in the dictation. It is a waste of the typist's time to sit with nothing to type because the tape has been allowed to run on while you have paused to light a cigarette, to think, or to answer the telephone.

Following up Letters

A chapter on letter writing would be incomplete without reference to the necessity to follow up our correspondence. Quite frequently our letters are not answered and some reminder system is needed to cope with this. Unfortunately, there is no automatic system that will ensure neglectful correspondents are prompted to reply and so some active inspection must be done at the sender's end.

One simple method is to keep a diary with notes under the dates when replies should be received. Another is to have a formal 'tickler' system in which a box file or similar receptacle is equipped with dated divisions. Carbon copies of the letters concerned are filed under the dates by which replies should be in. In both systems daily inspection is essential so that reminders can be sent promptly.

Memoranda

Memoranda are written communications intended for internal use only. The first thing to ask about a memorandum is: 'Is it necessary to write one at all?' In very many cases the answer will be 'No' because

MEMORANDUM	
From:	To:
Subject:	Date:

Fig. 16. A commonly used memorandum form.

the matter could very well be dealt with over the internal telephone. All too often the memorandum is looked upon as a defensive device to be used to avoid blame in the future—and an expensive defence it is to the organisation. A memorandum should be used only where the absolute accuracy of the written word is essential.

When a memorandum cannot be avoided it should be **brief** and to the point. Though the writer should not be discourteous, he has no need to use the same care in quality and politeness that an external letter requires. The matter should be dealt with in a direct fashion, without unnecessary embellishment, but the same regard to the precise use of words and the avoidance of ambiguity is as important in this case as it is in the writing of a letter.

A memorandum, like a letter, should deal with **only one subject**. Usually memoranda are written on standard forms which encourage this practice and a specimen of the most common type is given in Fig. 16.

Easy Reply Memorandum Forms

Various other designs which facilitate the sending of replies are, however, beginning to become popular. Fig. 17 shows one such form, which makes provision for a reply alongside the original message. This form also has a perforated strip at the top on which the names of the originator and the addressee are written. When he replies, the addressee

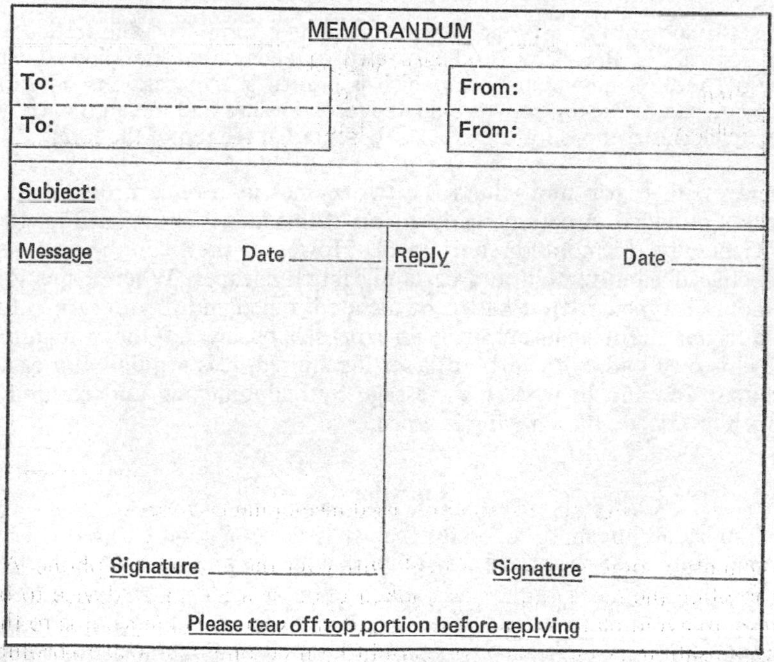
MEMORANDUM

To: From:

To: From:

Subject:

Message Date ____ Reply Date ____

Signature ____ Signature ____

Please tear off top portion before replying

Fig. 17. An improved memorandum form.

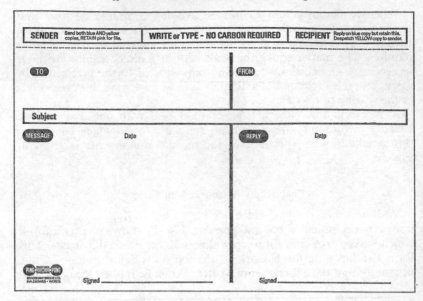

| SENDER Send both blue AND yellow copies, RETAIN pink for file. | WRITE or TYPE – NO CARBON REQUIRED | RECIPIENT Reply on blue copy but retain this. Despatch YELLOW copy to sender. |

TO   FROM

Subject

MESSAGE   Date   REPLY   Date

PING PONG   BRADSHAW BRODIE LTD. HALESOWEN · WORCS.   Signed —————————————   Signed —————————

Fig. 18. Specimen of a proprietary memorandum form. This illustration is by courtesy of Bradshaw Brodie Limited of Halesowen and shows their 'PING PONG' memorandum form which is printed in triplicate sets on self-copying paper. The top copy is blue, the second yellow and the bottom copy pink. Instructions for use are clearly set out at the top of the form.

tears off this strip and enters the two names in reverse order in the spaces provided. A commercial version of this idea is shown in Fig. 18.

Generally, memoranda are typed. However, they can be just as effective if hand-written and certainly much cheaper. When a memorandum is typewritten it has to be dictated, typed and then returned to the originator for signature: truly an expensive business. If the originator has his own pad, with carbon paper if required, it is a quick and easy exercise for him to write his message by ballpoint pen and certainly much less costly than having it typed.

Questions

1. What are the most important characteristics of a good business letter? Explain why these characteristics are important.   (ICSA, Part I)

2. Write a formal business letter based on the following instructions:
'You have been asked by your superior, Mr Jones, to write to one of his friends and business associates, Kenneth Smith of International Industries Limited, Northern Street, London. Mr Smith has become interested in

business communication and wants to know what are the most important principles of communication of which a professional administrator should be aware.' (ICSA, Part I)

3. What is the purpose of the memorandum or 'memo' in business communications, and to what points would you pay attention when writing a memorandum? (AIA, Foundation Part A)

4. Describe in detail three ways in which your executives could increase their output of correspondence.

5. Write a memorandum to members of your staff who use dictating machines giving them advice as to how they can increase their dictating efficiency and save typists' time.

15

REPORT WRITING

A Definition

According to the dictionary a report is 'an account given or opinion formally expressed, after investigation or consideration'. It will be seen from this definition that a report is reckoned to be formal, and is required to give an account of the matter covered or to state an opinion on it: sometimes both are required. In most cases, moreover, conclusions have to be drawn by the compiler of the report and, often, recommendations given.

Generally speaking, there are **two main types of report**, though every report will not fall neatly into one or other of these categories. The first is the **individual report**. This is usually expressed in the first person and is the kind used for internal routine reports and short reports on day-to-day matters. Examples of these are accident reports, organisation and method reports, sales reports and so on. In some cases, particularly where a great deal of figure information is included, a standard form is used so that variable data only has to be entered as in the case of the form letter.

The second type of report is the **general report**. This is more formal than the individual report and is generally written in the third person, though this is not always the case. Such reports are frequently composed for external or public circulation, and are often quite voluminous. Official reports of this nature sometimes run into two or more volumes bound in book form, with extensive indexes.

Basic Principles

Whatever form a report takes it will be subject to a set of basic rules or principles. These do two things: they ensure that the report is logically constructed and they encourage the writer to present his report in an accepted format. The principles may be summarised as follows:

(1) The report should have a **title**. This should be indicative of the content of the report, and clarity should not be sacrificed for brevity.

(2) The report should be **addressed** to the person, or body of people,

who are intended to study it. In a report destined for general public distribution, however, this is not considered necessary.

(3) If the report is addressed as in (2) it should normally begin with a **salutation**, e.g. 'Dear Sir', or 'Gentlemen'. No such salutation is required where the report is a regular routine one nor, of course, if there is no specific addressee.

(4) A statement of the **terms of reference** under which the report has been prepared is important, and this should be set out at the beginning of the report. In the case of regular routine reports, however, such terms will have been set down at the beginning of the series and need not be repeated unless, or until, they change. Neither are they required to be stated in a short internal report on any special matter, as the introductory sentence to the body of the report can cover this matter without undue formality.

(5) Some sort of **introduction** to the body of the report is useful to present the problem dealt with and, usually, to state under whose authority the report has been prepared. Often this need not be more than one sentence.

(6) The **body of the report** should contain the following:

(a) The nature of any investigations carried out;
(b) A statement of the facts discovered during the investigations;
(c) Clear arguments and opinions arising from the investigations and the facts uncovered by them.

In order to assist the reader to follow the report most effectively it is recommended that **headings** and **subheadings** are used for sections and paragraphs to indicate the various factors. This is helpful in all but the very shortest of reports. In long reports it is further recommended that the paragraphs be numbered for easy reference and as an aid to indexing in cases where the work is voluminous enough to warrant an index.

(7) The **conclusions** of the author or authors are normally called for, and should be the subject of a separate section under its appropriate heading. The case leading to the writer's conclusions should be clearly and logically put in as succinct a manner as possible commensurate with conviction.

(8) Frequently the **recommendations** of the writer are required to be stated. As with the conclusions, these should be separately put under the proper heading.

Lengthy reports may have the conclusions and recommendations given at the ends of the relevant sections of the body of the report, particularly where the report is a substantial one and each section has a chapter to itself.

At this point it should be mentioned that some authorities recommend that conclusions and recommendations be put immediately after the opening of the report and before the main body of the report. The argument here is that this is a position that enables the reader, especially one with limited time, to come to a quick agreement or disagreement with the report, and that he need then read only the body of the report on the investigations and the facts drawn out if he feels the need to substantiate his first opinion.

(9) Inevitably, it will often be necessary to include in a report various **charts, statistics, graphs** and **other supporting material**, and the position of these within the work is sometimes a problem. The guide here should be the ease with which the report can be read. If the supporting tables and so on are few in number they may be positioned by the text to which they refer. If, however, there are a large number of them and they interfere too much with the flow of reading, then they may be put at the back of the report as an appendix and reference made to them in the text itself. However, sometimes constant reference to an appendix can be very irritating, if not difficult, and this should be borne in mind when arranging the layout of the report. This problem, of course, presents itself only in the case of long reports.

(10) Where the **report** is **of a meeting**, the names of those present as members should be given at the head, under the title of 'Present'. Where there are non-members present their names should also be given at the head of the report under the title of 'In attendance'. Similarly, if the report is the result of the joint efforts of several people the name of each individual should be given.

(11) Where the report is a lengthy one a **table of contents**, and possibly an index, should be provided so as to make reference to specific topics as easy as possible for the reader.

(12) All reports should be **signed** by the author. If the report is the work of a team, the signature is usually that of the chairman. Most official reports, incidentally, are known by the name of their chairman, e.g. the Robbins Report on Higher Education.

(13) A report must be **dated**.

Planning and Preparing a Report

Terms of Reference

A report, especially a formal one, is always commissioned for a specific purpose, and the extent of the brief must always be clearly known by the investigator. This is given in the terms of reference, and these terms must never be exceeded. Where, during the investigation, pertinent matters are uncovered that go beyond the terms of reference, these must on no account be included in the report, but must form the subject of a supplementary communication.

For Whom Intended

It is necessary for the writer of a report to know for whom the report is intended and why it is required. This information will help the writer to decide which parts of the matter he has collected should be included in the report and which should be omitted. Such discrimination is an essential talent for any investigator or writer, and is highly desirable in the sphere of report writing. For example, if a report is required on a new machine tool, the board of directors of the company will be interested in different data from the works maintenance engineer.

Similarly, the language in which the report is couched will be different according to its destination. Highly technical language will be in order for the works engineer, but not for the board of directors.

Headings

As with other written communication, the report should flow logically from one point to another, and should develop in an orderly and easily understood fashion. With this aim in view it is of great assistance if the headings and subheadings of the various sections of the report are laid down first so that a proper framework is constructed. The writing of the full account can then be undertaken in the sure knowledge that a logical arrangement has been established. Further, this method helps to avoid the accidental omission of important points that have to be made.

Drafts

For any report other than a fairly brief one, it is almost always essential to prepare a draft first, so that it can be carefully edited before it is produced in its final form. In fact, a lengthy report may require more than one edited draft before it is considered satisfactory. Where the report is to contain any statements or opinions by experts, it is very necessary to have these verified by the experts, particularly in the context in which they are to appear. Drafts of these parts of the report will most certainly be required, therefore, to submit to the authorities in question for verification.

Meeting the Required Date

Not only is a report required for a specific purpose, it will almost certainly be required by a specified date. This must be known at the outset and must be met at all costs. A report that is not ready when needed is a valueless report.

Style

The style in which a report is written is important. It should be authoritative, and positive statements should be employed wherever possible. Negative statements should not be used unless there is no way of avoiding them. Particularly, if part of the purpose of the report is to stimulate action, positive statements will encourage a positive approach in the reader whereas negative statements are inclined to lead to apathy.

Presentation

The way the report is presented in its final form will depend upon its length, upon the number of copies required and, not least, upon the impression it is sought to have on its readers. It may be typewritten, duplicated or printed, therefore. A lengthy, formal report will normally be printed, and bound in book form, whilst a short, informal one may be duplicated and stapled together. If it is required to impress a potential client, a short, formal report on some project may be carefully typed, and bound in an attractive cover by one of the modern binding devices to be found in most offices nowadays. Presentation, then, is a matter of length and for whom.

A Specimen Report

The following is a specimen of a short, formal report. Examples of long, official reports are held by most public libraries and may be seen on request of the librarian.

> The Nonsuch Company Limited,
> Oldville,
> Anyshire.
> 30th October, 19. .

The Board of Directors.
Gentlemen,

Subject: Modernisation of Motorcar Fleet

As instructed I have investigated the condition of the motorcars now used by our salesmen, and have to report as follows:

Present position:	The fleet of motorcars used by our salesmen comprises 10 vehicles. Of these, two are over five years old, six are three years old and the remaining two were acquired six months ago: all are Ford Escorts of 1300 c.c. capacity.
Condition of vehicles:	The two oldest vehicles have done over 100 000 miles and are overdue for replacement. Of the six three-year-old cars, four have done over 60 000 miles and the remaining two nearly 50 000 miles. The two six-month-old vehicles have both done under 15 000 miles.
Other findings:	The six three-year-old cars are performing reliably at the present time, but are beginning to require constant maintenance to keep their performance up to par. Further, four of them will require an expensive major

overhaul in the very near future, and in the opinion of our maintenance engineer the other two are likely to be in this category within the next three or four months.

All eight salesmen driving the oldest cars have expressed dissatisfaction that they have not been allocated up-to-date vehicles in line with those driven by their competitors.

Recommendations: In order to modernise our salesmen's motorcar fleet, the eight cars of three years old and older should be replaced by current models of the same make and capacity. Competitive quotes should be obtained from three fleet dealers, and orders placed on the basis of best selling price coupled with best trade-in prices for our existing vehicles. Immediate delivery is desirable but not essential provided the delay is not more than two months.

Car Fleet Manager

Questions

1. Prepare a brief guide to the writing of an effective report. This should contain discussion of at least the following:

(a) how to approach the task of writing a report
(b) the characteristics of an effective report
(c) common weakness and problems that may be encountered in reports.

(ICSA, Part I)

2. You have to report on a new method of operation to the managing director who will assess whether it is likely to be of value to your organisation. Produce a report for him briefly describing the procedure (using your imagination) and assessing its advantages and disadvantages over the existing system.

(CIT, Intermediate)

3. What guidelines would you recommend to administrators who wish to ensure that their formal reports are examples of good communication?

Justify your recommendations in terms of underlying principles of communication.

(ICSA, Part I)

4. In the context of report writing it has been said, 'Write to communicate your findings and express your ideas, not to impress someone with your learning'.

Demonstrate your understanding of this quotation.

(AIA, Foundation Part A)

5. Describe the types and applications of reports. Select one type of report and outline its structure.

(InstAM, Dip. Part I)

16

FORM DESIGN AND CONTROL

The Need for Forms

An organisation works by communication, very largely recorded on paper. If variable information under fixed descriptions is frequently required it is most quickly and efficiently dealt with if the information is in the same fashion and in the same order on all occasions. Hence the use of forms. A form is merely a device which tries to ensure that all the information required for a particular purpose is provided, and that it is presented in the way and in the order in which it can most easily be used. This explains the increasing use of forms and the emergence of the skill of form design, for upon the use of forms, effectively designed, depends to a large extent the efficient operation of all kinds of enterprises—the tax office, the manufacturer, the haulier, the football pool.

Briefly, then, the use of forms makes the recording and presentation of data uniform. It enables information to be easily recognised, compared and, if necessary, further processed. Most procedures are based on a form or forms, and the form is now the basis for reporting and directing services. Consequently, a heavy responsibility rests on the form designer to provide forms that are appropriate to the task they are to perform and are at the same time easy to use and handle. This task requires skill and a good knowledge of the organisation's procedures and practices, as well as acquaintance with the circumstances under which the forms will be completed and interpreted or otherwise processed. First he has to be aware of what the form is required to accomplish—to provide hours of work for wages calculation, check lists for procedure control and so on—and second, how the form can contribute to the smooth operation of the organisation, remembering that it has been stated that the filling in of a form costs at least 20 times the value of the form itself.

Principles of Form Design

Whereas it used to be the practice for various departmental managers to design their own forms for use in their own departments, this is a practice that is now recognised as inefficient because such forms are drawn up from a very limited viewpoint, and increasingly design is centred in the hands of a form designer. In fact, his first task on being asked to raise a new form will be to consider whether a form is required at all. Specially designed stationery ties up money in stock and it may be that information supposedly required on a new form can just as effectively be provided by a memorandum or by other means.

Secondly, the need for a form having been established, it is possible that there is already in use, probably in another department, a form which could be amended so that it could be used for the new requirement as well as for its existing use. This saves stocking additional special forms, and also may mean that an entry made at one point may be used at another, instead of information having to be abstracted from one form and transferred to another. Copying, besides being a wasteful operation, is also one that gives rise to errors.

Thirdly, on being given the questions which are purported to be necessary on the form, the designer, from his own knowledge of the systems and in collaboration with the department concerned, will prune the contents so that only the essential questions are asked and redundant matter is eliminated. Here ruthlessness is necessary: every inessential entry must be cut out as being a waste of money (*a*) in producing the form itself and (*b*) in the time taken to complete and to interpret the unnecessary items.

Practical Considerations

The need for a new form having been established, and the essential contents agreed, the form designer now has to give consideration to the form itself. This involves a series of decisions that have to be made based on the following questions:

(1) **How should the entries be arranged?** A logical order will speed the filling in of the form and will help to avoid mistakes, especially if the information is new and not being taken from an existing record. A simple example is the entry of name and address. If this were asked for as 'address and name' the chances are that the number of forms completed giving the name first would be quite high, particularly if the forms were filled in by members of the general public. Similarly, where information has to be copied from other sources or forms, so far as possible the entries on the new form should be in the same order as the existing, otherwise the incidence of error by transposition of items will tend to be high.

(2) **Who will complete the form and by what means?** A manual worker using a pencil needs a different kind of document from the office worker using a typewriter. In the first case instructions must be particularly clear and simple and the spaces for writing large, whereas in

the second case the instructions may be brief and the writing space at a minimum. The wording of the question and the style of type are also matters of concern under this heading.

(3) **Under what conditions will the form be entered?** This will be particularly pertinent where the form has to be completed in the factory, or out on a building site. The substance of the paper, its resistance to dirt and damp, the size of the print, will all be determined to a large extent by this factor.

(4) **To what use will the completed form be put?** If it is to stand on its own for the communication of data then considerations as to means of emphasising certain areas may be needed: if it has to be used in conjunction with other forms, as a source document perhaps, then it needs to relate to them, particularly in ease of transcription and order of contents.

(5) **Are copies required**, and if so, how many? The answer to this question will determine the weight of the paper to be used, the manner of production having regard to the need for accurate registration of all the copies, and also the means of copying.

(6) **How will the forms be kept after completion?** This will have some bearing on the kind of paper used, and whether or not a wide margin needs to be left for punching or binding.

Having laid down the essential, basic principles of form design, it will be profitable to examine some of the points in greater detail.

Contents

Whilst it is necessary that only essential information should be included on the form, it is equally necessary that nothing essential should be omitted. In consequence, in settling what the form should contain a complete list of all probable and possible entries must be made, which can then be pruned so as to leave only the vital minimum. If the preliminary full list is not prepared there is a real danger that something of importance may be missed. When examining the contents, the order in which they appear must also be considered. It is sometimes urged that the most important information should appear first, with the other entries going down the form in descending order of importance, and this is, in general, a logical approach. Where material has to be copied from another source it helps accuracy if the form order matches the source order; original material must flow logically.

Putting the Questions

Here the designer must have firmly in his mind the type of person or persons who will complete the entries, as this will have a distinct bearing upon the manner in which the questions are asked and the style and type of language used. The wording understandable to a high-level manager may be incomprehensible to an operative on the workshop floor. Even the style of type may have some effect on understanding and interpretation. Ambiguity or vagueness should be avoided at all costs. Where instructions have to be given on filling in the form, it is accepted that these should be given at the beginning if at all possible. Reference to marginal notes or separate sheets for instructions should be avoided if at all possible. Answers should require the very minimum of writing, and if questions can be formulated to provide for 'yes/no' answers so much the better.

Means of Completion

The mode of entry has a very great effect on the spacing required for answering questions, and on the kind of paper used for the form:

Hand Entries: These may be by pen and ink, ballpoint pen or pencil. A smooth paper is needed for the first, but a rougher, and cheaper, paper may be used for the others. Spacing is very important here. The formal calculation for handwriting is an allowance of eight letters to the inch horizontally and four lines to the inch vertically, the actual spaces allowed being based on the expected number of words to be written.

Typewritten Entries: The material here should be hard-surfaced and reasonably smooth, but not glossy. Remember that erasures will be made and the paper must be able to stand up to this without either losing its surface or showing the alterations too conspicuously. Bond or bank papers are normally used, the former being the more expensive. Horizontal spacing is usually reckoned as 10 or 12 letters to the inch, depending upon whether the typewriter has pica or elite size type, these being the most popular sizes. However, other type spacings are available which give characters up to 20 to the inch, and if this kind of machine is to be used to fill in the form then answer spaces may be designed accordingly. Vertical spacing on typewriters is almost always six lines to the inch whatever the horizontal letter spacing.

Mixed Entries: Where entries are to be made by either hand or typewriter, or by both on one form, then the recommended allowances are eight letters to the inch horizontally and three lines to the inch vertically.

Other Machine Entries: Where entries are to be made by machines other than typewriters, the spacing requirements will follow those set by the equipment concerned, e.g. addressing machines, accounting machines or visible record computers.

Place of Entry

The chief concern here is the material. A stouter, more crease-resistant paper is needed where forms have to be used under factory or external site conditions than when they are used entirely within the office. In the factory they will pick up dirt and grease; on an external site they may be creased and folded and carried about in workers' pockets, as well as being subjected to damp and, possibly, wet. Fortunately, if the precise circumstances are explained, the paper suppliers will give advice on the exact type of paper required to suit any situation.

Lay-out and other Matters

The lay-out of a form should be as simple as possible, of neat and uncluttered appearance, and the type style should be clear. Headings should be in capital letters and/or underlined, and the title of the form should be prominent so that it can be easily identified.

Make _____	Model _____	Colour _____
Engine No. _____	Chassis No. _____	Capacity _____
Purchased _____	Purchase Price _____	Depreciation _____ %

This layout has nine starting points for entries

Make _____	Model _____	Colour _____
Engine No. _____	Chas. No. _____	Capacity _____
Bought _____	Price _____	Depreciation _____ %

This layout has only three starting points for entries, thus minimising tabulation

Fig. 19

It is frequently recommended that **entries** be made **across the page** where possible as this reduces the length of the form. This is particularly valuable where entries are being made by machine, because tabulating across the page is less time-wasting than returning the carriage to the beginning of the line and turning up the paper. However, if this design is adopted the various reply sections should be so laid out that they fall under each other going down the page, otherwise more time is lost in selecting the writing point than by returning the carriage. For example, Fig. 19 shows two alternative ways of setting out a plant record form, clearly indicating the value of lining up the tabulation points.

Column headings also need particular attention. Wide columns present no problem because it is easy to set the headings horizontally, but narrow columns often have headings set vertically so that it is necessary to turn the form round to read them. In such cases a splayed heading makes reading much easier—see Fig. 20.

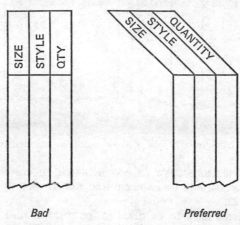

Bad   *Preferred*

Fig. 20. Splayed headings are easier to read in narrow columns than vertical headings. They can slant either way according to the requirements of the form.

It has already been suggested that **writing should be reduced to a minimum,** and the use of questions requiring ticks or deletions are alternatives that will save time in completing the form. Specimens are given in Fig. 21.

FINISH: ~~GROUND~~/POLISHED

FINISH: GROUND ☐

POLISHED ☑

Fig. 21. Deletions or ticks are quicker than written entries.

Where **additions** or **calculations** have to be carried out on forms, one or two points should be watched to minimise the possibility of mistakes:

(1) Wherever possible figures should be added in vertical columns rather than across the page. Cross-casting is more subject to error than vertical addition.

(2) Where figures have to be subtracted and the order is vertical the amount to be deducted should be below the gross figure. If subtraction is required horizontally it seems to be more natural to subtract from right to left.

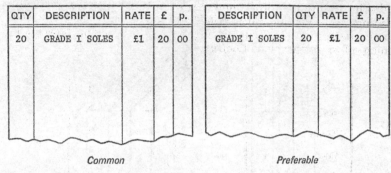

QTY	DESCRIPTION	RATE	£	p.
20	GRADE I SOLES	£1	20	00

Common

DESCRIPTION	QTY	RATE	£	p.
GRADE I SOLES	20	£1	20	00

Preferable

Fig. 22. It is obvious in which of these examples calculation is easier.

(3) Where extensions have to be calculated, as on an invoice, the quantity and rate should be adjacent and not divided by narration, as shown in Fig. 22.

(4) Where items have to be filled in for product and quantity, and the variety is not too great, omissions are avoided by having the item

Works order

COMPONENT	QTY
Side Panels	20
Rear Panels	5
Window Panels	2
Narrow Panels	–
Rear Posts	2

Invoice

DESCRIPTION	QTY	RATE	£	p.
Side Panels	20	£5	100	00
Rear Panels	5	£5	25	00
Window Panels	2	£6	12	00
Narrow Panels	–	–	–	–
Rear Posts	2	£4.10	8	20

Fig. 23. Two complementary forms showing printed items in same order.

descriptions preprinted. In this case it is essential that all complementary forms have the items printed in the same order, as illustrated in Fig. 23, otherwise mistakes of transposition are likely.

(5) Where a particular item, especially a figure, has to be picked out

from many, speed and accuracy can be assisted by emphasising such items in some way. Two very successful methods are to box round the item with thick lines, or to hatch the space lightly, as shown in Fig. 24.

(6) Where there are many columns of entries across the page—for example, statistical tabulations—every fifth and sixth row should be divided by a heavy line, lighter lines dividing the other rows. If there are no horizontal rulings a slightly wider space should be left between each fifth and sixth row. This helps the eye across the page and prevents it running off to another line of entries.

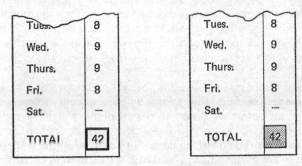

Fig. 24. Two methods of emphasising important information.

Finally, the question of paper sizes must be considered. Unless there are very strong grounds for doing otherwise, forms should be designed for standard paper sizes. Non-standard formats mean cutting paper to waste and extra cost, as well as leading to possible filing difficulties. Preference should be given to the international paper sizes, the most likely formats being A4 (210 mm × 297 mm) and A5 (148 mm × 210 mm).

Forms for Export Documentation

What has been written above is applicable to the design of any kind of form, from the simplest to the most complicated. However, organisations engaged in the export trade face a special problem in that forms for this purpose are both many in number and detailed in content. Efforts have been made, therefore, to simplify the documents concerned.

This has been done under the auspices of the Simplification of International Trade Procedures Board, more commonly referred to as SITPRO.

Anyone engaged in international trade is recommended to obtain a copy of SITPRO's publication entitled *Systematic Export Documentation*, in which will be found specimens of recommended forms for all export procedures, together with a great deal of technical advice on their production and use.

Control of Forms

Apart from the actual design of the forms, their issue, make-up and availability should also be a fixed responsibility and not left, as so often is the case, to heads of departments or supervisors. The job of forms control can be amalgamated with that of designer, or may be separate, depending very largely upon the size of the organisation. Where the functions are separate there is no doubt that the final authority should rest with the controller (by whatever title he is known). His main responsibilities will be to control the publication of forms and to ensure their most economical use, and to minimise the costs of production.

Under the heading of publication, he will make sure that **unnecessary forms** are **not produced** and that a form will be used only where necessary. Duplication of forms in different departments will be avoided, and forms will be circulated only to those needing them either for entry or for interpretation. To ensure efficiency in publication the controller will need to be aware of the office procedures as practised in his organisation and will need to know the purpose to which each copy of each form is put.

In order to avoid duplication and to identify each form, the controller will give each form a **code number**, and **maintain a file** holding a copy of each and every form used throughout his organisation. Repeat orders for forms from users should then be accepted only against the identifying code numbers. If the number of forms is very large it may be helpful for two files of forms to be kept, one in code order and one by form title.

Cost control embraces not only economy of use but also economy in the actual production of forms. Economy in use is achieved by ensuring that the number of entries required is at the minimum, as already discussed, that these entries are made in the quickest manner and that they can be read in the quickest way—the main features of good form design. Economy in production requires examination of paper and printing costs, and needs some knowledge of the different methods of production.

Finally, the controller will institute a **periodic review** of all the forms in use. Circumstances alter over the course of time, and occasionally it will be found that a form and the information on it have become redundant, even though the form is still being completed and circulated. If a periodic review is carried out such cases will come to light and can be remedied.

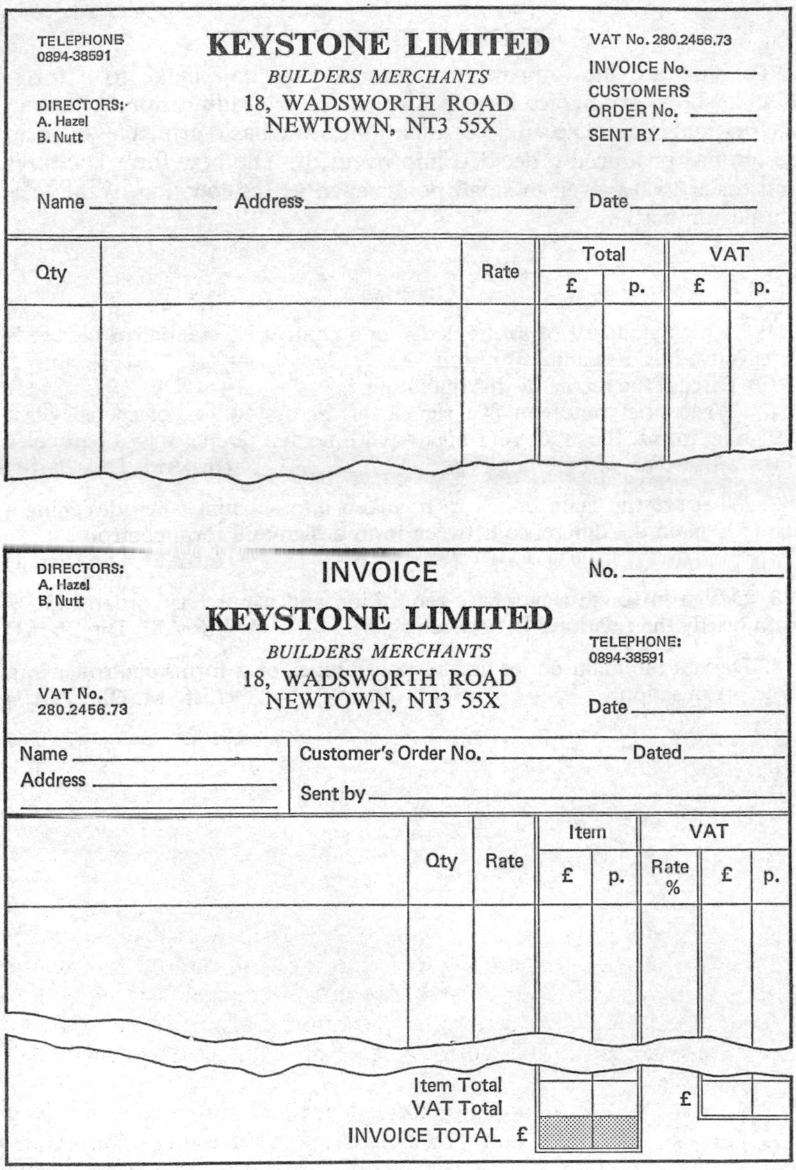

TELEPHONE
0894-38591

DIRECTORS:
A. Hazel
B. Nutt

KEYSTONE LIMITED
BUILDERS MERCHANTS
18, WADSWORTH ROAD
NEWTOWN, NT3 55X

VAT No. 280.2456.73
INVOICE No.
CUSTOMERS ORDER No.
SENT BY

Name Address Date

Qty		Rate	Total £	Total p.	VAT £	VAT p.

DIRECTORS:
A. Hazel
B. Nutt

INVOICE

No.

KEYSTONE LIMITED
BUILDERS MERCHANTS
18, WADSWORTH ROAD
NEWTOWN, NT3 55X

TELEPHONE:
0894-38591

VAT No.
280.2456.73

Date

Name
Address

Customer's Order No. Dated
Sent by

	Qty	Rate	Item £	Item p.	VAT Rate %	VAT £	VAT p.

Item Total
VAT Total
INVOICE TOTAL £
£

Fig. 25. Invoice form design. *Top:* invoice before modification. *Bottom:* invoice after modification. Note the clearer lay-out, form title, telephone number where it will not be hidden by possible corner fastenings, and other improvements.

A Specimen of an Improved Form

To illustrate the improvement good design can make to a form, Fig. 25 shows an invoice form before and after modification. Although the original is quite acceptable, attention to the basic principles of form design has produced a decided improvement. The new form is clearer and easier to use even in small points such as the location of the telephone number.

Questions

1. 'A high standard of forms design and control is essential to the needs of effective business administration.'
   (*a*) Discuss the merits of this quotation.
   (*b*) Write brief notes on five significant factors to be considered when designing forms. Illustrate your answer with textual reference to a particular form with which you are familiar. (InstAM, Dip. Part I)

2. What are the main points to be taken into account when designing a form? Explain the difference between form design and form control.
   (InstAM, Dip. Part I)

3. Design in rough a purchase requisition and a purchase order and explain briefly the relationship between them. (InstAM, Dip. Part I)

4. Discuss the main duties and responsibilities of a forms controller in a large organisation. (InstAM, Dip. Part I)

17

SOME ASPECTS OF WRITTEN LANGUAGE

Previously, we have examined the construction of different forms of written communication. In this chapter we look at various other aspects of this subject, and we shall begin with style.

Style

Style is an important element in written communication, but is extremely difficult to define. Very loosely, it means 'the way we write'. It is to do with the way we use words, the variety of our vocabulary, the length and rhythm of our sentences. Style is essentially a personal thing, like the way we walk and the way we eat, but nevertheless it can be improved by using thought and care. The use of long, ponderous sentences liberally laced with long and obscure words produces a dreary style that soon bores the reader. Replace the long words with those in more general use, and intersperse the long sentences with short ones, and immediately a brighter style emerges. Conversely, a style composed principally of short sentences constructed of words of one or two syllables presents a staccato effect that starts by being arresting but soon becomes irritating.

An example of a long sentence composed of long words, many not in everyday use, was given under the heading of Language in Chapter 2, and how dreary this sentence is. An example of the other extreme—short words and short sentences carried to excess—might be:

'The day was hot. The sun was strong. John took off his shirt. His back was wet with sweat. He could not walk much further. His feet were swollen. They began to ache. His boots hurt. How far was the next town? Six miles he had been told. Since then he had walked for two hours. Had he missed the way? His mouth was dry. His lips were sore. He must have a drink soon. His water bottle was empty. There was no sign of a stream. The pools were dried up. Why had he come out on such a day?'

At the beginning of this piece the staccato style grips the imagination, but before the end it palls. Without losing too much of the atmosphere the passage can be made to maintain interest and become easier to read by the use of long sentences in place of some of the short ones, so allowing the prose to flow more easily, thus:

'The day was hot. The sun was strong. John took off his shirt, revealing his back wet with sweat. He could not walk much further. His feet were swollen and aching and his boots had begun to hurt. How far was the next town? Since he had been told it was six miles on he had walked for two hours without sight of it. Had he missed his way? His lips were sore and his mouth was dry. He must have a drink but his water bottle was empty and there was no sign of a stream. Even the pools were dry. Why, oh why, had he come out on such a day?'

Perhaps more than anything, the **choice of words** influences style, and this is to a great extent governed by education, social environment and breadth of reading. One writer has estimated that the average educated person has a vocabulary of about 15 000 words which he understands. Yet the average person manages on about 2 000 words actively used and many people use considerably less. Further, 80 per cent of all that is written is accounted for by only 1 000 words. Because a person knows a large number of words, it does not mean that he uses them all in original communication. The greater proportion of them are recognised and understood when met in communication coming from others —books, newspapers and other media—and many are understood simply because their meanings are inferred from their context, or that their roots are recognised.

Vocabulary

English is remarkable in its ability to present nuances of meaning, but this calls for a wide, active vocabulary. It is, therefore, encumbent upon all who use the written word, including those who write reports, letters and other forms of communication, to increase their vocabulary so as to reduce the monotony of reading and to be able to present finer shades of meaning than would otherwise be the case. It must be remembered, also, that only rarely in English do two words have identical meanings. Thus, Chambers's Dictionary gives the synonyms of *pleasant* as *pleasing, cheerful, gay* and *facetious*, but it must be agreed that none of these substitute words exactly replaces the word *pleasant* in meaning, though in the first case the difference is very subtle.

Naturally, what has been said about vocabulary for writing applies equally to speaking, but here words come spontaneously and we are, therefore, less precise. When writing, for the most part, we have time and opportunity to select the exact word for our meaning. In verbal communication this can be done only for prepared speeches, lectures and in similar circumstances.

For those who are serious in their efforts to widen their vocabulary there are three valuable aids: these are a good dictionary, a dictionary of antonyms and synonyms and, for the really dedicated, Roget's *Thesaurus of English Words and Phrases*. The last publication is a very comprehensive survey of the English language, providing not only an exhaustive index of words and their synonyms and antonyms, but also relevant phrases.

Suit Your Style to Your Reader

Two things must be remembered when you attempt to reduce monotony in your writing. The first is the probable educational and technical level of your readers. A comparison of the styles used by the popular newspapers, such as *The Sun* or *The Daily Mirror*, with that employed by the so-called quality papers, such as *The Times* or *The Guardian*, will quickly reveal the difference in the two readerships. The second is that there is great variety in simple English words and recourse to long Latin- or Greek-based words is often unnecessary. In fact, it is often considered to be pretentious to use the latter. Unfortunately, however, it is also thought by some to signify intelligence or a good education, and so the use of this pretentious style is, sadly, becoming more common, and is tending to degrade the language.

It must be admitted that some writers adopt an elaborate way of expressing themselves, making use of many long words quite unnecessarily, to try to appear clever: sometimes they even reach the stage of being practically unintelligible. An interesting survey was carried out in America some years ago among some successful writers, asking them why they used such pretentious language. The replies were enlightening. Among them were the following: 'I use this kind of language otherwise my articles would not fetch so much'; and 'People would not think me knowledgeable if I did not write in this way'. One writer, when asked the meaning of one of his more obscure passages, could not even translate it himself! Since that time the situation in America seems to have become even worse, and there is a great deal of evidence that some British writers are following this example.

Technical Writing

Some difficulty is sometimes experienced in writing about technical matters. The approach here is to try to visualise your probable readers. If they are likely to be knowledgeable about your subject then it is usually safe to assume that they will understand the technical terms associated with it. In the case of readers not likely to be familiar with your subject matter it would be most unwise to presume that they will have any acquaintance with the relevant technical terms. Writing for such a readership can be quite a test of an author's skill with language. Quite frequently, fortunately, it is possible to use a technical term and explain it the first time, and thereafter assume the reader will understand it when it is subsequently used. In dealing with a photographic subject, for example, one might say, 'The depth of field—that is, the distance between the nearest and furthest points from the camera which is sharp when the lens is focused on any particular plane—is dependent upon the aperture—that is, the diameter of the opening of the lens. The smaller the aperture, the greater the depth of field.' Thereafter, in this piece, the author can confidently refer to both the depth of field and the aperture with the fair assumption that even a lay reader will understand the terms.

In general, the use of trade names as generic terms is to be avoided. Here again, though, such usage can help a lay person. Thus, the uninformed may be mystified by the description 'cylinder night-latch' but will readily understand 'Yale lock', though the compromise 'Yale-pattern lock' or 'Yale-type lock' might be more advisable, especially in a specification.

First or Third Person

Whether to use the first person or the third in writing sometimes poses a problem. In some cases there are accepted conventions, as in the writing of formal reports where the third person is normally employed. However, this manner of writing produces a stiff and often dreary style. If we wish our style to be alive and dynamic then we should use the first person which, by its very nature, indicates a measure of personal involvement. Consider these two examples:

The Board of Directors has given consideration to the holding of an office party again this year, but in view of the present economic difficulties, has decided against it. Nevertheless, the Board wishes to extend the compliments of the season to all staff.

Economic difficulties have forced us to cancel the usual office party this year. We are very sorry to disappoint you, but nevertheless wish you all a very happy Christmas.

(Signed) *Managing Director*

The first example, in the third person, is distant and cold, and bears no relation to the atmosphere that should obtain at Christmas time. It does, however, have authority and would seem to brook no argument. The second example, in the first person, brings some personal feeling into the message which makes it more alive.

Active or Passive Voice

The same remarks as applied to the use of the first or third person also apply to the active or the passive voice. The active voice is alive and tends to make the reader feel that he is being addressed personally: the passive voice often gives the impression that the reader is not personally involved but that he is a spectator in someone else's game. Contrast the following two examples:

When you are shopping in this supermarket would you please make sure that you use one of the baskets or trolleys provided.

Customers are requested to use the baskets or trolleys provided.

The first, in the active voice, positively invites the customers' co-operation: it is addressed directly to the shopper. The second, in the passive voice, lacks vitality and does not motivate the customer to comply with the request as an act of cooperation.

An argument often put forward against using the first person and against the use of the active voice is that they put the emphasis on the writer instead of on the subject. To some extent this is true, but in doing so the writer produces a positive feeling in his communication that is likely to result in a positive reaction in his readers.

Generally speaking it is found that the passive voice is used where formal communication is concerned—occasions such as official pronouncements, formal reports and the like. Informal reports entirely for internal circulation are often written entirely in the active voice, but a common construction is for the body of the report and the presentation of facts and findings to be in the passive voice, and the introduction, discussion, conclusions and, where given, recommendations to be in the active voice. This method gives authority to the factual part of the report and disassociates it from positive involvement by the writer, and at the same time indicates his personal involvement in reaching conclusions and the steps that led up to his decisions.

Similarly, the use of the active voice in letters rather than the passive voice gives a dynamic impression to the reader: for this reason the active voice is especially useful in the composition of sales letters. In fact, it is noticeable that there is a distinct trend in written communications, even in business letters, to use a more dynamic presentation. This is probably due, in some part at least, to the less formal attitudes that have become prevalent in modern society.

Positive and Negative Statements

When we consider the style in which to write a communication we should try to determine whether we wish only to give information, or whether we wish to influence the reader to take some positive action. It can be said that action flows from positive statements whilst inaction most usually results from negative ones. It is a common ploy by salesmen always to put questions to their prospective customers that require 'yes' answers, never questions that will evoke a 'no' response. The basis of this practice is to induce a positive attitude in the customer's mind so that he will think positively when the time comes to close the sale. Similarly, in any written communication that demands a positive reaction in the reader, the writer should try to generate this positive style so that the reader is influenced to be persuaded by the communication. This practice is not so important where a communication is for information only, but even in this case positive language is to be preferred to negative language.

Subjectivity and Objectivity

Almost all communication is subjective to some degree, and it is usually necessary to make an effort to be completely objective. What do we mean by these two terms? Being subjective means allowing our own opinion or attitude to colour our statements, perhaps to modify facts, whereas being objective requires us to forget entirely our personal prejudices and to communicate entirely on the basis of facts as they are.

If you say that a building is high, that is a subjective statement. To you the building may be high, but to a New Yorker it may be quite low. On the other hand, if you say that the building is 14 storeys high, this is an objective statement and your opinion does not enter into the communication.

There are times when subjectivity is useful and times when it is essential to be completely objective in our statements. If a customer is worrying about the delivery of his order he will be more impressed with an objective statement telling him precisely when his goods will arrive than any subjective statement about an expected delivery date. However, when we are communicating through advertisements or sales letters, and seeking to persuade or influence potential customers in favour of our products, then some subjectivity is necessary and, of course, expected. The facts about our goods will be embellished by our high opinion of them, and this must be communicated to possible buyers.

Generally speaking, it is accepted that objectivity demands an authoritative style of writing, using the third person and the passive voice, because objectivity tends to be impersonal, whereas subjectivity assumes the personal touch using the first person and the active voice. However, this is not necessarily so. 'I saw the boat strike the rock and watched it sink in five minutes' is an objective statement in both the first person and in the active voice. Conversely, no less subjective is 'Sue said that the temperature was rather high', even though it is written in the third person, passive voice.

Thoughtful use of both objectivity and subjectivity can help us produce in our written communication just the effect we want, matter-of-fact, persuasive, authoritative.

Sentence Structure

The structure of sentences plays a very large part in writing good, effective English. In particular, the order in which the words are placed affects the meaning of the sentence and writers often actually say what they do not mean to say.

The **normal word order** is subject, verb, object or complement. However, English is very flexible and by altering the order in which the words occur we can change the meaning of a sentence completely, or merely give a change of emphasis. As an example of the latter, compare the two following sentences:

(*a*) A professional qualification will increase your chances of promotion.

(*b*) Your chances of promotion will be increased by your having a professional qualification.

In sentence (*a*) the emphasis is on the professional qualification whereas in (*b*) it is on the chances of promotion.

There are a number of **words** that are **commonly misplaced** with the result that the author does not actually say what he really means. 'Only' is, perhaps, the most common of these words and we will now examine a few examples of its misuse. It is important that 'only' should in normal circumstances be placed nearest the word it qualifies, otherwise ambiguity can be created. Thus, consider:

'His rheumatism can only be relieved by the new drug.'

This can mean one of two things. Either the new drug can do nothing except relieve the man's rheumatism, or only the new drug can effect some relief. Strictly speaking, as written, the former interpretation is the correct one, but so common is it for writers to misplace 'only' that it is highly probable the second interpretation was in the author's mind.

Such is the flexibility of the English language, however, that we **may deliberately place a word in the wrong order** to make a statement more graphic than if the sentence structure were grammatically correct. 'The temperature will remain above 1°C only in the south of England' may be precisely correct, but it does not give the feeling of a land suffering from intense cold everywhere except in the south as does the sentence 'the temperature will only remain above 1°C in the south of England'. Strictly speaking, in the second sentence 'only' qualifies 'remain' and not 'south of England', but only a pedant would interpret it in this way.

The misplacing of words, and also phrases, is a common trap for the writer and there are many humorous examples of this fault. The remedy is simple. When you write, look at your work objectively and make sure that you have put the words in the order that will make the sense you are trying to convey. Formal grammar has no place in a book such as this. All that is really needed to ensure correct word placing is common sense and care.

The **importance of word order** can be illustrated by some examples of deliberate changes and their effects. Think about the following:

(1) 'I am not even going out tonight.'
(2) 'I am not going out even tonight.'
(3) 'Even I am not going out tonight.'

Only the word 'even' has altered its position, but each sentence means something different.

The Length of Sentences

Thus, the placing of words in sentences and the kinds of words you use need thought and care. Sentence length is also something that must be carefully considered. Almost all authorities on written English agree that short sentences are more effective than long ones in achieving clarity of expression. This is because short sentences make less demands on the reader for the retention of ideas in his mind. The end of a sentence gives the reader a short rest that enables him to digest the purport of the sentence he has just read. Long sentences, on the other hand, require the reader to retain in his mind the ideas expressed for a much longer time. Thus, the content of long sentences can be more difficult to assimilate because of the greater effort involved. The following is an **example of a long sentence** that illustrates this:

'In recent years the difficulty experienced in most districts in recruiting new staff to the clerical grade has considerably diminished and from recently published information from authoritative sources on the number of boys and girls who will reach the age of sixteen during the period 1980–1995 it is highly probable that there will be particularly in the years 1988, 1989 and 1990 a significant surplus of young people available for employment.'

As it stands this long sentence is clear but it is not easy to read. This is because it requires a number of clauses to be retained in the reader's mind until the end. Slightly modified, using shorter sentences to tell the story, it becomes easier to read and, therefore, easier to understand:

'The difficulty experienced in most districts in recent years in recruiting new staff to the clerical grade has considerably diminished. Moreover, information recently published by authoritative sources shows a considerable increase in the number of boys and girls reaching the age of sixteen during the period 1980–1995. These figures suggest that there will be a significant surplus of young people available for employment, particularly in the years 1988–1990.'

It can readily be seen that written communication can be made more readable and more easily understood by using short sentences instead of long ones. Where long, complex sentences have been employed the piece can be redrafted, using shorter ones, with a clear improvement in comprehensibility.

One of the contributory factors to lengthy sentences is the tendency nowadays to use **wordy phrases** instead of single words or short phrases. This habit is especially prevalent in American writing, and in the work of British authors who imitate the American style. It might be said that some writers will not use one word where several will do. For example, 'speak' becomes 'formulate a verbal utterance'. Even in the example just given of improving a long sentence, the second version could be further shortened by substituting 'clerical staff' for 'staff to the clerical grade', using only two words instead of five without loss of meaning. Below are given some examples of commonly used phrases that could be shortened to one or two words with a consequent reduction in verbosity:

Long (Avoid)	*Short (Preferred)*
In very few cases	Seldom
Has a tendency to	Tends to
It is obvious that	Obviously
In the vicinity of	Near
For the reason that	For
In the event of	If
Have a dialogue	Discuss
Take into consideration	Consider
It will be noticed that	(This phrase is usually superfluous)

It is also necessary to take care about the actual words we use in our communications. Just as there is a tendency nowadays to use phrases instead of words, there is also the tendency to use long words instead of short ones, a point that has already been mentioned. Some examples of these might not be out of place:

Long	Short
Assist	Help
Locate	Find
Procure	Buy
Commence	Start
Terminate	End
Elevate	Raise
Aggravate	Worsen

In considering the need to shorten our written communications, it is worth remembering that new developments and techniques in preparing these communications are all the time speeding up this process: as we saw in Chapter 14 some word processing installations are capable of between 200 and 300 words per minute. It makes nonsense of these advances if our actual texts are unnecessarily long because of the use of verbose language.

English Usage versus American Usage

It would be as well at this stage to remember that American usage of our language is very different from our own, and that the Americans are past-masters of long words and wordy statements. If we wish to be succinct and clear in our writing we must avoid their construction and keep to the suggestions already made in this chapter. The American language is overlaid with multiple prepositions and is very prone to verbosity. To avoid American word usage, phraseology and sentence structure is in no small measure to avoid wordiness and lack of clarity. However, American films, television productions, radio and textbooks are part of our lives and it is very difficult to avoid being influenced by their usage of our language.

Just one or two examples will illustrate the American way compared to the British way:

American	English
Meet up with	Meet
This point in time	Now; at present
Miss out on	Fail; miss
Regular	Normal
Figure	Think
Terminal	Fatal
Let up on	Stop; cease

Whenever you find a phrase that has two prepositions following each other—'lose out on', for example—you can be sure this is an American import and you should consider carefully whether this should not be rewritten in English. The American love for long words is also illustrated above. Each example has one syllable more than the English equivalent, and there are very many others such as 'elevator' for 'lift', 'compensation' for 'wages' and so on. An extreme example of American verbosity is that of naughty children being described as 'children who are not functioning well in a particular behavioural dimension'.

Despite these remarks on the American way with English, we must not forget that the Americans have also contributed some useful additions to our normal language which, whilst often not yet wholly accepted here in the written form, are nevertheless very much to the point. It is difficult, for example, to find a short substitute for 'meaningful', and though ugly, 'institutionalise' says a lot in one word.

In purely spoken language, the phrase 'You're welcome' has no British equivalent that conveys the same feeling.

It follows, therefore, that all Americanisms must not be condemned out of hand; the user must just be careful to be very selective. After all, English owes much of its richness and variety to imports from abroad.

Finally, we must remember that Americans often use different words from those we use to describe a variety of things, as the following short list will show:

American	*English*
Suspenders	Braces
Braces	Garters
Candy	Sweets
Subway (train)	Underground (train)
Sidewalk	Pavement
Gasoline (also Gas)	Petrol

Jargon

Most professions, sciences and trades develop a special vocabulary of their own which practitioners use and understand, and which may be incomprehensible to those outside these particular circles. This is known as jargon. Often the words and phrases used are technical and often they are a sort of shorthand for the convenient, rapid passing on of information. As jargon is the product of a specific activity its use amongst people practising that activity is perfectly legitimate, whether the communication is written or spoken. However, its use is best avoided when the specialist is trying to communicate with a member of the lay public, especially if the communication is in writing. When addressing other salesmen, it is perfectly in order for a salesman to discuss the 'cold canvas'. It would be quite wrong to use this expression to members of the general public because to them it would be completely incomprehensible. Similarly, a photographer using the term 'bounce flash' would be unintelligible to a holiday snapshotter. Where a communication is for a mixed readership the most sensible thing to do is for the author to provide a glossary of technical terms and professional jargon.

Another form of jargon is that which has become a custom in certain circumstances. This particular form has been the subject of much criticism from writers on English for a very long time. The most common examples are those used in business letters and include:

'Referring to your letter of the . . .'
'Assuring you of our best attention'
'Thanking you in anticipation of your kind order'

and there are very many more.

All of these phrases sound old-fashioned and none of them advances the message. It is for these reasons that experts in English wish them to be dropped. On the other hand, the more dynamic and direct approach recommended may seem to many business people to be lacking in politeness and courtesy, sentiments that are certainly displayed in the last two examples above. Furthermore, this jargon is used almost unconsciously by writers of business letters and often serves as a means of overcoming the inertia sometimes experienced in starting or finishing a letter.

So, while we might applaud the omission of the first phrase 'Referring to your letter . . .' in favour of plunging straight into the subject of the communication, we must be careful not to drop the second two without putting something courteous in their place, which will, in turn, become jargon. Compare the following two letters:

Dear Sirs,
Referring to your letter of the 12th April, we are pleased to quote you as follows:

2 'Maximillia' grates @ £25 each	£50·00
1 'Tudorite' surround @ £30	30·00
	£80·00

Prices are net delivered to your address.
Thanking you in anticipation of your kind order,

We are,
Yours faithfully
. . . .

Gentlemen,

Your letter 12.4.79

Our prices are as follows:

2 'Maximillia' grates @ £25 each, net		£50·00
1 'Tudorite' surround @ £30 net		30·00
		£80·00

delivered to your address.

Yours truly,

. . . .

Slang

Unlike some foreign languages, English has no central academy to regulate its use or its growth and it is thus constantly altering and being enlarged without deliberate reference to precedent. Yet few new words are deliberately coined. Often they begin as slang and gradually they become part of accepted language if they perform a real purpose and fill a lack, or they die. How they arise is hard to discover. A new situation needs a new means of expression, some writer or speaker tries to be different; a specialist group needs to name a new idea or a new device. Much slang would never, in fact, be heard or used by the public if it were not used eventually in films or plays, or other literary works.

Slang is not admissible in formal writing and herein lies a problem for the writer: when does a word cease to be slang and become acceptable? For example, the word 'job' is now used in formal communications of all kinds, yet not very many years ago it was a slang term and not admissible. Constant use in the spoken language and its adoption by the personnel profession and others has made its use legitimate.

Another problem for the author is to determine when an accepted slang word has gone out of fashion, because although slang is usually expressive it often has a very limited life. Among the slang expressions in current use, even in the written word, are 'escalate', 'breakthrough' and 'redundant' (in connection with loss of employment). At best they will become part of the language and acceptable in all written communications; at worst they will fall into disuse, when any writing containing them will sound very dated.

Clichés

These are hackneyed expressions, often figurative, that have lost their freshness through over-use. Nevertheless, they are the mainstay of a lot of writing, and whether to use them or not is a matter of opinion. Any alternative way of saying what they mean would frequently require many more words, and so lose the pithiness of their expression. On the other hand, a skilful writer should try to create new forms of expression to communicate his ideas, and avoid too much reliance on clichés.

Some examples of common clichés are:

'Part and parcel'
'Nest egg'
'Flash in the pan'
'Done to death'

They are expressive and brief. Could they be improved upon?

In one chapter it has been possible only to touch on the various aspects of written language, some of which, of course, also apply to the spoken word. Those of you who would like to go further into this study would find a very great deal of useful and appropriate material in *English Made Simple*, a companion volume to this.

Questions

1. What are the principles of style (choosing words, arranging sentences and paragraphs) which make for good reports and letters?

(CIT, Intermediate)

2. What is the difference between active and passive sentences? Give examples and say which you prefer and why. (CIT, Intermediate—adapted)

3. Discuss objectivity and subjectivity as qualities of communication. In what circumstances would you prefer one to the other? Does objectivity necessarily imply an impersonal style of writing? (CIT, Intermediate)

4. What is a cliché? Give four examples and suggest an alternative form of wording for one of them. (AIA, Foundation Part A)

18

THE SUMMARY OR PRÉCIS

The Need for Summaries

We are, in these days of swift and easy communication, in danger of being submerged in a sea of paper. Business managers, in particular, are faced with oceans of correspondence, reports, discussion papers and other forms of written communication all claiming attention. Similarly, there are endless streams of books and journals full of useful information which the manager should read, but for which he just has not enough time: in fact, there is a thriving section of the publishing industry that specialises in publishing abstracts of technical articles in an endeavour to keep the manager up to date in his field without his having to read through thousands of unnecessary words in the originals.

The skill to summarise or make précis of reports, articles and other written information is, therefore, a very valuable one, and this chapter is devoted to some simple rules applicable to this skill.

Simple Rules for Writing a Summary

First, the **subject matter.** It is not possible to make a sensible summary unless we fully comprehend the theme and subject matter of the source material. In order to do this it is necessary to read the original right through very carefully so as to gain a sense of its meaning and intent. At this stage refrain from making any notes: concentrate on understanding.

Secondly, **note-taking.** The next step is to read the original through a second time, underlining the passages that we feel are significant to the theme, making sure that important points are so marked and unnecessary points ignored. From these underlined passages we can now make notes from which to write up our summary. These notes should be in our own words, and not a repetition of the words and phrases occurring in the original. It is likely at this stage that we can condense the underlined passages by simplifying the language and using words instead of phrases. At all costs, however, we must preserve the meaning and intent of the original work, and care must be taken that we do not introduce any personal slant or bias into our notes.

Thirdly, the **first draft.** It is rarely possible to make a satisfactory summary or précis at the first attempt and so, using our notes, it is necessary to prepare a draft summary. This draft must be written from the notes we have made, and without reference to the source material. This ensures that the summary is entirely in our own style, and that we are not tempted to embellish it with any of the author's original turns of phrase: this might lead to a lengthening of our précis. This is not to suggest that we must rigorously exclude all wording and phrasing from the original, but it is usually wiser to include as little as possible.

Fourthly, the **first draft** must be **edited**. To do this we must first read through it carefully to ascertain that it is written in acceptable language, and that its length is within the limits set. At this point the difference between a précis written for an English examination and a summary written for business purposes must be understood. The examiner usually sets a word number limit, or a proportion limit (a quarter or a third of the original) as a target. On the other hand, a business summary must be as short as it possibly can be without sacrificing anything by way of purport or intent.

Having read our work and made corrections where necessary to improve our phraseology, language and so on, we must now **compare** our **summary with** the **original** to check that we have retained all the sense and meaning of the original, and that we have achieved a suitable length.

Finally, having edited our first draft, we may go on, if time permits, to write a **second draft** for further editing. However, such are the usual pressures of time, we shall probably now prepare our final, completed summary. The précis for an examination presents no problems: one copy will be written on our answer paper. Business summaries, though, may require further consideration. Often it is preferable to subdivide the summary with headings. These give the scope of the summary at a glance and, in some cases, may allow us to condense our summary even further. In addition, the summary may have to be produced in several copies so the matter of reproduction must have attention. Three or four copies could be photocopied from an original typing, but two or three dozen copies may entail the original being typed on to a duplicator master. If the summary is of a very long report and itself, therefore, runs into several pages, some form of binding may be necessary. Any instructions of this nature must be complied with.

A Worked Example

As an example of précis-writing, perhaps we could have a look at a question asked by the Institute of Chartered Secretaries and Administrators in one of their examination papers on 'Communication':

Using your own words as far as is possible, write a summary of the following passage of about 500 words from *The Times*. Use not more than 150 words. Supply a title and state the number of words you have used.

The growing awareness of consumer protection issues has focused fresh attention on advertisements and what can and cannot be said in them. It is argued that the consumer buys products on the basis of information contained in advertisements and that the information should be accurate and fairly presented. All sides of the industry are acutely aware that this has not always been the case. The history of advertising is littered with examples of false and misleading statements made in an (often successful) attempt to make people part with their money.

In most developed countries there is legislation to prevent outright dishonesty, and media proprietors, and others on whom some of the stigma inevitably rubs off, see it as in their own best interest to make sure that this is observed. There is, however, a wide area where advertisements which although not unlawful may be said to harm the consumer in some way, or may be considered undesirable on other grounds such as decency, taste or morals. It is that area which is coming under new scrutiny, especially in Britain. In the past year an existing code of practice agreed by advertisers and advertising agencies as well as by media proprietors has been strengthened. Starting in January a scheme to raise funds by a self-imposed 1 per cent levy on all advertisements except television and radio has come into operation to finance the new measures. Special voluntary regulations for alcoholic drink products have been introduced and a separate tobacco code is expected shortly. In Britain the scheme is administered by the Advertising Standards Authority, which is concerned to see that all advertising should be 'legal, decent, honest and truthful'. The voluntary regulations operate against a background of legal controls. There are more than 60 laws affecting either advertising in general or specialised areas of it in Britain. Among the most important is the Trade Description Act 1968, which prohibits false and misleading statements about goods and services, including their cost.

False and misleading statements are also a specific offence under French law whether published copy, visual or spoken word. The officials responsible for verifying infringements are empowered to require advertisers to substantiate their statements. If they cannot, the law makes provision for corrective advertising at the discretion of the judge. It is also forbidden under French law to make any comparisons with competitors' products, since that is seen as an infringement of article 1382 of the civil code which prohibits unfair competition. Neither of these requirements exists in the British controls. In Italy there is a voluntary code of advertising practice approved by the National Federation of Italian Advertisers and modelled on similar lines to that in use in Britain. The German laws on advertising are much more specific and restrictive. It is a legal requirement that advertising statements must be true. In addition advertisements must not refer to competitors either directly or indirectly, in a way that might interfere with the latter's competitive chances.

Suggested answer:

Advertising Controls

The Times reported that increasing consumer protection had led to a fresh examination of misleading advertisements to ensure that people were not falsely parted from their money.

Most countries had legislation against dishonest advertising: people in the profession appreciated that offences against decency, taste or morals were undesirable in the interests of both advertisers and customers.

A new scheme had started in January, financed by a 1 per cent levy on all advertising, except that broadcast, to enforce a strengthened voluntary code of practice. The Advertising Standards Authority would use this fund to ensure that all advertising was 'legal, decent, honest and truthful' as required by various British legislation.

Continental countries had enacted legal bans on untrue advertisements and *The Times* specifically mentioned France and Germany as having especially severe restrictions. In both these countries it was forbidden to mention competitors or their products, something allowed in Britain.

Total number of words in précis: 150.

Of course, there are many possible summaries that could have been written in answer to this question and the one above is not offered as the only solution. However, any answer must embrace the essential points of the original and bring out the essence of the piece.

Tense

It will be noticed that the tense used in the original piece was the present, whereas that used in the summary was the past tense. Some rules on this will, therefore, not be out of place.

First, it is usual to write a summary in reported speech—that is, indirect and not direct speech. Thus, the précis above started '*The Times* reported that . . .'

Second, the use of the past tense is customary where the original is written in the present tense. Where the original is already in the past tense the summary will make use of the past perfect. 'He ran', for example, will become 'He had run'.

It must be said, however, that these two rules are not universally held, and there is nothing intrinsically wrong in writing a summary in the present tense or in direct speech. Nevertheless, anyone attempting a précis in an examination could not be faulted if he or she used the customary method, whereas an examiner might take exception to the use of the alternative form.

Third, good English is essential, however much the original must be curtailed.

Summarising Correspondence

It is not unusual, particularly in business, for a summary of the contents of a series of letters or memoranda to be required. The problem is the same as that encountered in the writing of a précis, and the same rules apply. However, here we are dealing with a series of state-

ments and not a single, continuous piece of writing. The first step,
therefore, is to arrange the letters in order of date, to read them carefully, and to discard any that have no importance to the narrative, such
as acknowledgements of forms or letters. The next step is to list the
dates of the letters and to write beside these dates the essential content
of each letter. The summary is then completed by welding these notes
into a continuous narrative, ready for editing. Remember, good
flowing English is required and the urge to use stilted language in the
manner of a telegram, to save words, must be resisted.

A Worked Example

The following is an example of a series of letters and a summary
concerning M. Austine's policy excess:

The Letters

> 40 Pennylets Lane,
> Stoke Regis,
> Newshire.
>
> 4th April, 19..

Mr P. J. Alton,
20 Wembol Cove,
Woodville, Oldshire.

Dear Mr Alton,
 Referring to the accident in Stoke Regis on the 3rd April, when your van
hit the back of our car RLB 914 N when it was stationary waiting to turn
into Wellingford Street, I have put the matter into the hands of my insurers,
Commercial General Insurance Ltd, of 89 High Street, Stoke Regis.
 I am awaiting the quotation for the necessary repairs to our car, but mean-
while I am instructed by my insurers to claim on you personally for the excess
on my policy of £10.
 Any claim in excess of this amount will be made by Commercial General
Insurance Ltd.

> Yours truly,
> (M. Austine)

Modern Broking Services,
88 Social Road,
Woodville, Olds.

11th April, 19..

M. Austine, Esq.,
40 Pennylets Lane,
Stoke Regis, News.

Dear Mr Austine,
  We are in receipt of your letter dated 4th April addressed to our Client, Mr P. J. Alton, and are writing to advise you that it has been passed to his Insurers, the Domestic Motor Insurance Group, 77 Lower Hill Road, Islington. He is insured under their policy No. 7916721/18/3 and they will be dealing with any claim for uninsured loss which you may wish to make.

Yours sincerely,
(Modern Broking Services)

---

40 Pennylets Lane,
Stoke Regis,
Newshire.

12th April, 19..

Domestic Motor Insurance Group,
77 Lower Hill Road,
Islington.

Dear Sirs,
Your Client Mr P. J. Alton,
Policy No. 7916721/18/3
  I have been directed by Modern Broking Services of 88 Social Road, Woodville, Oldshire, to apply to you in respect of my claim for damages to my car, caused when Mr Alton's van ran into the back of it on the 3rd April last.
  My own insurers, Commercial General Insurance Ltd, of 89 High Street, Stoke Regis, have my completed claim form, but I was instructed by them to apply to Mr Alton direct for the £10 excess on my policy. No doubt you will be hearing from Commercial General, but meanwhile I should be glad of your cheque to cover the excess referred to.

Yours faithfully,
(M. Austine)

Domestic Motor Insurance Group,
77 Lower Hill Road,
Islington, London.

19th April, 19..

M. Austine, Esq.,
40 Pennylets Lane,
Stoke Regis, News.

Dear Sir,

Re: Our Insured—P. J. Alton.
Accident on 3.4.19..

Further to your letter dated the 12th April, entirely without prejudice we await sight of the receipted account in respect of your £10 Policy Excess, when further consideration will be given to your claim.

Yours faithfully,
(E. O. Silcote)
for Branch Manager.

40 Pennylets Lane,
Stoke Regis,
Newshire.

27th April, 19..

Domestic Motor Insurance Group,
77 Lower Hill Road,
Islington.

Dear Sirs,

Your Insured—Mr P. J. Alton.
Accident on 3.4.19..

Thank you for your letter of the 19th April.

Owing to domestic difficulties I shall not be able to put my car in for the necessary repairs arising out of the above accident until July or August.

I shall be happy to forward you the receipted garage account for the repairs after that time, although I expect my own insurers will want to see it first to make out their claim against you. An alternative suggestion is for you to clear my claim of £10 excess now, to get it out of the way, and we can deal with the full account when the repairs have been done.

Yours faithfully,
(M. Austine)

Domestic Motor Insurance Group,
77 Lower Hill Road,
Islington, London.

25th May, 19..

M. Austine, Esq.,
40 Pennylets Lane,
Stoke Regis, News.
Dear Sir,

Re: Our Insured—P. J. Alton.
Accident on 3.4.19..

Further to your letter dated the 27th April, in view of your remarks we are willing, in this instance, to deal with your claim for £10 excess immediately, without prejudice.

We, therefore, enclose our cheque for this amount and should be glad of your acknowledgement in due course on the accompanying slip.

Yours faithfully,
(E. O. Silcote)
for Branch Manager.

Summary of this Correspondence

Summary of claim for insurance excess made by Mr M. Austine on Mr P. J. Alton, resulting from Mr Alton's van running into the back of Mr Austine's car.

On 4th April Mr M. Austine claimed from Mr P. J. Alton the sum of £10 policy excess, arising from an accident on 3rd April when Mr Alton drove his van into the back of Mr Austine's car. Initially Mr Alton's insurers, the Domestic Motor Insurance Group, requested a receipted account for the repairs. On Mr Austine's protestation that he could not put his car in for repairs until July or August, however, the insurers sent him a cheque for £10 on 25th May.

It will be noticed that this summary gives all the essential information about this case and that it has not been necessary to refer at all to most of the correspondence. For example, reference to Modern Broking Services' letter has been completely omitted without detriment to a full understanding of the matter.

Questions

1. (*a*) What rules would you follow when preparing a précis of an article?
(*b*) What steps would you take before preparing the draft of a summary of some correspondence, and how would you subsequently proceed?

2. Using your own words as far as is possible, write a summary of the following passage of about 500 words from *The Times*. Use not more than 150 words. Supply a title and state the number of words you have used.

One of the most useful single devices yet invented for world development is an electronic eye in the sky, circling 567 miles above the earth. From its near-polar orbit the Landsat 11 land-scanning satellite, launched by the United States in 1975, scans the earth continuously, sending back a mass of information invaluable for agriculture, forestry, mineral exploration, mapping, land management and soil use. Scientists in the United States are using it experimentally to monitor and estimate yields, and to detect the presence of pests and disease often before the farmers themselves are aware of them. In little mapped and explored areas of the Third World it can indicate where mineralogists could profitably prospect for deposits of, say, copper. Its visual image of the earth's surface is so accurate that it can be used for small-scale mapping. Landsat 11 information can make a large contribution towards the production of more food in the world by showing untouched areas suitable for cultivation or grazing, or by indicating water courses and drainage systems which could be used for irrigation.

Landsat 11 is only one of a number of earth-scanning meteorological and other satellites now circling the earth whose future potentialities for the progress of man can still only be guessed at. The United Nations Food and Agriculture Organisation (FAO), quick to realise the value of satellite and aerial sensing, set up its own sensing unit in 1975 to pass on its benefits to member countries, particularly in the Third World. FAO experts are now experimenting with the use of data from Landsat and other types of satellite in the fight against desert locusts. A satellite cannot 'see' locusts but it spots the conditions in which swarms breed—the appearance of fresh vegetation after heavy rainfall in arid areas. This information can alert locust-prone countries to deal with the swarms before they set out to ravage vast areas of land. FAO has been using satellite data to track the progress of the Indian monsoon and is studying ways to monitor the growth of deserts. Work is in progress on a plan to enable scientists to predict crop yields by combining Landsat data with meteorological information. The future development of the plan depends largely on whether more accurate weather forecasting techniques can be achieved.

Satellites, however, are only the latest and most advanced of many remote sensing devices. Probably man's first attempt to gain information about the earth's unseen resources was water divining. Other techniques include magnetometry used by geologists and sonar soundings from ships. But the real breakthrough came with aviation and the development of aerial photography and radar. Aerial photography, whether from balloons, helicopters or high-flying aircraft, is still widely used and remains the best method for highly detailed work. The advent of colour and infra-red photography has increased its scope. (ICSA, Part I)

3. Summarise into not more than 100 words, the following article from *The Guardian*:

A fundamental and exhaustive review of all insolvency and bankruptcy laws in England and Wales is to be undertaken by an independent committee headed by Mr Kenneth Cork, the City's favourite liquidator.

Mr Edmund Dell, Secretary of State for Trade, announced the far-ranging review in a written reply in the Commons yesterday. Scottish insolvency laws are currently being reviewed by the Scottish Law Commission.

Mr Cork, who will be unpaid for his services apart from expenses, will head a committee composed of around a dozen representatives of the legal, accountancy and banking professions. A report is expected within two to three years.

Pressure for reform of the insolvency laws came to a head during the committee stage of the short Insolvency Bill currently passing through the Commons. The Bill reaches the third reading and report stage today and will raise the monetary limit for a debtor's petition from £50 to £300.

The basis of most bankruptcy law in England and Wales is the Bankruptcy Act of 1883 which established the £50 limit. The Blagden Committee looked at the problem in 1957 and the Jenkins Committee on Company Law which reported in 1962 suggested reforms in the insolvency laws. These were incorporated in the Tories' 1973 Companies Bill.

So a fundamental review is long overdue and there has been increasing pressure for reform in recent years, particularly from the Law Society and the Bar Council. Last night the Law Society welcomed the review committee and confirmed that the solicitors' body was strongly in favour of an extended look at the insolvency laws.

The Department of Trade has consulted about 40 bodies before announcing the Cork Committee, including lawyers, accountants, bankers and members of finance houses.

The underlying aim of the review is to streamline legislation on insolvency and in particular to bring together laws relating to corporate bankruptcy and liquidation and the bankruptcy of private individuals. Most Common Market countries adopt such a unified system and there is at present a draft EEC convention on bankruptcy laws under discussion.

(AIA, Foundation Part A)

19

SOURCES OF INFORMATION

There are very many occasions when we have to consult outside sources either to gather additional information or to check what we already have, and in this chapter we shall have a look at ways and means of doing this.

An ever increasing volume of information is published nowadays on every subject one can think of from accountancy to zoology, and each has its own standard works which should be the first to be consulted for basic knowledge. So rapid is the advance of knowledge these days, however, that it is necessary to supplement basic reading of standard works with consultation of other writings on the same subject. It is also essential to consult the latest editions of all publications.

The Public Library

The most convenient source of textbooks and technical works is the public library. A member of the British public library system has at his command the written knowledge of all the experts on every area of study that man has engaged in, and what is not on the shelves of the local library can be obtained from any other library in the United Kingdom or abroad. On the rare occasions when the local library is unable to borrow a required book from another library then sympathetic consideration is given to the purchase of such a volume. Such purchases can be authorised, naturally, only if a sufficient demand can be established by the librarian. However, this point seems to be liberally interpreted.

The Dewey System

Every library has a very comprehensive indexing system so that required books can be easily located on the library shelves. Almost without exception it is possible to look up a book under subject, author and in some cases title. The most popular indexing method is the Dewey system, in which broad subject areas are numerically classified. Specific subject areas are then subdivided within the broad classifications, and further subdivision is carried out as necessary until it is possible to pinpoint any particular book on the shelves. Where the Dewey system operates the indexes are usually supported by a numerical or classified index. On consulting the author or subject index one finds the Dewey index number, which, on reference, indicates all the books stocked in that area by the library in question.

In essence, the Dewey system is a simple one but, unfortunately, it was devised before the number of separate subject areas was as large as it is now: this has put something of a strain on the classification. It is a decimal system, the digits 0 to 9 each covering a specific division of knowledge. At one time study areas could be subdivided comfortably within the main ten categories, but the enormous increase in research and in the consequent expansion in the knowledge available in specific parts of subjects, and in the advent of new subjects altogether, have stretched the Dewey system considerably. An example will serve to make this clear.

It is only comparatively recently that management has become a study in its own right, and this study has brought with it an ever increasing supply of textbooks and other writings on the subject. In addition, many separate, specialised, areas of management study have developed demanding a special subcategory of their own. The Dewey system copes with this problem by first designating the general area of knowledge as a part of an existing division, and then progressively subdivides by category until, as far as possible, the final index number shows the precise contents of the book being indexed. Thus, business is designated as a technology, and the Dewey main index number for technology is 600. As a subdivision of technology, business is given the index number 50. Management, being a subject concerned with business studies, is then classified as a subdivision of business, and is indexed as 8. So a book on the general subject of management will be found under the index number 658. In order that a volume may be easily located on the shelves the librarian further assists the seeker by suffixing the Dewey number with the first three letters of the author's name so that, in theory, it should be possible to find the precise position of any book by the index number. *Management Made Simple*, for instance, will be located at 658 COV, the three letters being derived from the author's name, William F. Coventry.

Further modification of the index number will take place as the topics covered become more specific, the modification being in the form of additional digits placed after a decimal point. In this way, for example, a volume about management information systems and the use of the computer for this purpose has the index number 658.403, followed by the first three letters of the author's surname.

The use of the Dewey system to enable you to locate books in the library, therefore, seems quite straightforward: and it can be. A problem arises, however, where you have to look up a book the main classification of which is open to opinion. Communication is one such subject. This may be variously found under 000, 300 or 600 (modified to 658). When consulting the index, therefore, it is sometimes wise to seek the librarian's advice as to where to look.

Every member of the public, including children, has the right to belong to the public library and thus to borrow books according to the regulations of the authority running the library. Membership can be with the local library where the borrower resides, or can be in the district of work, or both, and charges are made only by way of fines should the book or books be kept beyond the date of return. However, all books are not available on loan, to be taken away. Such volumes, known as reference books, may be consulted only on the library premises. These include very expensive publications such as the better encyclopedias, large dictionaries, all kinds of directories and, often, the very expensive textbooks. Examples are Kelly's Street Directories, Wilson's *Bibliographic Index*, *Encyclopedia Britannica*, Kempe's *Engineers' Year Book*, and so on.

Copying Published Material

Bearing in mind that reference books may not be borrowed, many libraries offer **photocopying** facilities at very reasonable prices by means of which copies of essential material may be made. It is very important, in this connection, to have regard to the law of **copyright** and, in fact, the library will almost certainly ask you to sign a form to protect the authority in case of your infringement of an author's copyright. The law on copyright is very complicated, but unless you are going to do a significant amount of copying this need not bother you. Simply remember that you may make only one copy, and that for your own private study: it is an infringement to make copies for friends and colleagues as well. Further, you may copy only a reasonable amount of a book; this has been assessed as something in the region of 100 words. For any extensive copying it is essential to obtain the permission of the copyright owner, who may be the author, the publisher or even another party. If such permission is required, then the author should be approached, addressed through his publisher, or application made to the publisher direct. Most modern textbooks have an indication as to who owns the copyright.

Despite a reading list, despite Dewey, you may still find yourself at a loss when seeking information. This is the time to consult the librarian. The art or science of librarianship is highly developed today and librarians have a vast amount of knowledge at their fingertips of where to look for information. They also have at their disposal a number of specialised reference books that act as a guide to the most likely sources of information on any subject. Further, there are very few librarians indeed who will not do everything possible to satisfy even the smallest enquiries.

Technical Journals

Of necessity, however, all books on library shelves are out of date to some extent. Two main reasons contribute to this: (1) the length of time it takes to write, print, check and publish a modern book; and (2) the rapid technological changes that nowadays take place outstripping the ability of writers and publishers of books to keep pace. For most subjects, therefore, it is necessary to go to another source for the latest information, and generally speaking this is the technical journal. All professional and technical societies publish journals devoted to their particular speciality and, in addition, there are scores of such magazines put out by independent publishers catering for both the professional and the amateur practitioner. In addition, the so-called quality newspapers, such as *The Times*, the *Financial Times* and *The Guardian*, often publish authoritative articles on technical, financial, social and economic matters. Particularly when consulting articles in the press, however, a watch for conscious or unconscious bias must be kept. Or, put another way, care must be taken to distinguish between fact and opinion.

Whilst all journals and newspapers can, of course, normally be purchased through the usual newsagents and bookstalls, though often only from the larger ones in the cases of very highly specialised journals, most can also be consulted at any large public library. If a newspaper or magazine is not kept by the library you visit, the librarian can usually obtain a specific edition on request, or, at least, a photocopy of the article it is required to read. Herein lies a problem. With the wealth of periodicals available, how is it possible to make a sensible choice of which to peruse? Here our librarian can, again, be of great assistance. Most libraries hold one or more of the current periodical indexes, such as *Willing's Press Guide*, the *British Technology Index*, the *Guide to Current British Periodicals* and the *Times Index*, and the librarian will be able to discuss your precise requirements and to recommend selections.

Specialist Bodies

So far we have discussed printed sources of information, and in doing so we have also seen how much help may be obtained from libraries and librarians. However, we must also remember that the most up-to-date information on any special subject is most likely to be held by the professional or trade association or institution specialising in that particular subject. Thus, the very latest knowledge about accountancy is likely to be obtainable from the Institute of Chartered Accountants or the Association of Certified Accountants. Similarly, the current thought on industrial and personnel relations is likely to come from the Institute of Personnel Management. From such bodies, both fact and opinion will be obtained, as well as what are the possibilities for the future. Most professional and trade associations are quite willing to provide information and advice to non-members provided that the applicant is serious.

Apart from the specialist bodies referred to, facts and opinions may also be solicited from government departments, local authorities, educational institutions and commercial or industrial undertakings having interests in the subject under investigation. Experience shows, however, that information from these sources is usually more guarded and less forthright than that obtained from the other sources we have discussed. Other direct requests may, of course, be made to the specialist writers of textbooks and of articles in journals, addressing them through their publishers. Replies from such people are often very full and detailed, and sometimes they are willing to enter into limited discussion on the topic in question to the benefit of both parties. Care must, of course, be taken in such cases to watch for bias.

Abstract Services

For the very busy person, however, the very wealth of current printed information, and the number of sources of information now available, make the task of investigation almost impossible. Fortunately, a number of abstracting services have been established during the past few years that produce summaries of articles appearing in various specialist journals so that it is possible for the researcher to keep abreast of essential information without the need to read through long articles. Two such services are *Anbar Abstracts* and *Management Abstracts*. Most of these services require the user to subscribe on a yearly basis, but there are many public libraries who subscribe to them and so the infrequent enquirer can make use of his library service.

Making Notes

Tracking down your material is only part of research: making notes is another. This must be done methodically if the notes are to be of most use. The making of notes is a highly individual activity, and one person's method is not necessarily the best for someone else. However, it is possible to formulate some general rules and these are given below to assist in this important task:

(1) **Identify Your Source.** When writing up your material you will need to be able to identify your source. At the same time as you make your notes, therefore, you must, without fail, also note the author's

name and where you found the material (book, paper, journal, letter, personal interview), its title, and the date of publication or interview.

(2) **Verify Accuracy of Information.** Where possible, the accuracy of the information you are gathering should be verified. This is particularly important where you are recording figure information or matters of law. Such checking can be done by referring to another article, a standard work on the subject, or by consulting a specialist body or writer.

(3) **Fact or Opinion?** You must differentiate between clear fact and the author's opinion. The use of opinion is absolutely valid provided it is identified as such when final use is made of the material.

(4) **Permission to Quote.** If you wish to quote verbatim from a published work you should seek the prior permission of the author or the publisher. Similarly, it is courteous to credit the author of a piece if you mention his ideas or opinions without directly quoting him. In both cases your source should be mentioned as given in (1) above. If you find it necessary to quote from other works frequently then it would be wise to become thoroughly acquainted with the law of copyright as it affects this activity.

(5) **Methods of Making Notes.** The physical act of note-making is highly individual. Some researchers use bound notebooks, often the conventional shorthand notebook. Entries are made as they go and abstracted afterwards for assembly into logical order. Others use loose-leaf notebooks, often using one page for one item. This method enables the writer to sort his material easily without copying. Yet again, some investigators use index cards, employing them in the same manner as the loose-leaf notebook. Cards, having filing boxes available, are perhaps best used for long-term research.

(6) **Classifying Your Notes.** The matter of classification of material is important so that retrieval is quick and simple. You should, therefore, devise a system which will allow you to find the information you want from your notes easily and quickly. A useful method is to plan a number of headings derived from the manner in which you will seek the information. These can be under subject, author, source, publisher, date or any other heading that you think convenient. Any one item will then be entered in full under the major heading, and will be cross-referenced to this main entry under all other relevant headings. This may, of course, entail three or four, or even more, entries for each item. It will, however, ensure that no material is missed when your notes are written up, and will also provide more than one trigger for the retrieval of any single entry of information.

(7) **Excess of Material.** Remember that all research turns up much more material than can be used in the finished article. When finally selecting items for use in your ultimate report or other work, be ruthless

in discarding anything that does not properly bear on your subject and the theme you are developing.

Questions

1. Detail the services available to the researcher by the public library service.

2. Give examples of sources of information other than those provided direct by the library service.

3. To what points should you pay attention when taking notes from source material?

4. Suppose you have to find out about South America's transport systems, political systems, and trade. How would you collect this information from a library? (CIT, Intermediate)

20

VERBAL COMMUNICATION

The most common form of communication is, of course, verbal communication—talking to each other face to face. It is also, in most cases, the most effective, the reasons for which will be discussed later in this chapter.

Differences between Spoken and Written English

In English we have not one but two languages, the written form and the spoken form, and whilst they are drawing closer together nevertheless they are still distinct. Written language when spoken very often sounds pompous and spoken language when written may sound brash. One or two examples will make this difference clear:

Spoken: 'Any chance of you paying me, Sid?'
Written: 'We would like to draw your attention to our overdue account.'

Spoken: 'You've got the job.'
Written: 'You have been appointed to the position.'

Spoken: 'My wipers are up the creek.'
Written: 'My windscreen wipers have developed a fault.'

It will be noticed that the spoken language in these examples is not only much less formal than the written one, but that the two forms are not interchangeable unless the writing is very personal. When we speak person to person, our language will be more familiar than if we are writing: how familiar depends upon the person we are addressing. There are degrees of familiarity that we adopt, usually quite unconsciously, according to how well we know the other party and according to the status of the other person relative to ourselves. We will address a close friend quite differently from the way we address our managing director. Such differences are recognised universally, are accepted and, in fact, are expected. To ignore them may cause annoyance, pique, irritation or indignation. The more formal our relationship the more formal will be our speech, and the closer it will approach the written form. Referring to the third example above, we would use the spoken form to a friend but not to the company's chairman; but we might use the written style

142

to the latter. Thus, when we write we should take a lot of care about the words we use and the construction of our sentences so that our meaning is clear and unambiguous. We should avoid slang in any but the most personal correspondence. When we speak we are able to be much more flexible. We may make use of many expressions that would be out of place if written, the construction of our sentences may be quite loose and we may be deliberately ungrammatical if this will emphasise our point.

The Use of Facial Expression, Gesture and Inflection

Perhaps the main advantage that we derive from talking face to face is that we are able to reinforce our speech with facial expressions, gestures, voice inflections and other physical devices: meanings of sentences can easily be modified by putting the stress on different words in otherwise identical phrases or sentences. Let us consider a simple, short example:

'I am going out.' This is a plain statement of fact.

'I am going out.' The stressed 'I' suggests that the speaker does not care what the others are going to do; he is going out anyway.

'I am going out.' This indicates that the speaker is determined to go out whatever is said to the contrary.

'I am going out.' This suggests an argumentative state of mind where the speaker's intention is in danger of being frustrated.

'I am going out.' This is suggestive of the speaker being in a temper. These are his final words and he slams the door behind him.

To make these various meanings plain in written language the sentences would have to be completely restructured and many more words employed. It must be remembered that although underscoring has been used in these examples, this is not permissible in ordinary, formal writing.

In a similar fashion, meaning when speaking can be modified or reinforced by facial expression or gesture. 'Please be more careful' as it stands is a reprimand. It becomes a very gentle reprimand, or even no reproach at all, if said with a smile. Similarly, a straightforward 'I don't know' means just that. If the speaker shrugs his shoulders, or raises his eyes to heaven, when saying it he can be expressing exasperation. Body language is much discussed nowadays, and this involves, in the main, unconscious or automatic gesture. Such communication is most evident on the football field. When a player scores a goal he almost inevitably jumps in the air with clenched fist raised: an accepted and recognised gesture of pleasure and sense of achievement. This gesture is sufficient in itself without any vocal accompaniment. The orator uses physical gesture to drive his points home: thus, when he is making statements about which he feels very passionately he will pound the table or the lectern with his fist, or will raise a finger to heaven at the same time bringing his shoulder forward and up.

These are extreme examples of the use of gesture, but the use of the hands and shoulders is very common whilst speaking. The British, perhaps, use gesture less than most peoples probably because English lends itself so well to the use of inflections: someone once said that to gag an Italian it is necessary to tie his hands behind his back. Nevertheless, gesture is generally used by those who speak English and is a valuable adjunct to speech. Similarly, our stance and deportment can add meaning to our verbal communication and can also indicate our attitude to our correspondent. For example, if a person being interviewed for a new post slouches in his chair and speaks in a slovenly manner, however highly he is qualified, the interviewer will derive the impression that the interviewee is less than interested in the proposition.

Immediate Feedback

A distinct advantage of face-to-face communication is the fact that feedback is immediate. The speaker can ascertain by the other party's reactions, even if not put into words, how he is being received. Again, facial expression, gesture and stance will communicate the receiver's feelings. The ability to see what response is being evoked is valuable in that it enables the speaker to adjust and modify his approach so that he becomes more acceptable. He can change his argument, alter his language or even modify his tone to make his communication acceptable to the receiver. Each change in tactic will evoke a response that will indicate at once whether it is being successful. So significant is this aspect of person-to-person communication that final negotiations in practically all matters of importance are conducted on a face-to-face basis. This verbal encounter enables the parties to modify their approach on the basis of the other's reactions.

Drawbacks to Verbal Communication

Despite its undoubted merits, face-to-face communication has, of course, some disadvantages. First, the participants really **need** to have reasonably **quick responses**. Meaning must be quickly understood and appropriate replies quickly formulated. If meaning is misunderstood the communication may break down or may become directed into a wrong channel.

Second, spoken language is **not** generally **so precise as written language**. Because of its spontaneity less care can be taken to select the correct words and phrases, and unless the speaker has a particularly good vocabulary exact words will not come easily to mind. This is in contrast to the written word, when a suitable dictionary or other aid may be consulted to help achieve accuracy of expression.

Third, there is usually **no record** of the conversation, unless a shorthand note is taken or a recording made. This can lead to subsequent misunderstanding particularly where memory is not reliable.

Finally, many people find **difficulty** in **expressing themselves verbally**. Especially is this so if the parties are not of equal status. Nervousness, lack of an adequate vocabulary or any other impediment may cause them to lose their self-confidence and thus cause them to communicate ineffectively. Only experience can remedy this.

Verbal Instructions

It falls to the lot of many people to have to give verbal instructions to their staff and to their colleagues, and this is part of the problem of effective communication. The necessity to give instructions implies a measure of authority, and also requires an insight into the problems of attitude and motivation, and these aspects were dealt with in Chapter 7. The giving of instructions, however, has the advantage that it is face-to-face communication. To this extent the supervisor or manager may take special care to observe the reactions of the receiver of the instructions, both verbal and physical, and so is in a position to change his approach should this appear necessary. All the points made in this chapter also apply to this problem.

Discussion and Debate

In later chapters we shall discuss public speaking and meetings, both of which are very special forms of verbal communication. At this stage we must have a look at two other closely related forms of verbal communication which are a step beyond simple face-to-face communication: these are discussion and debate. Both of these involve face-to-face communication but there is a significant difference between them. In **discussion** the parties seek to **give and receive information** and ideas, to talk matters over on the basis of the points brought out, and to come to some mutually agreed conclusion. The participants in a discussion, therefore, adopt a flexible attitude and acknowledge the need to give and take so that a reasonable conclusion can be arrived at.

Just the opposite is the case **in a debate**. Here the **speakers have already formulated their decisions** on the matter to be debated and their task is to endeavour to persuade their opponent to their way of thinking by means of skilful argument. Each participant will have a properly prepared speech on which much previous research has been done, and full notes of this will be used whilst he is talking. A debate has definite rules of procedure which must be strictly adhered to and the proceedings are conducted under the authority of a properly appointed chairman. There is much cut and thrust in a debate, but little of the give and take that is evident in a discussion. The purpose is to find weaknesses in the opponent's line of argument and so upset his case, and to persuade specially appointed adjudicators to agree with one point of view or the other. Perhaps we could define a debate as a series of prepared and persuasive talks that are modified as the debate progresses in accordance with the counter-arguments of the other side.

Naturally, a proper discussion requires some preparation to be done, but this involves making notes of the principal points to be brought up in the discussion with supporting evidence to reinforce the argument: set speeches are not prepared beforehand. Essentially, **a discussion is to reach a solution to a problem: a debate is to score a victory.**

Argument

Under discussion and debate we have mentioned the question of argument, and a few words on this subject would not be out of place.

It must first be understood that no argument can stand up unless the **subject** of the argument is **clear** and **unambiguous**. Therefore the subject must be absolute and must be definable: in drawing a definition we will discover how clear-cut our idea of our subject is. This will enable us to clarify our thinking and to round down our topic to manageable proportions.

Next we must provide ourselves with **authoritative supporting evidence** for our case, personal, third-party, or both. Such evidence must be acceptable to the other party in the argument, and to any adjudicators if such are appointed. Any weaknesses in our case must also be investigated and noted, and convincing reasons worked out for minimising their effect on the argument as a whole.

Finally, we must work out how we are going to present our case; whether we are going to argue deductively or inductively.

Deductive argument is probably the surest way to achieve acceptance of a proposition as it rests on an already proven rule. An established principle is cited as the basis of our case, and this is irrefutable. Our aim is then to marry our proposition to the rule—that is, to prove within reason that the established rule governs our proposition. A very great part of English case law has been achieved by deductive argument —in other words, the success in showing that the case in question is covered by a previously decided case which has become law by precedent.

Argument by induction is another approach. Here a law has to be established upon which the argument is to be based. If a large enough number of facts and established conditions can be discovered, then the argument stands a good chance of being won. In considering inductive argument, one must remember that all natural laws which now form the basis of deductive reasoning were originally formulated by inductive reasoning. For example, it is a natural law that the application of manure results in superior crops than when no manure is applied. This was known long before scientific investigation proved it. The land worker found that every time he spread manure his crops benefited and by inductive reasoning formulated the rule, or practice, that manuring improved cropping.

We can also **argue from cause and effect**, which is a little like inductive reasoning. An effect can be observed from an identified cause and it can be argued that such a cause will result in a similar effect on a future occasion. For instance, if workers' wages rise then prices will go up. As Sir Harold Wilson is reported as having said, 'One man's pay rise is another man's price rise.' So in an argument against wage rises one could put the point that such a rise would result in higher prices and, hence, lower sales. Similarly, one can argue from effect to cause. To be on safe ground in using this form of argument, frequency of repetition of the cause and the effect is important, when it approaches inductive argument.

These notes on argument refer principally to formal debate and argument, but can, of course, be applied equally well to informal argument.

Questions

1. What advantages does verbal communication have over the written form? When would you consider it the more desirable method in dealing with labour relations? (CIT, Intermediate)

2. What would you say are the main drawbacks in verbal communication within any organisation? (AIA, Foundation Part A)

3. 'Group discussion plays a vital role in modern business.' What is its importance and what can it achieve? How can an administrator ensure that informal group discussion is being used effectively and appropriately in his organisation and what gains would he achieve by this? (ICSA, Part I)

21

THE TELEPHONE

Advantages of the Telephone

Use of the telephone as a means of verbal communication is so commonplace that we seldom think objectively about this valuable device. Perhaps this explains why it is so often used badly. The telephone offers a means of verbal communication without a personal meeting; it is swift, person to person and universally accepted. It also provides immediate feedback and thus enables both parties to check the quality of the response, so giving the opportunity for a modification of approach if necessary, and for the correction of errors in understanding.

Using the Telephone Effectively

The initial requirement when using the telephone is to establish identity. In order to do this when making a telephone call, the caller should ask the person who answers to verify his identity and should then announce who is calling. Before any conversation takes place it is important that the right people are connected. When a telephone ring is answered it is important to state at once the telephone number followed by the name of the person answering. Wrong numbers are not unknown, and much time, not to mention money, can be wasted in starting conversations with the wrong people.

The reproduction produced by the telephone does usually leave something to be desired and the result is some distortion of the words being transmitted. To overcome this defect it is necessary to stress consonants slightly more than in ordinary speech, to talk a little more slowly, and to prevent the voice dropping in tone at the ends of sentences. This is not to say that speech should be laboured; just a little more distinct than in everyday talking.

Inaccuracy over the telephone is also a product of distortion. Unless care is taken some words, particularly names, and some figures may be misunderstood. A name such as 'Knifton' may be heard as 'Niston', and the numbers 'five' and 'seven' may easily be mistaken for 'nine' and 'eleven' respectively. In fact, all numbers should be very carefully verified when given over the telephone. Many people well versed in

148

telephone usage have their own ways of overcoming these difficulties; for example, 'five' is frequently pronounced as 'fife', and 'seven' enunciated very deliberately as 'se-*ven*' rather than the more slovenly 'sev'n'. Similarly, key words and key phrases in the conversation should be checked to make sure that they are properly understood—a clear advantage of the immediate feedback available by using the telephone. Very often, despite great care in diction, a word or words cannot be understood. In such cases it is usual to spell the offending word or words, but here, again, difficulties arise because some letters sound alike, for instance 'm' and 'n'. To solve this problem we can use a **phonetic alphabet**, in which each letter is represented by a word whose initial letter is the same as the one to be identified. Any easily recognisable words may be pressed into service though British Telecom does, in fact, have a recommended phonetic alphabet, which runs as follows:

A = Andrew	B = Benjamin	C = Charlie	D = David
E = Edward	F = Freddie	G = George	H = Harry
I = Isaac	J = Jack	K = King	L = Lucy
M = Mary	N = Nellie	O = Oliver	P = Peter
Q = Queenie	R = Robert	S = Sugar	T = Tommy
U = Uncle	V = Victor	W = William	X = Xmas
Y = Yellow	Z = Zebra		

The use of such alphabetic codes is, of course, quite common where accuracy is essential though the identifying words used may vary. Thus 'P, Peter' and 'I, Isaac' become, in aircraft control work, 'P, Papa' and 'I, India'.

Courtesy

One remarkable effect of using the telephone is that some people tend to forget the rules of common politeness. To such people the telephone seems to have an inbuilt irritant that causes them to lose their tempers very much more easily than they would if they were talking face to face. Very often, however, and particularly in business, the telephone is the only personal contact that the parties have and very wrong impressions may be given if one or the other exhibits a shortness of temper which is really uncharacteristic. It behoves us, therefore, to speak with due courtesy when using the telephone, and to resist any temptation to lose our tempers or to be impolite in any other way. Such behaviour can be harmful to relations between the parties and, in business, can lose customers.

Saving Time on the Telephone

Time is money on the telephone, and whereas this may not be of great significance in private and social telephone conversations, it must be carefully considered when business calls are in progress. Brevity is, therefore, an important factor in communication by telephone, particularly so if the other party is paying for the call. To say the least it is discourteous to prolong such a call unnecessarily. If you are making the call, then care should be taken to have to hand all the information you wish to discuss, preferably noted in logical order on paper. If you have questions to ask, you should make sure that you have all the necessary factors to put to your correspondent, so far as you are able. If information or queries arise that need clarification from another source, say a file, then it is often preferable to terminate the present call and ring back later. This eliminates costly and unnecessary waiting whilst the search takes place. It is one of the unfortunate omissions from our telephone apparatus that it is not possible to recall the party at the other end if he has moved from the telephone. If, therefore, either party is requested to 'hang on' it is wise to indicate that the waiting party will terminate the call if the wait becomes prolonged. In this way a dead telephone indicates no discourtesy.

Equally, time should not be wasted on irrelevant chitchat, though this is not to say that the customary courtesies should be omitted.

A small aid to save callers' time, and one that is being increasingly adopted by the more efficient firms, is to have the writer's telephone extension number shown on all outgoing correspondence. If, then, the receiver wishes to telephone in connection with the letter he knows at a glance what extension to ask for and so can avoid the frustration of waiting whilst the correct extension is found. Similarly, attention should be paid to the placing of the telephone number when note headings are designed. When the number is printed in the top left-hand corner, for example, it is often obscured by other papers pinned to the letter in just that position. The telephone number is, nowadays, just as important as the postal address, and should be shown just as prominently.

The Switchboard Operator

Little attention is given by most organisations to the importance of the telephone switchboard operator: yet she (or he) has more influence on the goodwill of the organisation than any other employee of similar status. Often the telephone operator is the first contact an outsider has with a firm, and from the reception he gets he will form an impression of the firm to its benefit or to its detriment. Further, this first impression will probably be the one that will last. Consequently, great care must be taken in the selection of a switchboard operator and in the training that is given. Many organisations train their own operators; for those who do not have this facility British Telecom will provide operator training on the user's own premises.

Courtesy and friendliness are the prime requisites of a telephone operator, coupled with efficiency. Some people are quite impolite to telephone operators, sometimes to the point of rudeness, especially when numbers or extensions are difficult to obtain. Of course, this is quite reprehensible behaviour, but nevertheless operators must have that type of temperament that can take this in its stride, and they must be unfailingly polite. Efficiency is also important. It is not efficient, however, to answer a call quickly by announcing the firm's identity, often quite abruptly, and then to put the caller on 'hold' for an indeterminate time. Not only is it not efficient, it is also ill-mannered and costly to that caller.

Efficiency means dealing with calls quickly, smoothly and pleasantly. One of the greatest aids to an operator's efficiency is the availability of an **up-to-date extensions directory.** Where people move their positions in an organisation the switchboard should be informed immediately so that incoming calls may be dealt with without frustrating delays whilst the new extension number is sought. If a job is taken over by another person who will henceforth be responsible for the former occupant's work, then the operator should have this information so that callers may be informed of this fact. It is also helpful if the operator is kept aware of the absences of extension users, however short, and of alternative extensions through which likely matters can have attention.

Nothing has been said in this chapter about the many telephone services and types of installation British Telecom can provide. This is because the range of both is very wide indeed and particular problems need particular solutions. It can be said, however, that British Telecom is both flexible and helpful in the provisions it can make. It is recommended, therefore, that **any telecommunication problem** that presents itself **should be taken to British Telecom** for discussion and recommendation: in this way the most efficient installation can be planned and fitted.

Questions

1. What are the uses, advantages and limitations of the telephone in industry? (CIT, Intermediate)

2. Telephone charges are steadily increasing. Draft a circular to all members of your office suggesting ways in which they might reduce these costs. (ICSA, Part I—adapted)

22

PUBLIC SPEAKING

Many of us, at some time or other, are asked to address an audience, especially if we have some special knowledge of a subject. The first attempt at public speaking can be an unnerving experience whether we are talking to a group of acquaintances and colleagues or whether we are addressing an audience of total strangers, and some guidance is necessary to overcome this apprehension and to increase confidence and effectiveness.

Some General Points

The first step to a confident, well delivered speech is **knowledge of the subject**. Usually you will be asked to speak because you are specially fitted to do so, you have studied the subject more thoroughly than most, or you have had superior experience of it. Consequently, your audience will expect you to be expert and to have a firm grasp of your topic. Any evidence that you have gaps in your knowledge will lose their confidence, and so it is essential that you examine the extent of your knowledge and repair any omissions that you find. In particular, if you wish to take a controversial stand on something it is doubly necessary to be quite certain of your ground. Questions are almost certain to be put to you and your authority over your subject will be open to question if you are not able to deal with them confidently. The problems associated with research were dealt with in Chapter 19 when sources of information were discussed. Your subject must be researched thoroughly before you expose your opinions to an audience: this is the first step to being able to put your points over effectively.

Next, it is desirable and very helpful if you **know what kind of audience** to expect. What is the extent of their previous knowledge of your subject? Are they familiar with the technical language of the subject and its jargon? Are they attending the talk out of general interest, or are they hoping to gain some specific technical knowledge? Are they coming because they wish to or have they been coerced? How are they likely to receive you? How many are expected? What is their social and educational background? Replies to these questions will help you to aim your speech at the right level, and to use the most effective language, to achieve understanding and acceptance. There is a maxim 'teach the students and not the subject'. This means that a speaker should take as much interest in his audience as he does in his subject, and applies to public speaking every bit as much as it does to teaching.

Notes

Very few speakers can deliver a first-class speech without notes in one form or another and so you must not be reticent about taking notes on to the platform with you, and be seen to be consulting them. The problem lies in the manner of your notes. They are needed as memory aids and to keep the talk flowing logically from step to step, and to avoid omission of important points. There are four basic ways in which to prepare a speech, which are as follows:

Writing the speech verbatim. This is not to be recommended for various reasons. First, a read speech is almost always boring to the listeners, and the speaker is often more concerned to keep his place on the page than to keep his speech lively and vital. Second, he has to keep his eyes on his notes and loses the eye contact that is so important to keep an audience involved with the subject. Third, written language is more stilted than spoken language and the speech is therefore likely to lose freshness and spontaneity, especially if the speaker has taken time during the preparation to 'polish' his work. Fourth, if the speaker loses his place there may be an embarrassing pause whilst he finds it again, in which case the thread of the speech is broken, or he may, on restarting, omit a sentence or two and so cause misunderstanding.

Writing out the speech and memorising it. This is even worse than reading the speech. In addition to the disadvantages of a written speech as mentioned above, there is the additional hazard of forgetting part of it. Furthermore, even a written speech can be attuned to an audience if necessary, but this is exceptionally difficult with a memorised one and leads to complications in delivery when attempted.

The extemporaneous method. Here no attempt is made to write down full notes; instead, headings are prepared of the principal parts of the speech and brief notes are added below them. The actual speech is composed as delivery is made, the headings and notes helping the speaker to remember the items and facts he wishes to bring to the audience's attention, and ensuring that he presents them in a logical fashion. Speeches given in this manner are likely to be lively and vital and to retain the interest of the audience more fully than the two previous methods.

Impromptu speaking. Strictly speaking this should not be included in preparation of notes, because no notes are prepared. Simply, the speaker delivers his speech without benefit of any notes at all, and often without any preparation beforehand. Speaking in this manner can be successful only when attempted by a very experienced person who has absolute control over his subject. It is not to be recommended to anyone of only average ability, and certainly not to a beginner.

One note of caution; whichever method of note preparation you adopt, always read out statistics and similar figure information: never trust your memory.

Preparing a Speech

Having looked at the question of the content of your speech, and how you should prepare your notes, we must now examine the steps required in the actual preparation of the speech. These can be enumerated as follows:

(1) Fix the **purpose and aim of the speech**. Is it to be informative, persuasive or evocative? Is it intended to offer new knowledge, to examine existing knowledge or to alter current thinking? Is it to instruct, to train or to further interest? Answers to these questions will set the tone and pattern of your speech.

(2) Ascertain, or fix, the **length of time** you are to speak.

(3) **Gather your ideas,** as suggested at the beginning of this chapter.

(4) Write your **main headings** and fill in with the outline of your talk, as explained under the section 'Notes'.

(5) **Familiarise yourself** with the **main pattern** of what you will say, guided by your notes as in (4).

(6) Endeavour to **set time limits to each section** of your speech. This will enable you to ensure that each part is given its appropriate quota of time. More important, it will help you to avoid over-running your total allotted time or, worse still, to avoid running out of material before your allotted span.

(7) Ask yourself whether your talk could be more informative or more entertaining if you used **some form of visual aid**, rather than relying entirely on your speech. (Visual aids are discussed in Chapter 23.)

(8) Leave time for **questions**.

In preparing your speech you will have to decide exactly how you will write your notes, and this is a matter of personal preference. Some speakers write their main headings and pertinent brief information on small cards, one card to a heading. The usual size for such cards is 5″ × 3″ and they should be written on one side only. They are easy to carry and easy to use. However, as they are separate, loose records, they can be dropped and become out of order, or individual cards can be mislaid or lost. Such events do not encourage a good speech. Other speakers use sheets of paper, often A4 size, and these can be stapled together to avoid mixing up the sheets or losing any.

As to setting the time limits to the sections of your speech, this is simply done by means of a chart as illustrated in Fig. 26. As will be seen, each heading is allocated a specific period of time by the clock, and

Title:	Communications	
Date	Time	Venue ....
Timing	Topic	Aid
10.00 - 10.15	Introduction - Dictionary definition	----
10.15 - 10.25	Two-way nature of communication	Chart on O/H projector
10.25 - 10.40	Factors affecting communication	Hand-out
10.40 - 11.00	Perception and experience	2" x 2" slides
	and so on	

Fig. 26. Specimen scheme for a talk.

where visual and other aids are to be used these are noted against the section heading in a column ruled for them. Inspection of this chart before the meeting will act as a reminder of what aids must be available, and the various times should be marked on the actual notes to be used for the speech. As a planning aid, this chart can be invaluable.

It cannot be overstated that the greater the care taken in preparing for a speech the better the speech is likely to be.

Delivery of your Speech

However thorough your preparation, however carefully you have made your notes, the success of your speech will succeed or fail very largely on your delivery, so let us examine some ways in which this matter may be handled.

There is a tendency, especially when speaking in public for the first time, to stand up and plunge into your speech straight away, and this is difficult to resist. In most cases this is a mistake. A brief preliminary pause before speaking gains attention and helps to dispel initial nervousness, and a steady start to your talk helps you to acclimatise yourself to your audience and to your environment. **Do not be tempted to rush things** at the initial stage.

Be sure of your opening words and **speak decisively**: rehearse them if you wish. An authoritative start alerts your audience and causes them to treat you seriously. It is essential to capture your audience's attention at the very beginning: it is difficult to capture it later.

However nervous you feel, **try to relax**. This is not always easy, but if you try to appear to be relaxed, and think that you are relaxed, then you will lose a great deal of your tension, and after a while you will actually feel relaxed. However, it must be admitted that some tension is helpful because it keys you up to your task and makes you more alert and lively, so enhancing your speech.

Always **face the audience** and **address them all** by letting your eye rove over the gathering. Do not concentrate your attention on one section only of the audience; they are all interested in what you have to say. A table or a lectern is often provided for the use of a speaker. This is a convenience but can form a barrier between the speaker and those he is addressing. Often a better rapport can be formed between the speaker and his audience if he stands in front of the table or lectern and so becomes part of the assembly. Notice how performers on the stage approach close to their audience, and notice what effect this has.

Use the kind of **vocabulary** that your **audience will understand**, and do not use long and unfamiliar words unnecessarily. For the sake of variety you may feel the occasional use of such words justified. In such cases, do be sure of their meaning, looking them up in the dictionary if need be. There is a great deal of slovenly language used nowadays, particularly on the radio and television, and this is to be avoided. Do not judge the meaning of a word by its sound—look it up. An example of the common misuse of a word by broadcasters is the use of 'decimate' to mean severe destruction. It does sound like that, but it actually means 'to kill every tenth person'.

On the other hand, provided you do not make crass errors, **do not worry** unduly **about grammar**. Use the style that comes naturally to you; small grammatical mistakes are acceptable in speech even though they are not in written language. Pay attention to obvious errors and double negatives, and avoid such Americanisms as 'meet up with' and 'this point in time'. Equally, do be sure that you are not ambiguous; be clear and certain.

Remember that **20 minutes** is commonly thought of as the **limit of** uninterrupted **concentration**. Consequently, your speech should allow for some form of quip or sideline to break it up every now and then. This will refresh your audience and revitalise their concentration.

The Voice

Some speakers, new to the task, worry about their voice, but they should not. It is one of the hardest things in the world to change your style of speech, your tone, pitch, accent or inflections, and should really be attempted only by someone who plans to spend a considerable part of his time in public speaking. Without a concentrated course of training, what happens when an attempt is made to modify the voice is that the speaker concentrates on voice production, listening to himself as he talks, and loses the thread and sense of his speech. In any case, most audiences appear to welcome variety. However, there are some simple rules that can be profitably remembered to improve your speech:

(1) **Enunciate clearly and deliberately.** Slovenly speech is often not intelligible, and if you are talking to a large gathering, certainly will not carry to the back row. A rate of delivery slightly slower than normal in ordinary conversation is also helpful in making yourself understood.

(2) **Do not drop your voice** to an inaudible pitch at the ends of sentences.

(3) Remember what was said in Chapter 20 about **stressing words in sentences**, and how altering the stressed word alters the meaning of a sentence. This can be used to good effect in public speaking.

(4) If you have a particular **defect in your speech try to remedy it**, but if you cannot do so **do not let it embarrass you**: try to steer round it. Thus, if you have difficulty in pronouncing certain words or phrases use others instead. For instance, if you find the word 'abstruse' difficult to say then use a substitute word or phrase such as 'difficult to understand'.

Your Hands and Mannerisms

Two other aspects of the presentation of a speech involve the speaker's hands and his mannerisms. First of all the hands. Though many new speakers become selfconscious about their hands the usual advice is to forget them. However, this is often not possible until some experience has been gained, so what can be done? First, there is no harm at all in thrusting one in your pocket, though as you warm up to your subject it is not likely to stay there: in fact, at that point you will forget your hands altogether.

Then, you can use them for making gestures. Appropriate use of the hands can reinforce your words and generally assist in bringing home your points. All great speakers have considerable fluency of gesture. However, your gestures must have meaning and you should avoid the aimless waving about of your hands and arms.

Your hands can also be occupied in holding your notes: this neatly solves the problem.

Mannerisms also cause a new speaker concern, particularly as so many authorities on public speaking make a point of condemning them. Unfortunately, these authorities never spell out how a speaker can overcome his mannerisms whilst at the same time concentrating on his speech. The answer is do not let your mannerisms worry you: forget them, they are your trade mark. The only exception to this advice is if they are offensive, distracting or particularly pretentious. In such cases special efforts must be made to modify them. If you suspect that your mannerisms may be unacceptable then it is wise to rehearse your speech in front of a frank friend, or in front of a mirror. Your fears may be allayed, or you may see the need for some modification of your presentation.

Under the term mannerism may be included the 'ers' and 'hms' that so frequently pepper the speeches of many people. These expressions can be extremely irritating to some listeners, and should be avoided at all costs. The solution is simple: you must be thoroughly acquainted with your subject and your preparation must, equally, be very thorough. Notice how some public figures are able to speak without this hesitancy, and how much more authority their speeches carry over those who cannot speak so fluently.

Questions from the Audience

Whether you allow questions during your talk or reserve a period for them at the end depends upon the circumstances of the occasion and upon your own wishes. Questions during the course of a speech frequently upset the pattern of thought and logical sequence. Questions at the end are more conducive to the delivery of a smooth flowing speech and are less likely to throw the speaker off balance. However, if questions are to be left to the end it is essential that sufficient time for proper consideration of both questions and answers is made available. If question time is too short or is curtailed the speaker's authority or sincerity may be doubted.

Despite the fact that question time is provided for at the end of a speech, inevitably there will be a question or two put by some member or members of the audience during the discourse. The wisest course to adopt in this situation is to suggest to the questioner that his point will be discussed at the end of the speech in accordance with the arrangements. If the interruption persists then you must appeal to the chairman and rely on his dealing properly with the matter. No attempt should be made to answer the question as this will encourage further questions and your speech will be disrupted.

Interruptions, generally, can cause something of a dilemma until, at least, you become accustomed to dealing with hecklers. Several measures are available, some more effective than others depending upon the circumstances. You can:

(a) Ignore them. This can sometimes be difficult, especially if the heckler has a powerful voice, or has support from others in the hall.

(b) Appeal to the chairman if the interruptions are persistent. As a final resort he may cause the offender or offenders to be ejected from the gathering.

(c) Use the interruptions to emphasise a point you have made, though this needs skill.

(d) Promise to deal later with the point being made.

(e) Ask that the question be deferred until proper question time.

(f) Give a crushing rejoinder. This, again, needs very great skill.

Dealing with questions, and with hecklers in particular, demands experience more than anything. Anyone new to public speaking is likely to find question time more trying and more demanding than giving a speech, but after some practice will also find it more rewarding.

Audience Apathy

At the beginning of this chapter it was stressed that a speaker must have a rapport with his audience. If this rapport does not develop very early in the talk then the audience is likely to become bored or apathetic. In consequence it is essential to discover the mood of the audience directly you start speaking so that you can adjust your approach to evoke a response. If your audience is immediately responsive and sympathetic then you have no problem, and you can attune your talk to them without difficulty. On occasions, however, you will find your efforts received without interest, unsympathetically or even with hostility. In such cases all you can do is to feel your way through the first few minutes trying to judge the mood of the people and trying to find ways of adjusting to it so that they become receptive. There is no rule-of-thumb method of doing this: a lot depends on your own personality. Sometimes a joke will thaw them out; sometimes a direct reference to their lack of response. It may be necessary to depart for a moment from your speech and touch on a current topic of general but not very deep significance.

Do not forget that **lack of response may** also **indicate lack of understanding.** If you suspect that this is so, look at some of the faces in the audience to see whether they bear puzzled expressions or exhibit other signs that indicate that the audience does not understand you. To confirm your suspicion, or to disprove it, ask individual members whether they understand what you are saying, and if they do not then be prepared to speak a little more slowly and to alter your language to suit the new situation. Do not ask the audience as a whole, as this will usually evoke no response.

Whatever you do to evoke audience response, however, you must at all times show good humour. On no account must you match bad humour with bad humour, nor hostility with hostility. Where lack of understanding is present, patience is usually required.

The points made in this chapter deal, in the main, with the problems of speaking in public. However, it is good to remember that the same approach applies where the speech is to be made to a small private gathering; only the scale is different.

Questions

1. What advice would you give to someone who, for the first time in his life, had been invited to give a lecture? Your advice should include both how to prepare and how to deliver the talk. (ICSA, Part I)

2. You are the Training Officer in a large transport undertaking and have been asked by your Managing Director to devote some attention to the need to improve effective speaking of your middle range managers when addressing groups of workers or the general public.

Set out *in summary form* a lecture you would give on the subject covering all the essential points as you see them. The full text of the lecture is not required. (CIT, Intermediate)

3. You are to give a speech of welcome to a group of foreigners who are on a visit to your firm. Their knowledge of English is adequate for everyday purposes but is far from perfect.

(*a*) Write in note form the points you intend to make in your speech.

(*b*) Explain what steps you will take to make sure your speech is fully understood by the visitors. (ICSA, Part I)

4. List the more important matters to which a speaker should pay attention if he wishes to maintain the interest of his audience.

(AIA, Foundation Part A)

5. In oral communication it has been said that to be effective 'the quality of the voice must be right'. In order to ensure that this is so to what points would you particularly pay attention while speaking to an audience?

(AIA, Foundation Part A)

23

PRACTICAL VISUAL AIDS IN PUBLIC SPEAKING

More often than not a speech or lecture can be made more interesting, and also more easily understandable, by the use of a visual aid. There are a number of such aids available and all of them are comparatively simple to use.

The Chalkboard

The most common visual aid, of course, is the chalkboard, or blackboard as it is more commonly known. Its primary use is to emphasise important words and headings in a talk, and in this way it aids the audience's understanding and memory. Difficult and technical expressions can also be shown visually with immense advantage for the listeners. Some practice is necessary to be able to use the chalkboard with confidence, but it is a skill well worth acquiring. Of course, writing on a chalkboard entails turning your back on your audience for a short while so you must stop talking whilst writing, otherwise your listeners will miss some of your words. Despite statements to the contrary, it is just not possible to face your audience and use the blackboard at the same time. The simplest way to overcome this problem is to write only a short statement at a time, and constantly turn round and talk to the audience thus maintaining verbal contact with them. With a little practice it is comparatively easy to write legibly and in a straight line, remembering to write large enough so that those in the back row can read what is on the board.

Diagrams and line drawings can also be made on the chalkboard though a speaker with no artistic ability may hesitate to attempt any sort of sketch. This lack of talent can be overcome by preparing the graphic work on the board before the arrival of the audience, either in chalk as a finished product or in pencil which can be chalked over during the speech. If the latter method is adopted the pencil marks will be visible only to the speaker and it will appear as though the drawing were being done without any aid. Whichever method is adopted, the graphic work can of course be done by a more gifted colleague.

White chalk is the usual medium to be used, but it must not be forgotten that chalk is available in a range of colours, which can be used with good effect for some purposes.

The Overhead Projector

The second most popular visual aid is, probably, the overhead projector. This is a very versatile instrument which has a very powerful light source and therefore requires little or no dimming of the light in the room or hall in which it is being used, provided the screen is situated in not too bright a position. Further, portable models are available as well as the more usual standard models.

This projector requires transparencies for projection, which are normally pre-prepared on 10 in. × 10 in. pieces of acetate. These may be written or drawn on by hand, using spirit-based felt-tipped pens or the appropriate wax pencils, or may be prepared by using self-adhesive letters, or cut-outs from self-adhesive, coloured transparent plastic material. A great variety of informative images can be made by hand in this way. Further, using two or more acetate sheets and preparing only parts of an illustration on the different sheets it is possible, by laying one on top of the other, to build up an image in front of your audience, often with telling effect.

In addition to transparencies prepared by hand, it is possible to make them on a variety of photocopying machines, though in such cases the images will be black only. The two most popular methods of making transparencies by photocopying are infra-red and dual-spectrum. The former has a restricted image sensitivity, and will copy only from originals having a metal or carbon content. Inks and colours made from vegetable pigments will not produce a copy and this must be borne in mind when preparing the original. The dual-spectrum method is able to produce transparencies from any kind of original but is slower and more expensive than the infra-red method. Neither method will reproduce photographs. If it is desired to make transparencies of photographic images then this can be done by either the reflex method of photocopying or by diffusion transfer. Both methods produce high-class results.

Most overhead projectors also have the facility to use a roll of clear acetate which may be pulled across the platen of the machine by rotating a small handle. This enables the projector to be used in place of a blackboard, using felt-tipped pens or suitable wax pencils. The advantage here over the chalkboard is that the speaker is able to face his audience and to continue his discourse whilst he is writing. The overhead projector has a very short throw, which means that it is used from the speaker's position and not from somewhere at the back of the audience. Another advantage over the chalkboard is that it is free of chalk dust, which can be a nuisance when using the blackboard.

Other Alternatives to the Chalkboard

Another visual aid device used in place of the chalkboard is the **flip pad**. This consists of a pad of sheets of plain, substantial newsprint fastened at the top and used on an easel or other suitable stand. The writing instruments employed are usually felt-tipped pens, and the pages are flipped over the top of the pad as they are used and their purpose completed; or they may be torn off and discarded. As with the overhead projector, material may be pre-prepared, and can thus be used repeatedly during different speeches. The use of felt-tipped pens also avoids the nuisance of chalk dust.

Another substitute for the chalkboard is the **'magic' writing board**. This is merely a board of smooth white plastic material which is written on by felt-tipped pens, and which can be cleaned with a damp felt or cloth rubber. Provided the pens used are water-based these boards are fairly successful, and by providing a coloured image on a white ground are, perhaps, easier to read than a blackboard.

Two other substitutes for the chalkboard, but requiring previously prepared material, are the **magnetic board** and the **flannel (or felt) board**. The former consists of a sheet of ferrous metal, suitably painted, to which pre-prepared cut-out images backed with small magnets will adhere. The cut-outs can be moved about at will and so this method is particularly suitable for showing evolving illustrations, such as traffic problems or the siting of buildings. The sheets are usually painted a dark colour and so chalk can be used on them to provide static images around which the magnetic cut-outs can be positioned. Flannel boards perform a similar function. Here the backing is flannel or felt, and the cut-outs are of similar material, often in bright colours. The cut-outs adhere very easily and firmly to the backing and are easily moved about to show an evolving situation.

The Episcope

Often we would like to display on the screen an illustration of which we have only an opaque copy, and thus it is unsuitable for the overhead projector without having a transparent copy made. The answer to this problem, whether the illustration is a single sheet or a page in a bound book, is the episcope. This is a projector with a very powerful light source which can project any opaque original. However, it has one very serious drawback. Because of the optical requirements necessary to be able to project the material there is a severe light loss in the process and, therefore, the room in which the episcope is used must have a particularly efficient black-out; any significant ambient light dims the image on the screen. Nevertheless, for some occasions—for example, the projection of reproductions of small paintings—this device can be invaluable. It has a sister machine, the epidiascope, which projects transparencies as well as opaque images.

The 35 mm Projector

Probably the most popular form of projector is the still projector that shows 2 in. × 2 in. slides—that is, slides made on 35 mm photographic film with which everyone is familiar. The measurements 2 in. × 2 in. refer to the size of the actual mount of the transparency, the picture itself being 36 mm × 24 mm, or a little less than $1\frac{1}{2}$ in. × 1 in. Naturally, these slides have to be made in advance of any talk. They can be purchased ready-made or they can easily be made specially for the purpose of the speech by anyone with even a modicum of experience with a 35 mm camera. Ready-made slides have the advantage of first-class quality but in many cases it is very difficult to find those that fit exactly the requirements of the speech. In such a case it is often necessary to modify the speech to accommodate what slides are available. Specially prepared slides may or may not be quite the quality of those that can be bought ready for use, but lack of quality is often made up for by the greater suitability they have for their purpose.

The advantages of the 2 in. × 2 in. projector are that it produces a very high quality image, and the slides are light and portable and may be sorted and re-sorted into any order for subsequent use. On the other hand, this projector does need some dimming of the ambient light level for a good screen image. Further, in order to provide a reasonably large picture the projector has to be a fair way from the speaker. Unless, therefore, the instrument is an automatic one which can be controlled from the platform, it is necessary to have a projectionist to operate the projector with the attendant problems of perfect understanding between him and the speaker. Many a speech has been spoilt by misunderstandings between these two people. In addition, the dimming of the house lights and the intervention of the operator can at times break the rapport so carefully built up between the speaker and his audience. Finally, it is essential that slides be spotted so that they are projected the right way round and the right way up. A slide projected upside down is embarrassing for the speaker and breaks the continuity of the talk. The spot is the universally recognised means of identifying the correct viewing side and correct way up of a transparency. Holding the slide as it should be viewed, the spot is marked on the left-hand bottom corner of the mount. When the slide is inserted for showing the projectionist takes it with his thumb covering the spot and places it in the carrier with the mark at top right and facing the rear of the projector.

Film Strips

Film strips are, in effect, slides on 35 mm film in continuous strips. It is customary for the frames to be half the size of slides—that is, 18 mm × 24 mm. Though it is possible for film strips to be made by the speaker specially for his individual speech, it is more usual for film strips to be borrowed or bought from an organisation specialising in this material, when the strips are accompanied by appropriate guide lecture notes. Naturally, it is open to the speaker to alter and modify these notes to suit his particular requirements. However, it is not possible for the film strip frames to be sorted or rearranged, so to this extent there is a limit to any modification. Like slides, film strips require a dimming of the ambient light and the projector cannot be operated from the platform. Further, they cannot be advanced automatically, neither is it easy for a third party to operate the projector, so it is usual for the speaker to show the strips himself. This entails his being down with, or even behind, his audience so this method is suitable only for small groups. To overcome these difficulties peculiar to film strips it is, of course, possible to cut them up into single frames and mount them in the same way as slides. However, they are smaller than the standard slides. This means that if it is required to show them to a large audience it will be necessary to change the lens on the projector to one of shorter focal length to obtain the same size picture as that produced by a 2 in. × 2 in. slide, as moving the projector further from the screen will result in a reduction of picture brightness.

Moving Films

Moving picture films may occasionally be of use as a visual aid to a speaker but as a rule are of dubious value, unless they are indispensable for illustration. Of course, there is no other way to show the motion of an animal or a machine to an audience except to use a motion film, and here the film should be specially made to be most effective. In the usual case, however, a special film cannot be produced and recourse has to be made to a film library. Material from these sources can be less than satisfactory as an adjunct to a speech, though it can be very useful as the primary means of communication, the speaker's contribution being merely commentary on the film and dealing with questions from the audience. Another very important point is that the moving film can very easily overshadow the speaker unless he is extremely skilled in the use of this aid. The objections mentioned in connection with the still projector of the necessity for low ambient lighting and the introduction of a third party for projection apply in greater measure to the motion film.

Videotape Recorders

The reproduction of videotape recordings as a visual aid falls into the same category as the motion film, with the possible exception that individually made material is somewhat less difficult to produce. Immediate playback of a record during production gives much greater opportunity for correction than does the taking of a motion film record, where the film has to be sent to a laboratory for processing and some time elapses before the results can be judged.

Closed-Circuit Television

Closed-circuit television has little place in ordinary public speaking, but can be useful to demonstrate processes or experiments to audiences too large to view them easily as they are carried out on the platform. In such instances the main problem is the correct placing of monitor screens about the hall so that all sections of the audience obtain an adequate view.

Tape Recorders

Though not a visual aid, mention must be made of the tape recorder. In certain limited areas, such as the discussion of dialects, language or drama, the tape recorder can assist the speaker as can no other device. It needs no darkened room, it is a natural extension of the speaker and does not overshadow him, and it can be stopped, started and replayed as often as required. With a very large audience, it is even possible to have extension loudspeakers round the hall so that everyone has a chance to hear properly. Material for the tape recorder is usually individually produced and normally causes few problems.

If you decide that you can make profitable use of one or more of the visual aids in your public speaking, then you must give very careful consideration as to the types to be employed and how to make the most effective use of them. Remember, a visual aid badly used is worse than using no visual aid at all. With the possible exception of the chalk-board, they all require careful preparation or careful selection of material, and adequate time and attention must be given to these matters well before your speech is due to be given.

Questions

1. What is a visual aid? Give the advantages and disadvantages of four types of visual aid. (CIT, Intermediate)

2. You have been asked to present a short talk to a group of managers. This will mean that you will have to refer them to many figures and statistics.

What methods of visual presentation could be used? Describe and compare their characteristic features   (ICSA, Part I)

3. 'Talk and Chalk—the first audio-visual aids.'

(a) How would you explain to a friend who has been invited to give a lecture the advantages of a blackboard as a visual aid? What advice would you give him on its most effective use?

(b) What do you consider are the disadvantages of this form of visual aid?
(AIA, Foundation Part A)

4. What are the main advantages and disadvantages of using a projector and slides in a business presentation?   (AIA, Foundation Part A)

5. What are the main forms of audio-visual aid now available to the professional administrator? Select *one* of these and describe its most important characteristics.

What advice would you give to an administrator who wishes to use this aid effectively during a talk on administrative techniques to a group of managers?
(ICSA, Part I)

24

INTERVIEWS

Defining an Interview

An interview is a face-to-face verbal exchange which endeavours to discover as much information as possible in the least amount of time about some relevant matter. In business, interviews are used for a variety of purposes which include recruitment of staff, hearing staff grievances and complaints, disciplinary action and many other matters chiefly concerned with management/staff relations. However, the term interview may be used for any two-way verbal communication where one of the participants has some sort of authority over the other, or is in some other way in an advantageous or superior position. This obtains, for example, when a sales representative sees a potential customer or a reporter visits a prominent or notorious person with a view to publishing a report of the conversation.

Authority may be overt, as in the case of an employer interviewing an applicant for an appointment, or it may be by way of some special superiority over the interviewee, such as special knowledge as in the case of a counselling interview. In many instances the interviewer needs to have positive skills in diplomacy as well as social skills to carry off an interview successfully—for example, where the meeting is for the dismissal or reprimand of an employee, or where the other participant is an angry, complaining customer. Such interviews should not end with a feeling of rancour in either party.

The Elements of an Interview

In order that the interviewer may derive the utmost benefit from an interview much care must be exercised before and during the meeting. It might be said that there are four elements to a successful interview: planning it, conducting it, making assessments during it and at its conclusion, and making a decision based on factors brought out by the interview.

Proper planning must be carried out prior to the meeting, as without a clear plan the interview will probably be less than completely successful. The purpose for holding the interview must be definite and certain. What, precisely, do we wish to find out? What sorts of questions should

169

we put to the interviewee and in what order? How are we going to put them? Which is the most suitable place to hold the interview?

Many interviewers prefer to have a structured interview—that is, one in which a specific list of topics with, perhaps, important questions, is prepared, probably on a form that can be completed as the interviewee answers. Others are content with a list of headings that act as a guide during the meeting, but which, nevertheless, keep the interview on course. Either method is preferable to an interview where the interviewer has no plan but asks questions as he thinks of them. Such an interview is likely to miss many important pieces of information that will allow of a well-considered decision.

The interview should be **conducted in accordance with the plan** that has been previously formulated. However, the plan must be viewed as a flexible guide rather than a rigid set of rules, and it must be modified as circumstances require during the course of the interview. An interview is a human situation. This being so, the personality of the interviewee must be taken into account and accommodated so far as the other requirements of the interview will allow. Only in this way will the most benefit be gained from the interview. It must also be remembered that in most cases the interviewer is in a position of command, and this fact produces different reactions in different interviewees.

Assessment is not, generally, something that happens at a particular point in an interview: rather is it the result of continuous appraisal from the moment the interview begins. Information will be gathered from the interviewee during the course of the meeting, adding to the knowledge being gained bit by bit. Gradually an assessment emerges based on this knowledge and on the impression made by the interviewee through his personality, his attitude and his apparent motivation. When this moment of final assessment is reached the discussion should be terminated; no useful purpose can be served by prolonging it and in some cases further conversation may interfere with the clear decision already made. In the case of the salesman/customer interview, for example, the customer may quite well be talked out of his favourable assessment of the product if the salesman continues to expound its virtues after the buyer has made up his mind to buy.

Decision on the course of action to take normally comes very soon after the final assessment. Sometimes the decision comes simultaneously with the assessment. The temptation to arrive at a conclusion during the course of assessment, and before the termination of the interview, should be firmly resisted, because in such a case a verdict is probably being taken before all the evidence has been presented. The decision should be objective: if it is made without the full information being presented it will probably be in some measure quite subjective, perhaps influenced by the interviewee's dress, his accent or other personal trait.

Where possible, the interviewee should be informed of the decision at once, otherwise he should be given the result as soon after the meeting as possible. In the latter case it is courteous to tell the person concerned when he may expect to hear the outcome of the interview. However, if the announcement of the decision is to be delayed it is most unwise to give any hint as to the possible outcome in advance. In the case of an applicant for a job, for instance, hopes may be raised that subsequently have to be dashed to the ground.

So important is the question of interviewing skills that it is advisable to look at some of the techniques that help to make a successful interview.

1. The Environment

Except for certain circumstances, such as a salesman/customer interview, all interviews should be held in private. All possible steps should be taken to avoid interruptions, such as informing the telephone switchboard operator to avoid putting telephone calls through, and asking colleagues to respect your privacy for the duration of the interview. Interruptions, even minor ones, can reduce the effectiveness of an interview by impeding the flow of thought and inhibiting conversation. Where a series of interviews has to take place, such as in the selection of an applicant for a job from among a number of interviewees, sufficient time should be allocated for this purpose and be made sacrosanct.

The physical arrangements are also of extreme importance, and must be such that they put the interviewee at his ease. The room should be pleasant and evenly lighted. The chairs should be businesslike but comfortable, and preferably the same for each party. Both people should be able to see each other easily. The interviewee should never be at a disadvantage as against the interviewer. He should not be positioned so that he faces a window directly, thus putting him fully in the light whilst the interviewer is less well lighted. Such a condition simply makes the interviewee feel selfconscious and puts an obstacle in the way of the free flow of conversation. Where possible there should be no physical obstacle between the two people, such as a desk, as this tends to produce a barrier against the free flow of thought as well as a barrier in the physical sense. Rather, if a desk is necessary to the interviewer, the interviewee should be seated at the side of it.

2. The Interviewer's Behaviour

Because he is in control of the interview, the interviewer has a position of authority and this he must be at pains not to abuse. He must, therefore, be especially careful to put the interviewee at his ease and to

give him confidence. The interviewer's attitude should be one of understanding and of wanting to be of assistance. Above all, the interviewer
must not be overbearing, thus creating apprehension or nervousness in
the mind of the interviewee. Neither must the interviewer abuse his
position by putting personal and irrelevant questions. Unless the
interviewee has a calm and relaxed mind communication will be
hindered and the interview will be less than successful.

3. Information Flow

The purpose of an interview is the gathering and interchange of
information, and this can come about only if a smooth, two-way
communication is established from the very beginning. Mutual trust
and confidence are essential, as is a relaxed and friendly atmosphere.
One way to generate these conditions is for the interviewer to introduce
a non-controversial topic of mutual interest at the start of the interview and so establish a rapport between the parties. This will make
subsequent conversation much easier and will lessen any nervousness
the interviewee may feel. The questions to be asked during the interview should have been decided upon during the planning stage; the
form in which they are put will be governed by the circumstances that
develop during the interview.

It must be remembered that it is desirable to **check the answers and
information** that the interviewee gives during the interview, though this
requires tact. There are a number of ways of doing this. For example, a
question may be put in a different manner at a later point in the interview and the response checked with the previous answer. A response
may be referred to again, casually, later and re-examined; or an alteration of approach may be adopted round a topic. It is important,
however, not to give the interviewee the slightest impression that his
integrity is doubted: his confidence must be maintained throughout.

4. The Theme of the Interview

An interview is an exercise in the meeting of minds, as mentioned
earlier. If this is successfully achieved, as it should be in a fruitful interview, then there may be a tendency to discuss interesting topics irrelevant to the objectives of the interview. This must be resisted firmly,
except, perhaps, at the beginning of the meeting when it is necessary to
induce a friendly and relaxed atmosphere. Thus, the purpose of the
interview must be kept firmly in mind throughout the discussion, and
no extraneous subjects allowed to intrude. If the interview has been
carefully planned this should not be very difficult. An unstructured
interview, however, may allow the conversation to wander off the point

with the result that insufficient information is gathered about the interviewee and a conclusion come to based on inadequate data. More often than not such a situation results in decisions being taken that prove unsatisfactory.

Behaviour the Interviewer Should Avoid

The effectiveness and success of an interview depend almost totally on the behaviour of the interviewer. At the beginning of this chapter we looked at some of the things he should do, and we must now examine some of the things he should avoid doing.

(1) He should **not let his personal reactions** to the interviewee **influence his assessment**. In particular, first impressions should not be allowed to colour the interviewer's attitude, otherwise a great deal of the objectivity of the interview will be lost. An open mind as to dress, accent, physical appearance and mannerisms must be maintained unless any of them is fundamental to the objective of the interview.

(2) The interviewer should, at all costs, **avoid asking leading questions** which could indicate to the interviewee what answers are expected: not, for example, 'You can do a trial balance, can't you?', but rather, 'How far can you take the books of account?'

(3) **Too much talking by the interviewer** is **detrimental** to the interview. This is not an uncommon fault, but must be resisted. The interviewee must be allowed to have his say fully and without having to compete for time with the interviewer.

(4) Conversely, the **interviewer** must **not be guilty** of **being taciturn**. If he is uncommunicative the interviewee may be hindered from speaking freely, or may feel compelled to talk too much to avoid embarrassing pauses. In either case the interview will be less than effective. The interviewer is in charge of the interview and it is his responsibility to keep it flowing along his planned course; this means that he must make a reasonable contribution throughout.

(5) Just as it is necessary to avoid putting leading questions, so is it important **not to give information that can give an indication** to the interviewee what sort **of attitude** and **response are expected** of him. At a job interview, for instance, if the interviewer extols the special virtues of the previous occupant of the post, the interviewee may be inclined to claim the same virtues.

(6) The interviewer should very carefully **avoid constantly interrupting** the interviewee's answers and comments, or cutting them short. In addition to resulting in a less than fully effective interview, this practice may also cause the interviewee to feel that the interviewer has little interest in him or his views. A personal rapport must be generated

and maintained all through the meeting, and this includes showing the interviewee that he has the interviewer's interest all the time.

(7) No questions should be put that can be answered simply by 'Yes' or 'No': the interviewee should be **required to express himself fully** at all times.

(8) The interviewee has as much interest in the interview as the interviewer, otherwise he would not be there. The interview should not be closed, therefore, without giving the **interviewee the opportunity to seek all the information** he feels **he needs.** Failure to do this frequently results in misunderstanding and subsequent grievance.

Staff Selection Interviews

A large proportion of the interviews that take place are concerned with the selection of suitable staff, and effective communication at such interviews is of considerable importance for both the employer and the potential employee. In order to try to draw from the applicant all the information that is necessary to make a wise staff choice the personnel profession has formulated a number of interviewing topics with this in mind. Called the 'Seven-Point Plan', it embraces the following seven points:

1. Physical Make-up

Is he agreeable in his bearing, in his speech and in his appearance? Does he appear to suffer from any defects in health or physique that might make him unsuitable for the position?

2. Attainments

Where was he educated? Did he acquire any educational qualifications? If so, what were they and at what level? What relevant training and experience has he had?

3. General Intelligence

What standard of general intelligence does he display? To what extent does his career to date give evidence of his general intelligence?

4. Special Aptitudes

What special talents does he have? Has he, for instance, an aptitude for the use of words, for mathematics? Does he possess any special manual dexterity?

5. Interests

What sort of non-professional interests does he have? Are these activities practical, socially biased or intellectual?

6. Disposition

Does he give the impression of being self-reliant and self-disciplined? Does he appear to be dependable? Would he mix well with other people? Is he argumentative?

7. Circumstances

What are his family and domestic circumstances?

If appointed, would he find the journey to the company's premises easy and reliable?

Would the vacancy for which he has applied be advantageous for his future career and personal development? Would his appointment to this particular position be of benefit to the company?

It goes without saying that it is quite impossible to obtain precise information on these seven points at an interview, and only an opinion can be formed about each. If a series of interviews can be arranged, or if social contact outside the interview can be organised, such as a lunch or a visit round the company's premises, then a deeper insight into the candidate's attributes can be achieved.

It is, also, as well to remember that the interview is an imperfect instrument, but it is the best that has yet been devised for the purposes for which it is used. We can make the most effective use of the interview by observing the points made in this chapter. We should also keep in mind other principles of effective communication such as using language the interviewee can understand, making sure that there is a logical development of questions and discussion, and that sufficient time is afforded for complete answers to questions.

Interviewing Panels

Often interviews are conducted not by one person, but by a panel of two or more people; especially is this so when an important vacancy has to be filled. Usually, of course, the various members of the panel have differing interests in the applicant.

In essence, the principles appertaining to interviewing by one person also apply to interviewing by several. However, it must be recognised that the presence of a **panel** makes the proceedings very much **more formal** and usually places a greater strain on the interviewee, who finds it much more difficult to relax in the presence of a panel than he would in the presence of a single interviewer. Great efforts must be made, therefore, to relieve the increase in tension likely to be experienced by the applicant and to lessen his nervousness in this situation.

Further, there is every **advantage** to be **gained by structuring** the interview. Each member of the panel will, in all probability, be expert in his own field and will be anxious to put questions on particular points appertaining to his special interest. Unless the interview is structured, and understood to be so by all concerned, there is the risk that the interviewee will be assailed by questions from all sides with little or no logic applied to their order or content. In such circumstances the applicant may quite easily become confused or, at least, tense, and be quite unable to show himself in the most favourable light. Under such conditions, in a competitive interview, it is quite possible that a less than satisfactory decision may be made by the panel, with the reward going to the candidate with the strongest nerves rather than the one with the highest ability for the position. Undoubtedly, however, much can be done to ease the situation if the panel is under the control of a firm and understanding chairman.

Questions

1. What are the main characteristics of a properly organised and well-conducted interview? How can an interviewer apply these characteristics in order to monitor and improve his/her performance?   (ICSA, Part I)

2. The effectiveness of an interview depends almost totally on the behaviour of an interviewer. What things should the interviewer avoid doing while interviewing a prospective employee?   (AIA, Foundation Part A)

3. What are the particular merits of panel interviews as opposed to interviews conducted by just one individual?

(AIA, Foundation Part A)

4. List four different purposes for which an interview may be regarded as an appropriate means of communication and in each case comment briefly on the objective of the interview.   (AIA, Foundation Part A)

5. What are the basic problems which affect both the interviewer and the interviewee in a job regrading/promotion interview? How would you as the interviewer ensure that the interview was fair and objective?

(InstAM, Dip. Part I)

6. 'What matters at an interview is not what is said, but how it is heard.' How far do you think this is true?   (ICSA, Part I)

25

MEETINGS

A Definition

Meetings have been defined as 'the gathering together of two or more persons in order to discuss matters of common concern, in order to arrive at a decision or promulgate a policy'. This definition covers all types of meeting—the formal, the informal and the statutory meeting. It also explains the principal purpose for holding a meeting: that is, to have discussion about a matter or number of matters, and if necessary to come to a decision about any action to take. A meeting, therefore, has the same aims as an interview. Where it differs is that all participants at a meeting have equal status and that group decisions or opinions are required to be formulated.

Many company meetings are statutory, being required by the Companies Acts. Such meetings include the Annual General Meeting, perhaps the best known of company meetings. Here the shareholders are given information about the progress of their company over the previous financial year, are asked to elect or re-elect members of the board of directors, and are asked to approve the rate of dividend the directors have decided to declare. The Annual General Meeting is the only time that shareholders can voice their opinion about the directors' conduct of the company without taking specific action under the various sections of the Companies Acts giving them rights to call special meetings.

Outside the requirements of general law or of statute there are many other kinds of meetings, some of which have executive powers and others that possess only the power to advise or to suggest action. Except for the very informal meeting, which is often completely unstructured, every meeting should have some sort of framework within which to work. The rules that govern a meeting will normally be laid down by the body responsible for convening it, but in some cases power is delegated to the meeting to formulate its own rules.

Kinds of Meeting

Before looking at the ways in which meetings are governed, however, we should examine the four important categories within which most

177

meetings fall, and which may affect the way in which any particular meeting is conducted.

1. The Meeting to Inform

Some meetings are called not to discuss a problem and seek a solution, but rather to inform the members of a decision already made and, possibly, to obtain their consent. Often the meeting takes place to ratify what has already been done, just to regularise the situation. It is highly likely that discussion will take place about the problem and explanations given for the decision, but it is unlikely that the decision will not stand. It may seem that such a meeting is autocratic. Very often it is. However, in other cases it may be that a decision has had to be taken in an emergency that arose before the meeting and there was no time to call a meeting. In such instances it may still be necessary to inform the members and to obtain their formal approval.

2. The Meeting to Persuade

A persuasive meeting is one called in order that a member may put a proposal, which he then seeks to persuade the meeting to adopt. The point before the meeting may be one of policy or of strategy, and it is the intent of the proposer to influence the members to accept his proposition. His role is that of persuasive advocate and his aim is to 'sell' his idea.

The two types of meeting mentioned above are positive meetings. In both there is a single-minded purpose: to inform or to persuade. Alternative propositions have really no place at such meetings. We have now to consider the two other categories, which are far less clear-cut.

3. The Consultative Meeting

Here there has been no previous decision taken, neither is it intended to persuade the members to a particular point of view. Instead, a problem is put to the meeting for discussion. In this way the knowledge and experience of the members can be called upon and brought to bear on the problem so that a satisfactory and generally agreed solution may be found. A good chairman is essential to this kind of meeting in order that all members may have a reasonable opportunity to put their views and have them properly considered, and so that the meeting is not dominated by just one or two members.

4. The Enquiring Meeting

This type of meeting seeks to acquire information, and so may be said to be an extension of the consultative meeting. Here the convener searches for ideas and information, and he may very well act as a catalyst to bring out suggestions. Discussion and debate will be freer than at a consultative meeting, and usually more wide-ranging.

Making a Meeting Effective

To be of any value a meeting must be fully effective. If it is not fully effective it has been a waste of the time of several people. If these are salaried officers of a company, a considerable expense may have been suffered as well. In order to avoid failure or only partial success there are certain steps that can be taken by the leader and convener of a meeting:

(1) The **objectives** of the meeting must be made quite clear to those invited. The topics to be dealt with must be given in precise terms so far as this is possible so that members are quite prepared for proper discussion.

(2) Members must be given **adequate notice** of the meeting, and a prepared agenda should be provided.

(3) The **accommodation** chosen for the meeting must be suitable; it must not be cramped for the number expected, it must be comfortable and as free from noise as possible, and efforts must be made to avoid interruptions. Such items as writing materials and ashtrays should be provided.

(4) The **time** of the meeting must be convenient for all concerned, and its probable duration specified.

(5) The **leader** of the meeting must be adequately **prepared**. He should have in advance all the information and material he knows he will need to deal with the proposals to be put, and he should anticipate possible questions and arguments so that he can meet them with confidence.

(6) He should acquaint himself with the **kind of people** who are to take part in the meeting and try to gauge their likely attitudes so that he is prepared for their response and likely participation. Of course, in the case of very many meetings, the members will already be known to each other through previous acquaintance.

If these six points are given proper attention, then the meeting should start off in the right way and there is every chance that it will be successful and effective.

The Conduct of a Meeting

The actual conduct of the meeting whilst it is in progress is equally important. It is upon the leader of the meeting that the burden of successfully running it falls. He may or may not be called the chairman, depending upon the size and type of meeting it is, but whatever his title he should pay attention to the following points:

(1) The **chairman's authority** must be **unquestioned**. Where a member seeks to dispute this authority or to defy it then the chairman must be firm and not allow himself to be overruled.

(2) It is up to the **chairman to set the tone** of the meeting. Members should be at ease with one another, and it is the chairman's duty to ensure this. If necessary he must ensure that members who have not met before are introduced to each other.

(3) The **purpose of the meeting** must be outlined right at the start, despite the notice and the agenda, by a short speech by the chairman.

(4) He must do his best to **ensure that members make useful** and positive **contributions** to the matters being discussed. Unhelpful and unconstructive remarks and criticisms must be checked, but useful criticism should be encouraged.

(5) **Discussion** should be kept **to the point**. Members' interest will be lost if the chairman allows irrelevant argument to develop, and loss of interest will lessen the value of the meeting.

(6) Useful discussion can take place only in an atmosphere of **good humour**. The chairman must, therefore, prevent any sense of acrimony or bad temper from developing. The way he does this will depend upon his own temperament and personality, but in the event of serious bad feeling he must be seen to be completely impartial.

(7) A **meeting must move** forward all the time, logically, from point to point. Too much time must not be spent on one aspect of a discussion to the detriment of the time available for other aspects, neither must aspects already discussed be allowed to be revived later in the argument. One of the skills demanded of the leader of a meeting is to be able to keep discussion flowing logically and at a pace commensurate with the arguments put up and the previously agreed duration of the meeting.

The Appointment of a Chairman

There is no standard procedure for the election of a chairman for a meeting: this will depend entirely on the regulations of the body concerned. If the meeting is an informal one comprising only a very few people it is highly probable that no formal chairman will preside. In such cases leadership of the group often arises naturally, or one person takes on the task at the invitation and mutual agreement of the remainder.

In the case of formal meetings, however, a properly appointed chairman is essential, and the Courts have ruled that a meeting is not legally constituted unless a correctly appointed chairman presides over it. Failure in this respect would lead to all the business conducted at such a meeting being invalid. In some cases the chairman holds office by virtue of his being chairman of a superior body—for instance, the chairman of a company is usually also chairman of the board of directors. In other cases the chairman is elected by the members at the first of a series of meetings and holds this office for a prescribed period— for example, the chairman of a social club.

Where the office is a continuing one, it is usually provided in the regulations that the members may vote for the resignation of an unsatisfactory chairman before his term of office has expired, and for the appointment of a new chairman. Similarly, it is also usual to find that the regulations require the meeting to choose a chairman from among its members present if the official chairman has not arrived at the meeting after a predetermined time (sometimes as short as five minutes). The term 'chairman' is, of course, merely a description of the office, and a woman may act in this capacity, when she is usually addressed as 'Madam Chairman'.

The Duties of a Chairman

To act as an effective chairman of a meeting is not a light task, but there are certain recognised duties and powers possessed by a chairman to help him in his duties. The chairman should:

(1) Be satisfied that his own **appointment** is **valid**.

(2) Ensure that the **meeting** is **properly convened**, validly constituted, and that those present have the right to attend.

(3) Make sure that a **quorum** is present.

(4) Ensure either that the **minutes** of the **last meeting** have been circulated and **read**, or that they are read at the current meeting. This having been done, he should seek the agreement of the members present that the minutes are a true record of the last meeting and then sign them.

(5) See that items are taken in **agenda order**. This does not, of course, prevent the meeting altering the order if it so wishes provided the majority of members agree.

(6) Give those who wish equal **opportunity to speak** on any subject on the agenda as it arises. In doing this, the chairman should try to encourage shy members to voice their views, at the same time curbing those who are verbose.

(7) In the case of dispute, **act fairly** and impartially.

(8) **Reject matters** that may be introduced that are **outside the agenda** or not within the jurisdiction of the meeting. The last item on practically all agendas is 'any other business'. This should not be per-

mitted to be taken as an excuse to bring up matters quite outside the business of the current meeting, unless of a very trivial nature.

(9) **Maintain proper order** during the proceedings and break up any unruly disputes between members. Most rules allow the chairman in such cases to adjourn the meeting for a short while for tempers to cool.

(10) Insist that all **motions, amendments** and **remarks are addressed to the chairman.** No direct communication between different members of the meeting should be allowed and offenders should be asked to put their remarks 'through the chair'. By this means the meeting as a whole is kept in the discussion and also some of the heat is kept out of arguments.

(11) **Put motions and amendments** to the vote of the meeting and pronounce the results.

(12) See that **voting** is carried out **in strict accordance with the regulations** of the meeting. Where there is no formal vote, as often happens at informal meetings, the chairman will pronounce the 'sense' of the meeting.

(13) In the event of equal voting, and where the regulations allow, **use his casting vote.** Contrary to popular belief, a chairman does not have a casting vote as a right: this has to be given him by the regulations. Where such a vote is allowed and is used the chairman must exercise the utmost discretion. It is, in fact, usual for the chairman to vote in such a way as to retain the status quo.

(14) After each discussion, **summarise** the sense of the arguments for the benefit of the meeting.

(15) If **another meeting** is to be held obtain the agreement of the members as to its **date and time.** This is, of course, not necessary where a series of meetings is planned to be held on specific dates.

(16) **Declare the meeting closed** at the end of the business, or if a valid quorum has ceased to exist through the departure of one or more members. The chairman has the prerogative to close the meeting, though the members may request that he does so.

(17) Make sure that **adequate notes** are taken during the meeting so that proper minutes may be written up. These notes may be taken by the chairman himself, but are more often made by the secretary, who will be responsible for actually writing the minutes.

In addition to the points mentioned above, the chairman also has power to have disorderly members expelled from the meeting and to adjourn the meeting if he finds it impossible to restore and maintain proper order.

The rôle of chairman, clearly, is a very onerous one. On him falls the full responsibility for the success and smooth running of the meeting. Some chairmen are weak and allow discussion to ramble on, often without regard to agenda or time. In such cases frequently only the most vociferous members are heard. The opposite situation occurs when the chairman is domineering or arrogant, and imposes his own views on the meeting. In such circumstances it is impossible for balanced discussion to take place.

Standing Orders

Many formal meetings are governed by specific regulations as to procedure, called 'standing orders'. These rules are designed to provide a procedural framework for the meetings concerned and are particularly helpful to members who may not be familiar with the conventions governing the conduct of meetings. Standing orders help to avoid misunderstandings, provide specific rules for most circumstances that may be met during a meeting, and generally assist in ensuring that the event will run smoothly and effectively.

Standing orders are usually formulated for the benefit of the particular meetings for which they are designed. However, there are some rules that are common to most standing orders and these are as follows:

1. The Quorum

The quorum shall consist of .... members, entitled to attend and to vote.

No meeting shall be considered as valid unless a quorum is present continuously throughout the whole of the duration of the meeting.

If at any time a quorum is not present or maintained, then the meeting shall stand adjourned on instructions from the chairman.

2. Notice of the Meeting

Seven clear days' notice must be given in writing to each and every member entitled to attend at a meeting, whether or not such member is entitled to vote.

3. Order of Business

An agenda must be prepared and circulated with the notice of the meeting to every member entitled to attend.

The business before the meeting shall be dealt with in the order set out on the agenda unless it be altered by agreement of the members. Such agreement shall be signified by a simple majority on a vote by a show of hands.

No business not included on the agenda shall be considered by the meeting, but by agreement with the members such business may be carried forward for the agenda of a future meeting.

4. Chairman's Ruling

The chairman's ruling on any matter shall be final. However, should any ruling be challenged by not less than 25 per cent of those present and entitled to vote then the ruling shall be put to the vote on a show of hands. The decision shall be by a simple majority.

5. Speeches

Members shall at all times address the meeting through the chair.

No member may speak on any motion more than once, except with the permission of the chairman. Nevertheless, any member who has spoken on the original motion may also speak on any amendment.

Speeches must be addressed strictly to the content of the motion or amendment before the meeting, and shall be immediately terminated if so directed by the chairman.

6. Motions and Amendments

All motions must be in writing and must be submitted to the secretary of the meeting not less than fourteen days before the date on which the meeting is to be held.

Amendments to motions before the meeting shall be put in writing and handed to the chairman, who will read them out to the members. All motions and amendments shall have a proposer and a seconder. The chairman may act in neither capacity.

Amendments must be put to the vote before the motions they seek to qualify. If an amendment is carried, the amended motion shall be put to the meeting as the substantive motion. If an amendment fails then the original motion must be voted upon without further discussion.

The chairman shall not allow any amendment that is merely a negation of the original motion.

A motion, having been carried, shall not be the subject of further discussion at the same meeting.

7. Voting

Voting shall be by show of hands and the chairman's decision on the result shall be final, subject to standing order 4 above.

A motion shall be deemed to have succeeded if it obtains a simple majority of the votes of those present and entitled to vote. There shall be no right of proxy.

In the event of a tie in voting the chairman may, at his discretion, use his casting vote. Should the chairman decline to use his casting vote in the event of a tie then the motion shall be deemed to have failed.

Any member entitled to vote may abstain if he thinks fit.

8. Unruly Behaviour

If any member acts in an unruly manner, uses unseemly language or interrupts a speaker without permission of the chairman, or if he refuses to obey the chairman when called to order, then he shall be required to leave the meeting. Neither shall he be allowed to return unless and until he gives to the meeting an acceptable apology.

Should this expulsion reduce the number of members to below the required quorum, the meeting must stand adjourned notwithstanding an apology.

9. The Adjournment

The chairman may adjourn the meeting as and when he considers it necessary. Similarly, any member may move the adjournment, when the motion must be seconded and put to the meeting. However, if at the time the motion for the adjournment is put a previous motion is being discussed, no member who has already spoken on the latter motion may move the adjournment.

These nine rules are only examples of what may be found in standing orders. Many other regulations may be included, such as the selection of speakers, right of reply, procedure in the event of the non-arrival of the chairman and the action to be taken in any circumstances likely to be encountered by any particular meeting it is sought to regulate.

Committee Meetings

Committees are a familiar phenomenon of most organised bodies nowadays. The reasons are not far to seek. First, a great deal of expert knowledge is required to deal with even the day-to-day work of large organisations, and second, the governing bodies of most organisations have little time to attend to detailed matters about which a fair proportion of their members have insufficient expert knowledge or experience. Hence, a board of management or other governing body may appoint specialist committees to deliberate on various matters for its information, guidance and counsel. Thus a large commercial enterprise may have a Capital Budget Committee to advise the board of directors on matters of capital investment, a local authority may have a Housing Committee to deal with the specialist matters involved in housing the needy.

Committee Membership

Members of specific committees may be members of the parent body which appoints the committee, or may be specialists directed or invited to the committee because of their particular knowledge, experience or qualifications. Generally speaking, then, committee members may be said to be expert in their fields and are appointed because of this very fact. Committees, of course, operate by holding committee meetings and any authority they have is derived from the fact that they do conduct their business in concert at meetings. Individual committee members have, as a rule, no individual responsibility or authority.

A Committee's Authority

A committee's authority is prescribed by the parent body that appoints it, and the limits to this authority are laid down by the terms of reference agreed at the time of the committee's formation. At no time may a committee exceed either its derived authority or its powers under these terms of reference. For the most part a committee's powers are limited by the simple reason that it has the authority only to consider, to report and to recommend; it has no executive power. Thus, usually a committee makes its reports to its parent body, together with its findings or its recommendations, and it is only the parent body that has the power to take action on the recommendations. A Planning Committee may recommend the demolition of a row of old houses and the building of a block of flats, but the power to put these recommendations into effect lies with the full council.

Nevertheless, some committees do have executive powers, though these may be confined to non-controversial matters, or to matters on which specific limits may be set. For example, a Finance Committee may have the power to authorise expenditure up to a limited sum but not beyond.

Standing Committees

Some matters for which committees are formed are of a continuing nature. Into this category would fall Finance Committees, Planning Committees, Share Transfer Committees and many others whose business is part of the day-to-day work of the organisation to which they belong. Such committees are called 'standing committees' and are, of course, of a permanent nature, though their actual membership may change from time to time. As stated previously, individual members have no status; theirs is a collective power arising from their acting together in a committee meeting.

Ad Hoc Committees

Often, however, a committee is appointed to look into a particular problem or project, and when work on this matter is completed and reported upon, the committee is disbanded. Such a body is known as an '*ad hoc* committee'. The same rules apply to the *ad hoc* committee as apply to the standing committee in regard to authority and powers.

Control of Committees

A committee is, of course, really an extension of the main assembly and the principal body remains responsible for the work of the committee. Consequently, it is essential that the main body has the means of exercising control over the committee. In very many cases this does not pose a significant problem, because the committee is composed of members of the main body, or has a majority of such members. Where, however, the committee is composed of persons who are not members of the main body, or where members of the main body sitting on the committee are in a minority, then some positive steps must be taken so that control is exercised by the responsible body. Particularly is this so if any of the committee members seem to be out of sympathy with the official policy of the main board. In such cases effective control of a committee can be exercised by following the suggestions set out below:

(1) When the main body appoints the committee its resolution to put this into effect should state clearly and precisely the terms of reference under which the committee will carry out its duties. Equally, the committee's powers should be precisely defined, with limits to those powers clearly stated.

(2) The chairman of the main body should be *ex officio* a member of the committee, preferably but not necessarily its chairman.

(3) Care should be taken that members appointed to a committee are, on the whole, sympathetic to the aims and policies of the main body. However, it should be appreciated that a little dissent can be very beneficial in discussion.

(4) Any person who is likely to dominate the committee, however well qualified he might be, should not be appointed unless his inclusion is unavoidable.

(5) The committee should be required to submit promptly to the main body the minutes of each meeting as they are prepared. The same remarks apply to reports that the committee is responsible for preparing.

Committees are a very necessary aid to the work of principal bodies and they help very significantly in the making of well considered and effective decisions.

Subcommittees

A committee is often helped by the appointment of a subcommittee. This is a subdivision of the committee. It is formed to deal with matters within the terms of reference of the committee that the selected members of the subcommittee are especially equipped to consider. Usually a committee has the power to appoint its own subcommittees, but where this is not so the necessary authority must be sought from the main body. Only very rarely has a subcommittee executive power; its function is to investigate the matter it is formed to consider and to report to the full committee.

Notice of Meetings

All formal meetings require notice to be given to all those who are entitled to attend. Failure to do this leads to the possibility that the business conducted at the meeting may be declared invalid. Failure to give notice to even one person entitled to attend may invalidate the meeting and its business. This is, therefore, a very important matter.

The notice that has to be given is laid down in the rules or standing orders governing the meeting, and such regulations must be rigidly observed. For example, if seven clear days' notice is required, this means what it says, and the day of sending the notice and of its receipt are not counted in the required seven.

However, whilst the failure to give adequate notice, or any notice at all, to a few members carries the danger that the meeting may be declared invalid, if the members so affected attend the meeting they may waive their rights about notice. In this case the meeting will be considered valid. Similarly, if the notice to all the members of a meeting does not meet the strict requirements of the regulations and is, therefore, not a proper notice, nevertheless the meeting may be declared valid if all the members so agree.

Finally, even the Courts do not construe the rules of notice absolutely rigidly, as was shown by a decision in 1961. In this case a company held a meeting of shareholders with a view to a reduction of capital. A few members were accidentally overlooked and received no notice, but the Court held that this did not invalidate the resolution passed to effect the desired reduction of capital. Nevertheless, it is very unwise not to follow the rules as to notice very carefully. Any doubt as to the validity of the business carried on at a meeting can cause delays in putting decisions into action and may, in serious cases, lead to expensive litigation.

Meetings that are held regularly, such as directors' meetings, committee meetings and the like, do not, strictly speaking, need formal notice. However, it is usual to send a notice, nevertheless, as this acts as a reminder at least. Similarly, if the date of a subsequent meeting is agreed at a meeting, again no notice is strictly required, but is usually sent.

The Agenda

Every formal meeting needs a guide so that its business is carried forward positively and in an orderly manner, and so that no item that should be considered is omitted. The guide prepared for this purpose is the agenda. This is merely a list of the matters to be put before the meeting for discussion and decision. Tradition has given the agenda an accepted format, starting with, in most cases, 'Apologies for absence', followed by 'Minutes of the last meeting' and then 'Matters arising'. Then follow the new items to be considered and the agenda finishes with two time-honoured items, 'Any other business' and 'Date of the next meeting'.

Naturally, every agenda is not prepared precisely in this fashion. Many omit reference to apologies for absence, and others itemise the matters in the minutes of the last meeting to be considered, instead of requiring the chairman to go through those minutes item by item putting each to the meeting for consideration. The latter method can be a great time-waster, and often encourages discussion to start on a matter already decided at the previous meeting. Such discussion must be firmly

```
                    NOTICE OF MEETING


         A meeting of the Safety Committee will be held on
         14th May, 19.., at 3.30 pm in the Committee Room

                        4th May, 19..


                         AGENDA


         1.    Apologies for absence.
         2.    Minutes of meeting held on 12th February, 19..
         3.    Matters arising.
         4.    Provision of fire extinguishers in Paint Store.
         5.    Recruitment of Safety Officer.
         6.    Any other business.
         7.    Date of next meeting.
```

Fig. 27. Specimen of combined Notice of Meeting and Agenda.

stopped by the chairman. Again, if there is not to be a subsequent meeting, then the last item—'Date of next meeting'—will not arise.

It is usual for the notice of a meeting and its agenda to be combined, and a specimen is given in Fig. 27.

Methods of Voting

Except at very informal meetings, when the chairman may 'sense' the desire of the meeting and record this accordingly, all meetings need some method of voting so as to determine the will of the meeting. How voting shall take place will be laid down in the regulations governing the meeting, but may be one or more of the following:

(1) **By Acclamation.** In this method the chairman first asks those in favour of the motion to express this by saying 'aye' and then those against to say 'nay' or 'no'. His decision is made by assessing which acclamation has the greater volume.

(2) **By Show of Hands.** This is the common method of voting, and is the accepted method at common law subject to regulations to the contrary. Each member has only one vote. The chairman is responsible for counting the hands but may be assisted by tellers.

(3) **By Poll.** A poll is carried out by members casting their votes on paper. A poll is a common law right, and may be demanded by any member validly present at the meeting. Unlike the previous two methods of voting, in a poll each member has a number of votes according to his interest. Thus, shareholders in companies have as many votes as they have voting shares. A poll may be held immediately on demand, or may be held at a later date. It is usual to require voting by poll to be done in person so that a poll at the meeting allows only those present to cast their votes whereas if it is held later other members may also take part.

(4) **By Ballot.** This is similar to a poll, but is a secret vote. Usually a ballot paper is used but in some cases the more old-fashioned method of casting votes by balls—white for 'aye' or black for 'nay'—is employed (hence the term 'black-balled'). Where the membership of an organisation is large and all are entitled to vote, then sometimes a ballot is taken by post.

If a poll or a ballot is held after voting by acclamation or by show of hands, the decision by poll or ballot overrides the previous vote. As stated previously, if the voting is even the chairman may, if he has one, use his casting vote to produce a decision, in which case he normally votes so as to leave things as they were. However, it must be stressed that a chairman has no right to a casting vote unless this is given him in the regulations. Where no casting vote is provided for and there is even voting then the motion concerned is lost.

The voting procedure is complete only when the chairman has declared the result. When a motion has been passed at a meeting by a valid vote, it may not again be raised in discussion, neither may it be rescinded, at that meeting.

Finally on voting, most rules provide for a simple majority to pass a motion. However, this is by no means universal and sometimes a specific percentage majority is necessary for a decision to be validly made.

Minutes

Meetings are held to determine action, to formulate policy or to make decisions. This being so, it is essential that the business of the meeting be truthfully and accurately recorded. This is the function of the minutes. However, they are not a report of the meeting, and will not normally record argument and discussion, but solely decisions reached.

Like the agenda, minutes have a conventional format. They are headed with the title of the meeting concerned, its venue and the date and time it was held. The names of those attending will be shown, with apologies for absences. In recording the business done, practice varies from body to body. Some minutes contain only the bare resolutions that have been passed, whereas others will include names of proposers and seconders. On occasion, though rarely, brief accounts of the arguments leading to the decisions are included. Where a resolution requires action by a named person this fact will generally be stated, as will any descriptions required to ensure the identification of sites, materials and so on.

When minutes are written up, the agenda of the meeting is used as a guide, and generally the secretary responsible for the minutes makes suitable notes on his or her copy of the agenda during the meeting. Each item in the minutes is numbered and in order to ensure that all items are included from the very beginning, thus providing a complete historical record, they are often numbered consecutively following on from one set of minutes to the next. This is particularly important where minutes are kept in loose-leaf binders, as it is reasonable proof than none is missing.

Signing the Minutes

It is usual for the regulations governing meetings to provide that the minutes be signed by the chairman of the next succeeding meeting. This is perfectly proper and simple where meetings are held at dates not too far apart. However, where there are long intervals between meetings it is

Minutes of the meeting of the Safety Committee
held on 14th May, 19.., at 3.30 pm in the
Committee Room.

Present: A. Dorritson   (Chairman)
                  B. Sideley
                  F. Bothamstone
                  S. Sydnie

In Attendance: J. Comely   (Secretary)

322. Apologies for absence were received from Messrs.
      A. Anville and B. Burdock.

323. The minutes of the meeting held on the 12th February,
      19.., having been previously circulated, were taken
      as read. They were signed by the Chairman as a correct
      record of that meeting.

324. **Matters Arising**
      A tender has been accepted for the installation of
      sprinkler valves in the General Office and work is
      due to start on the 1st June.

325. **Fire Extinguishers for Paint Store.**
      It was agreed that an additional four fire extinguishers
      should be purchased and installed in the Paint Store.
      Mr Sydnie was instructed to obtain tenders from three
      suppliers for consideration at the next meeting.

326. **Recruitment of Safety Officer**
      It was agreed that a Safety Officer should be recruited
      as soon as possible. Mr Dorritson will instruct the
      Personnel Department to draw up a suitable job
      specification with a view to advertising this post.

327. **Any Other Business**
      The low level of lighting on the stairway in the old
      building was brought up by Mr Sideley. Mr Sydnie
      promised to look into this matter and report at the next
      meeting.

328. The next meeting will be on the 30th July at 3.30 pm.

                        CHAIRMAN

Fig. 28. Specimen Minutes.

more sensible for provision to be made for the signing prior to the next meeting. In either case, once signed the minutes become the legal record of the business transacted at the meeting to which they refer and must on no account be altered. Where the minutes are signed at the next meeting it is usual for the chairman to have the secretary read the minutes, or to have them circulated previously and taken as read. He then asks the meeting to confirm that the minutes are correct before he signs them. By 'correct' he means a truthful and accurate record of the business transacted: this is not an invitation for any item to be reopened, which would be quite irregular. Should any member disagree with an item in the minutes it is for him, with the permission of the chairman, to put a motion to the current meeting so that the item concerned can be overturned by a proper vote if this is the wish of the meeting.

Where meetings are held at regular intervals it is common for copies of the minutes of the previous meeting to be circulated with the notice and agenda for the next one. This gives the members the opportunity to study them and to formulate any questions necessary under the agenda item 'Matters arising'. It also provides a record of the meeting for those members who were unable to attend.

A specimen of a common form of minutes is given in Fig. 28, based on the specimen agenda shown earlier in this chapter.

A Glossary of Meetings Terms

The procedures in connection with meetings have a vocabulary of their own. The main terms used are set out below.

Addendum An addition to a motion. Really an amendment and often so called. The term 'rider' is often used instead.

Ad hoc Literally 'for this' (purpose). An ad hoc committee is one set up for one special purpose on completion of which it is disbanded.

Adjournment A temporary cessation of a meeting. A meeting may be adjourned only in accordance with the rules of the body concerned, and reasons for this action have been discussed earlier in this chapter. When the meeting is resumed, be it hours, days or weeks after the adjournment, it is considered to be the same meeting and not a new one. Hence, any resolutions passed at the first sessions may not again be raised.

Agenda	The programme of a meeting—the list of items to be considered.
Amendment	A proposed alteration to a motion already before a meeting. An amendment must be voted on before the motion it seeks to alter, and if passed must be incorporated in the main motion. It must not just negate the motion.
Carried	A motion is said to be carried when it is passed by the meeting.
Casting vote	This is a vote often given to the chairman of a meeting to avoid an impasse in the event of even voting on a motion. A chairman has no right to this vote unless it is authorised by the regulations governing the meeting. It is usual for it to be used to preserve the status quo.
Closure	When discussion on an item of business has been going on for an undue length of time any member may try to curtail the discussion by moving the closure. To do this he puts the motion to the meeting (seconded if necessary) 'that the question be now put'. If this is carried then the motion or amendment before the meeting must be voted upon without further discussion.
Co-opted member	Someone who is invited to serve on a committee of which he is not a member, but who, by his special knowledge, may be able to contribute significantly to it.
Ex officio	Such a member serves on a committee not because he has been elected, but because of his position or the office he holds. For instance, a group accountant will serve on a Finance Committee by reason of his position in the company. The term means 'by virtue of office'.
Lie on the table	If a meeting passes a resolution that a certain matter 'lie on the table', then this decision means that it will be left in abeyance more or less indefinitely, and that no action will be taken upon it.
Minutes	These are the official records of the business transacted at a meeting. When they are signed by the chairman as a correct record, which is usually done

at the next meeting, they become the legal *prima facie* evidence of the proceedings of the meeting to which they refer. They also constitute the authority for any actions to be taken by virtue of decisions made at the meeting.

Motions

This is the correct term for proposals put before a meeting. Having been passed they are called 'resolutions'. However, it is quite common for the term 'resolution' to be used both before and after a proposal has been accepted.

Nem. con.

In full *nemine contradicente*, this term is used to indicate that a motion has been approved without any votes being cast against it, one or more of those present having abstained.

Next business

If for some reason, such as inconclusive discussion, it is decided not to put a motion to the vote, a member may propose 'that we proceed to the next business'. If this is carried the motion before the meeting will be dropped and the next item on the agenda will be put up for discussion.

Out of order

When there is a breach of the regulations governing the meeting, the person in breach is said to be 'out of order'. It is the chairman's duty to call such a member to order.

Points of order

These relate to questions concerning breaches of procedure or of the conduct of the meeting. Any member may put to the chairman for his ruling any question about possible non-compliance with standing orders, about the absence of a quorum, about irrelevant remarks, unseemly language and so on.

Proposer

One who puts a motion for consideration of the meeting. Any motion must be put through the chairman, and must be submitted in accordance with the regulations governing the meeting.

Proxy

Where the regulations allow—which is not common except at company meetings, where the law requires it—a member entitled to attend and vote at a meeting may appoint and send a substitute, who is known as his proxy.

Quorum   The number of members required to constitute a valid meeting. This minimum number is laid down in the rules governing the meeting.

Resolution   The correct term for a motion that has been passed by a meeting. Sometimes used to mean a motion, particularly in connection with company meetings.

Seconder   One who supports a proposal put to a meeting. The rules of a body will establish whether or not a seconder to a proposal is needed, but this is usual. The main advantage of the use of a seconder is that it avoids wasting a meeting's time on the discussion of a proposal that has the support only of the proposer.

Sine die   This means 'without date'. A meeting is said to be adjourned *sine die* when no date has been decided for its resumption.

Standing orders   These are the permanent rules by which a meeting is governed. They are normally established by the governing body which the meeting serves, and may usually be altered only by that body in general meeting.

Substantive motion   A motion that has been amended. A substantive motion may be further altered by other amendments if it is the will of the meeting, but must never become a direct negation of the original motion.

Ultra vires   This is the Latin for 'beyond one's powers'. A meeting is acting *ultra vires* when it attempts to discuss matters outside its terms of reference or beyond the purposes for which it was constituted.

Unanimously   A motion is carried unanimously when all the members of a meeting have voted in its favour. Where all votes are in favour but there are abstentions the term used is *nem. con.* (see above).

Questions

1. How does a committee differ from its parent body? Draw up the main standing orders for a joint consultative committee.   (CIT, Intermediate)

2. Explain the meaning of the following terms often used at meetings:
Ad hoc; addendum; casting vote; *ex officio*; lie on the table; *nem. con.*; quorum; *sine die*; *ultra vires*; unanimous.   (ICSA, Part I)

3. Various types of meeting take place in companies and business organisations. Included in these types are: the meeting to inform, the meeting to persuade, the consultative meeting and the enquiring meeting. Describe each type of meeting in sufficient detail to demonstrate your understanding of the differences between them. (AIA, Foundation Part A)

4. 'To be of any value a meeting must be fully effective.' What are the characteristics of an effective meeting?

How can an administrator prepare and conduct meetings to ensure they possess these characteristics? (ICSA, Part I)

5. What powers are usually given to a chairman in respect of normal business meetings? (AIA, Foundation Part A)

6. How important is the role of chairman in ensuring the effectiveness of a committee? (ICSA, Part I)

26

PUBLIC RELATIONS, ADVERTISING AND THE MASS MEDIA

If we are to consider communication fully we must not omit a brief look at public relations and advertising, and at the mass media.

Public Relations

The Institute of Public Relations has defined public relations as 'the deliberate, planned and sustained effort to establish and maintain mutual understanding between an organisation and its public'.

It is the function of public relations, therefore, to create a feeling of goodwill in an organisation's dealings with its customers and with the public at large, to foster trust in its integrity and generally to ensure that the company has an attractive image in the outside world. The creation of goodwill and trust does not stop with the general public: it has become an established practice also to promote the same atmosphere among a company's workers. Having created a good image for the concern, however, public relations has the continuing task of maintaining this image, sometimes in the face of adverse behaviour by the organisation.

The Need for Public Relations

The need nowadays for a specialist public relations function is not far to seek. In the past most businesses and other organisations were relatively small, and very many were managed either by the proprietors themselves, or by those who had a strong family interest in the enterprises. Good customer and staff relations were created and maintained by these people as a matter of self-interest as well as by a personal concern in the success of the organisation. Very many employers took a paternal interest in their staff and the goodwill thus generated spilled over from the staff to the customers. Such goodwill brought with it the loyalty of the workers to their firm and a genuine desire to serve the firm's customers to the best of the staff's ability. Thus, these proprietors and managers were their own public relations officers, though they never thought of themselves as such. Staff, also, were engaged in the public relations exercise by virtue of the rapport that formed between employer and employee.

The growth of business enterprises caused by the need for more and more capital quite beyond the means of the owner-manager has resulted in the need for the employment of specialist managers who, for the most part, have no financial stake in their company. This has led, in turn, to vast, impersonal enterprises where the workers have ceased to identify themselves with their company in the same way that they did in the past. This lack of strong, personal involvement has given rise to the lack of personal interest displayed by many workers, including sales staff, in their customers and the impression the customers, and the world at large, receive of the enterprise. The sheer size of many companies means that it is virtually impossible for management to control the behaviour of the staff to customers and others.

The good reputation of an organisation and its goodwill are built up only after a long period of time, and with much effort, but they are destroyed very quickly indeed. Even relatively minor faults can harm a firm's reputation, leading to loss of customers and thus to loss of revenue and profit. An uncooperative attitude by a member of the sales staff, an impolite response by a telephone operator, can result in bad customer relations. A complaint dealt with ungraciously, particularly if the complainant feels it has been dealt with unfairly, can have an adverse effect on an organisation's reputation that may linger long. Furthermore, it takes longer and much harder work to recover a lost reputation than it does to create one.

Hence the positive efforts that are made to foster good public relations and to maintain a good public image: these are the sphere of the public relations officer.

Accomplishing the Public Relations Task

However, the public relations officer is charged with more than the protection of the company's good name in dealing with criticisms of company behaviour; he is also responsible for explaining his organisation's policies and actions as they affect the social environment generally. Particularly where the physical environment is concerned, he will take every step possible to meet objections with rational explanations, and will have to pacify pressure groups of one kind or another, some of whose members may border on the fanatical.

The rôle of the public relations officer is not only a defensive one. A great deal is done in a positive way to enhance the company image, and large companies devote substantial funds to many activities unconnected with their businesses. Many of the major enterprises sponsor all sorts of public events in sport and the arts, and can be said to have taken over the rôle of the wealthy patron in many cases. The John Player League and the Gillette Cup are but two sports examples. Other activities include the production and free loan to interested bodies of films illustrating various aspects of the firm's business and its concern with the environment, the provision of speakers for various clubs, conferences and other meetings, the production of brochures and magazines such as *Know Britain*, issued by Trusthouse Forte, and the publication in the press of letters and articles intended to explain the company's activities and to enhance its image. Perhaps one of the best known of public relations exercises is the literary lunch.

The function of the public relations department is not directly to sell. Its purpose is to show the world that the firm concerned is socially aware and socially responsible. At the customer level the purpose is to indicate the company's desire to serve the customer to the best of its ability, and in this respect it is hoped that sales will ultimately result. To carry out these tasks the public relations officer will use all the media available to him. At national level he will probably take space in the national newspapers and magazines to put his company's case, or he may make use of the advertising facilities offered by the Independent Broadcasting Authority. Where his organisation is intending to carry out some activity that could be construed as adversely affecting the environment at a local level he may put his case in the local newspapers, or call local meetings; or do both. In both situations he may also write letters to the newspapers on the topic in question. Matters involving individual customers, or individual people, will probably be dealt with on a personal basis by letter or by interview.

For favourable publicity, particularly if more directed to the marketing effort, he may organise conferences of interested parties probably supported by suitable films. To promote his company's image as a helpful organisation, particularly if the products are hobby items, he will make lecturers available to clubs and interested societies to explain the use of his company's goods, and these talks will almost always be supported by appropriate slides, films and other publicity material. This is very widely done, for example, with photographic goods, where organisations such as Ilford Limited and Kodak Limited have panels of lecturers who attend camera club meetings, demonstrating their companies' products and answering queries concerning the use of materials and apparatus. Exhibitions and advice centres are an extension of this service.

The Credibility of Public Relations

The credibility of the practice of public relations has frequently been called into question. Often it is seen as just an exercise to excuse some action that has been taken, or is proposed to be taken, by a company for its own benefit and to the detriment of its customers or to the public. As with all human activity, the public relations function is not all good nor is it all bad. Where the practice is used genuinely to inform and explain in an honest fashion, then the public are prepared to trust it. Where, however, public relations officers endeavour to explain away some disadvantageous act or practice then this firm will certainly lose credibility, and the public will be loath to believe its honesty in the future.

Advertising

Unlike public relations, advertising is directly concerned with selling the goods or services of a company. In the main it is concerned to perform three functions:

(1) It seeks to **inform the public** what goods or services the company can provide. Because of the diversity of a company's activities it is not usually possible to convey information on its whole range, and advertisements normally concentrate on one product or service at a time. Thus, in advertising motorcars, the advertiser usually concentrates on one model only.

(2) The second function of advertising is to **persuade potential customers** that they need the particular product or service being advertised, and that, in particular, it is the product of the advertiser that will best fill their need. In this respect it can be said that advertising tries to create a demand and then the advertiser seeks to satisfy it by persuading the public that he can do this better than his competitors.

(3) Thirdly, advertising seeks to **maintain customer loyalty.** It does this by convincing the customer that he has made the right choice in the first place, and that future purchases from the same source will continue to give greater satisfaction than purchases from other sources.

It is in the area of persuasion that advertising attracts most criticism, and where the integrity of the practice is most in doubt. Communication here is very much to the emotions, rather than to reason. The intrinsic qualities of the product very often take second place to what the use of the product is supposed to do for the customer. Thus, the use of a certain perfume by a woman will make the men's heads turn; or the smoking of a certain cigar by a man will make him more attractive to women.

This aspect of advertising is 'selling dreams', and is most evident in the world of cosmetics and similar products. It is much less common in the selling of industrial goods, such as machines, though even here it does occur. For example, an advertiser may try to show that the installation of his particular machine will cut costs and thereby increase profits, rather than demonstrate the superior qualities of the machine itself.

Advertising, then, is a **direct effort** to create and increase sales. It can be undertaken in many ways. The **traditional medium** of advertising is the **press**. In both newspapers and magazines a significant proportion of the contents consists of advertisements of various kinds, from full-page displays to small, classified announcements. The independent **television** channels are probably the **most effective** avenue for advertising, as they provide both moving images and colour. The costs of television advertising are very high, however, and this medium is most suited to consumer goods.

Commercial radio in Britain is also a vehicle for advertisements and there are, of course, certain continental radio stations, such as Luxembourg, that carry English-language programmes supported by advertisements in English. Other media are advertising slides and short films in cinemas, and posters and direct mail advertising. Cinema slides and most of the short films are usually devoted to shops and businesses in the locality of the cinema showing them, though films are occasionally sponsored by nationally known concerns. Posters really come under the heading of reminders and are frequently used to support advertising campaigns in other media. Few people stop to read a poster so its impact must be immediate, which means that it should evoke the retrieval of material already absorbed from elsewhere, such as from a magazine.

Direct mail advertising is commonly used in certain industries such as reference book publishing, but is rather unpredictable in its results. A 10 per cent response in enquiries from a mail shot is considered to be very good, but the conversion to orders may be as low as 1 per cent of the enquiries. Problems can also arise because of out-of-date mailing lists, when a proportion of the circulars is returned because the addressees have moved away. Nevertheless, direct mail advertising can be cheaper than other forms of advertising and so the low response may be acceptable.

Akin to direct mail advertising is the insert in magazines. Again, this method is frequently used by publishers, particularly those offering technical or professional books, when the inserts are stuffed between the pages of the appropriate trade and professional journals.

Local newspapers also carry inserts from local tradesmen of all kinds, particularly to announce the start of sales or special offers. This method offers inexpensive access to possible customers for the local shops and businesses. There has also grown up, over the last few years, the free area newspaper that carries advertisements from various businesses in the locality, and which is financed out of the revenue obtained from the advertisers. Such newspapers are delivered to householders throughout the neighbourhood and carry, not only advertisements, but also helpful and interesting articles on a variety of topics.

Similarly, there are **monthly magazines** and **weekly papers** devoted to special interests and circulated only to people with special connections: these are free to the recipients and are paid for out of the proceeds of the advertisements they carry. Such specialist publications, of which *Computer Weekly* and *Business Systems & Equipment* are two examples, include a large number of articles of particular interest to their readers concerning both developments in equipment and items of general interest.

Advertising is a form of communication and so the same rules apply here as apply to other methods of communication. The language must be right and the vocabulary appropriate to the market it is hoped to influence. The medium must be appropriate and the timing must be suitable. Most important, however, is that the advertisement must evoke a willingness to read it and understand it. It must also generate a favourable response in the mind of the reader (or viewer) and engender a feeling of trust in the advertiser and in the goods advertised.

Choosing the Advertising Medium

The choice of the appropriate medium is probably more important in advertising than in any other form of communication. That being so, we must examine the factors that will influence the choice of medium by the advertiser.

(1) The **market** aimed at is of utmost importance. This includes both the kind of product or service being offered and also the social stratum it is desired to influence. It would be appropriate to offer a cookery book in a women's magazine but not in a magazine devoted to angling. Similarly, an advertisement for a Rolls Royce would be more successful in *The Times* than in the *Daily Mirror*.

(2) Is the **market** a **local** one, **or** is it a **national** one? A local newspaper would serve the former quite adequately, as would the local cinema. For the national market a national newspaper, either daily or Sunday, an appropriate journal or magazine or even television would be appropriate.

(3) **Are** the **names and addresses** of potential customers **easily available?** If so, then the use of direct mail advertising could be considered. Despite the low response rate, this form of approach does enable the advertiser to aim precisely at the customers he hopes to interest.

(4) If the product or service offered lends itself to a **visual or moving** display then the production of **slides or moving films** might be considered appropriate. Depending upon the nature of the offer, and whether it is local or national, presentation of the slides or films could be made in local cinemas, loaned to interested societies or clubs for restricted markets, or shown on television.

O. & M. Supplies Unlimited

OFFICE MACHINES•STATIONERY SUPPLIES
18 Office Road
EVERYTOWN
Oldshire
Telephone: 0398 - 77889

ECE/OMS

18th May, 19..

Newbuilders Ltd.,
Brick Lane,
CONCRETEVILLE, News.

Dear Sirs,   MONEY DOWN THE DRAIN

    Have you ever considered how much of your money
ends up in the waste-paper basket?   It can be a considerable
amount if you are using an out-of-date photocopier.

    We have just received a consignment of the most
advanced plain paper copiers from Ecknor Photocopiers which
are designed to cut down wasted copies to the irreducible
minimum.   Not only that, but as they use standard bond paper,
the same as your typist now uses, there are no storage costs
for specially coated or sensitive materials, nor even for
special plain paper: you already have suitable paper in stock.

    Think of the convenience of being able to run off
copy specifications and other documents quickly and at next
to no cost!

    To demonstrate one of these new machines in your
own office would take us very little time: may we do this
for you?

Yours faithfully,
O. & M. SUPPLIES UNLIMITED

A. FOTOMAN,
Manager.

Fig. 29. Specimen direct sales letter.

(5) Consideration must, certainly, be given to the **response** enjoyed **from the various media in the past**. It is important, when employing a medium, to try to find some means of assessing its effectiveness. In newspaper and magazine advertising, where replies are sought direct, it is a simple matter to include a coding in the address to identify the source—for example, 'Dept.S.T.' for the *Sunday Times*. Direct questions to customers about how they heard of the product or service are also a ploy sometimes used. In general advertising, however, it is extremely difficult, if not impossible, to identify where sales and enquiries are generated, particularly if several media are used simultaneously.

(6) The selection of a medium may sometimes be constrained by the amount of **money allocated** for advertising. A calculated assessment of the expected gain in revenue against the proposed advertising budget must be made so that the utmost benefit may be extracted from the advertising expenditure. The effectiveness of television advertising is beyond question, but it is extremely expensive. A very large potential market is, therefore, essential to make it an economical proposition.

(7) Another consideration in the choice of medium is whether it is desired to increase **sales to existing customers, or** whether to try to attract **new ones**. There is a subtle difference between the various media even, ostensibly, serving the same kind of people. Two apparently similar magazines, for example, may have two entirely different readerships. Careful comparison of, say, *Popular Gardening* with *Amateur Gardener*, or *Woman's Own* with *Woman's Realm*, will illustrate this point.

The **production of advertisements** is a **specialised** and expert undertaking, and is best left to those who have the knowledge and skill to prepare effective material. This applies equally well to the circular sales letter, which is only too often left to someone in the sales office who is supposed to have a flair for it. The effective sales letter must be short, certainly not more than one page unless it is very skilfully composed, and must command attention from the very first line. It must be fully informative and must create in the reader's mind a desire to buy. A reader soon loses interest if the letter is vague or difficult to understand; if it is over-long he may not finish it. The rules appertaining to letter-writing, and set out in Chapter 14, apply equally to the writing of sales letters. A specimen of a direct sales letter is given in Fig. 29.

The Mass Media

In any examination of effective communication a brief look at the mass media is essential. The first to come to mind is probably the newspaper.

Newspapers

Newspapers have been with us in Britain, in one form or another, since the early seventeenth century. Until fairly recently, however, their effect on the bulk of the population was very limited for the simple reason that most people were illiterate. It was not until the latter part of the last century, with the introduction of compulsory education, that the ability to read became widespread, and even then the road to literacy was long and slow. Nevertheless, with the increasing numbers of the public able to read, the demand for newspapers, magazines and books gradually rose until today it is accepted that the majority of the population will have access to all forms of printed matter.

Unlike some other forms of mass media, print requires some effort from the reader to receive the communication: he must physically take up the paper or the book to read it. He has consciously to make the effort to absorb the meaning of the words. Consequently, newspaper editors feel it necessary to make a positive and determined effort to attract the attention of the potential reader. In pursuing this aim they made use of eye-catching headlines, often in large bold type, of so-called glamour pictures, and of similar devices. This form of activity is at its most lurid in the popular press, but even the 'quality' papers are not beyond reproach in this direction in the effort to increase circulation.

Vivid headlines and an exaggerated writing style in order to dramatise events and excite the reader have inevitably led to a debasement of our language, and to the habitual wrong use of words because of their sound rather than their true meaning. Two common words come readily to mind to illustrate this trend: 'photogenic', which really means 'generating light', is now used to describe a person, usually female, who is photographically attractive, and 'decimate' which, literally, means 'to kill every tenth person' is now used to indicate almost total destruction of a fighting force or other similar group.

Magazines

Magazines, like newspapers, have to appeal to a vast public to pay their way, and so have to adopt similar practices to newspapers to maintain and increase circulation. However, generally speaking their treatment of the English language is less abusive than that of certain papers, and their efforts to attract readers are often concentrated on eye-catching covers and cover designs. Further, as the majority of them are slanted to a particular readership with a specialist interest, the need for a garish attraction is less.

Radio

Radio is a very potent mass medium, and has the advantage over the printed word that its audience does not have to be able to read, and so it can penetrate to all sections of the community, literate or not. Further, it can be listened to without the need for exclusive concentration. This, of course, constitutes a danger. Whereas certain tasks, particularly of a manual nature such as knitting or decorating, can be carried on at the same time as the radio is listened to, certain other activities can leave only a part of the mind free to receive the radio broadcast, and thus an incomplete picture of the broadcast may be received. In the latter conditions erroneous impressions may be retained, giving rise to false conclusions from the subject matter purveyed. Furthermore, the radio is often used as a background, a sort of sound wallpaper, of which the recipient is only dimly aware. True, this relates mainly to music of various kinds, but it does mean that when the broadcaster wishes to attract attention he has to make a special effort. To do this he often uses what is known as a 'jingle', accompanied by a 'racy' style of speech. This 'racy' style has led, as with newspapers, to a debasement of the language, and nowhere is this truer than in the broadcast advertisements put out by the commercial stations.

Television

It can probably be said without fear of contradiction that the most influential mass medium is television, because it combines both sound and moving pictures. However, it is not just radio with pictures, but a medium in its own right. The marriage of sound and sight, projected on a small screen and taken right into the home, has an impact not provided by any other form of communication. Once switched on, the television seems to rivet the attention of the viewer as no other medium can, and most people seem unable to switch it off even if they do not like the programme being broadcast. Further, it demands almost exclusive concentration, unlike radio, and also appears to command much more authority than either ordinary sound broadcasting or the press. The addition of colour to the picture has also increased its attraction.

Because of the competition in the United Kingdom between the three television channels, especially between the two controlling bodies, the fight to attract attention is even fiercer in television than it is in radio. Thus we find that in this medium the language has been distorted and debased even more than with radio and the press. Whilst a great deal of this can be laid at the door of the advertisers, the journalists and playwrights are not free from blame. An added problem of language usage in television is the fact that much of the material shown originates in the USA, where English usage is different in many respects from its usage in Britain. Further, many of the programmes made in this country are produced with an eye to the American market and so transatlantic speech patterns are adopted to make the material more attractive to the Americans and Canadians.

It must also be remembered that both radio and television use the language of speech, which is much less formal than written English, and which includes slang and other unconventional expressions not normally acceptable in the written word. In fact, we are becoming so exposed to the spoken word over so many hours of the day that many people are beginning to find it almost impossible to write formal English even where this is necessary.

Other Forms

Other forms of mass media that are available for those who seek to communicate with the public at large are the theatre, the cinema and books. All of these demand a conscious act on the part of the recipient to indulge in them. Thus, it is necessary to journey to the theatre, to buy a ticket, and to give up two or three hours to see the show. The cinema requires similar actions on the part of the film-goer, though he may not have to travel so far to see the show of his choice as the theatre-goer does. The reader of books must either visit his bookshop or his local library, make his selection, and then be prepared to spend a considerable time in reading the book he has chosen. This form of mass communication probably demands more concentration from the receiver than any of the others. The need to attract audiences and readers has led to a debasement of standards in the theatre, the cinema and in authorship as it has in the other media that have been discussed.

With all the mass media, much of the debasement of standards of all kinds is, of course, due to the fact that the content is directed to audiences who do not wish to think or to analyse, but only to absorb.

It must not be forgotten that **mass communication**, for the most part, **is one way only**: it provides information and tries to persuade, but receives little feedback from its audience. To encourage some response, newspapers include correspondence columns for letters from their readers, and the radio and television promote discussion programmes, often inviting comments from listeners and viewers. Request programmes are also put on as much to sound out audience response and numbers as to provide programme material.

The Influence of the Mass Media

Much argument has raged over recent years as to the way the mass media, particularly television, can influence public opinion, public attitudes and public behaviour, and to what extent this takes place. A great many people do believe that television does influence general behaviour patterns and there are others who contend that television merely mirrors what is actually taking place and does not positively change the way people act and think. Evidence for either point of view is available from sociologists and others. However, it is true that perception is influenced by stored experiences and impressions, whether they be first-hand or second-hand. Second-hand experiences are provided by all the mass media, not only television, and it seems obvious, therefore, that they must have some effect on perception and, hence, on attitudes and behaviour.

Some experts go further, and suggest that the mass media can even condition the public. In support of this they point to the rise of the Nazis in Germany in the 1930s. The propaganda machine of the National Socialist Party made extensive use of radio, film and newspapers to condition the German population to their dogma, and their success cannot be denied: 'The big lie, often repeated, will ultimately be believed.'

Business Management and the Mass Media

Except for advertising their wares, and announcements of a public relations nature, the mass media have limited use for business management. Nevertheless, television and the newspapers, especially the local ones, have been pressed into service on occasion to communicate with employees when the more usual means have not been available. Thus, messages to recall striking workers have been put into local newspapers, and at least on one occasion, have been the subject of an announcement on television. Another example is that of companies involved in takeover bids trying to influence shareholders either to accept or reject the scheme.

The problems and challenges presented by mass communication are difficult and exciting, and range well beyond the constraints set for this book.

Questions

1. How does the practice of public relations differ from consumer and industrial advertising? Do you think this practice is nowadays losing its credibility?   (CIT, Intermediate)

2. Explain the advantages and drawbacks of (*a*) press advertising, (*b*) TV advertising.   (ICSA, Part I)

3. What are the main forms of mass media which exist in your locality? What are the most important differences between these forms? Select ONE and discuss how a professional administrator can make use of it.
(ICSA, Part I)

4. Press releases are now a regular feature of most company Public Relations programmes. Enumerate the points which you feel are of importance in the preparation and submission of press releases.

(AIA, Foundation Part A)

5. Describe the various ways in which the Press can be of help to a business or industrial organisation. (ICSA, Part I)

6. With reference to *one* form of the mass media, discuss the following:

(*a*) What are its particular characteristics which are relevant to the professional administrator?

(*b*) How can the professional administrator ensure its effective use by and good relations with his company? (ICSA, Part I)

27

EFFECTIVE READING AND EFFECTIVE LISTENING

A work on communication would be incomplete without some mention of the arts of reading and listening. Communicators must receive information as well as give it. This chapter is, therefore, devoted to these two important activities.

Reading

When discussing the question of reading many people first consider the speed at which the reading is done. An efficient reader, they say, reads fast. However, the activity of reading cannot be taken in isolation and must be related to comprehension. A shorthand writer may take notes at 200 words per minute, but this is pointless unless they can be transcribed. The average person reads at something like 200 to 300 words per minute and at this pace he will comprehend about 75 per cent of the content of what he has read. If he decides to read faster the chances are that his comprehension will fall because he will concentrate on raising his reading speed instead of concentrating on the content of the author's work.

Therefore, efficient reading consists of a combination of speed and understanding, and increasing one at the expense of the other will not lead to efficiency.

There is, of course, some relationship between efficiency in reading and the purpose for which we are doing it. We are more likely to read quickly and comprehend fully and promptly something that interests us greatly than something which is irksome to us. If we do not find what we are reading of interest, then our reading will probably be slow and comprehension low. Other things that affect reading speed are style of writing, kind of typeface and, to many, even the kind of paper used.

However, there are certain things we can do to enable us to read faster and to improve our reading efficiency. The most important one is to understand the physical activity of the eye when we read. The eye does not travel along the line of print in a continuous manner; if it did that we should see nothing but a blur of words. What it does is to stop, take in a word or phrase, and then move on, and it does this all the time we are reading. In fact, it acts in the same way as a movie camera or projector, where the film is constantly stopping and starting

211

so that there is produced or projected a series of still images snapping on and off at speed.

At each rest the eye sees a segment of print—the visual span—and this segment is assimilated and passed to the brain for interpretation. One way to increase reading speed is not to move the eyes faster, but to widen the visual span. There are various devices that encourage this spreading of the span, but with practice it can be done without such assistance. Start with a piece of print in narrow format, such as a newspaper column. With practice you will find you can encompass the whole width of the column without sideways movement of your eyes, focusing them in the middle of each line. In such circumstances your reading speed will increase to the extent that you need to read only down the column. Check all the time, though, that your comprehension does not suffer.

From the newspaper column you can go on to narrow printed pages, such as paperback books, perhaps starting by dividing the lines up into two segments only. The wider your span the more quickly you will be able to read without loss of comprehension.

Having increased your visual span horizontally, the next step is to try to assimilate two lines, and then three, vertically, because your eyes' peripheral vision extends upwards and downwards as well as sideways. This is, to be truthful, rather more difficult for the simple reason that reading horizontally means there is some relationship between the words and phrases whereas vertically this may not be so. You must remember that it is not only the eyes that are involved in reading—the brain has an important part to play in it as well. Therefore, what the eyes see and transmit to the brain must be decoded and processed by the brain. Where there is a relationship between words the brain can deal with the matter speedily; if there is little association, or none, the brain will not react so quickly.

Many people, when they read, vocalise: that is, they say to themselves, either audibly or inaudibly, the words and phrases they are reading. Some readers even mouth the words. Such activity slows down the reading speed and is some hindrance to comprehension. In order to achieve greater efficiency in reading every effort should be made to assimilate the meaning of what is being read without repeating inwardly the actual images. Grasping, mentally, whole phrases and whole lines of writing is of great assistance in losing the habit of vocalising.

Concentration

To read with understanding it is necessary to concentrate. Concentration is the essence of comprehension, but is sometimes difficult to achieve. The reason is, very often, that the reader is looking at the words whereas he should be looking for the meaning. Vocalising, either inwardly or by mouthing the words, very often causes loss of concentration as more emphasis is being given to the words themselves than to their meaning. Aids to concentration, apart from freedom from outside distractions, are an interest in the matter being read, and a motive for reading it. Without one or the other of these, concentration is likely to be difficult to achieve.

Skimming

Skimming is a skill that should be acquired by the person who aims to be an efficient reader. To skim does not mean to read carelessly or without motive. Essentially it is a practice to be indulged in as a prelude to the serious study of a written work. It consists of allowing the eye to move quickly over the page, picking out important words and phrases as it goes, and of skipping inessential statements and information.

The manner in which a reader skims is purely personal, and his success relies to a large extent on his ability to spot key words and phrases on sight. Some readers will move their eyes quickly down the centre of the page, using their peripheral vision to assimilate the beginnings and ends of lines, whilst others will glance down the page diagonally.

Skimming is not meant to replace serious reading but is used to obtain a general grasp of the sense of a piece. It is thus helpful in ascertaining whether the material is going to be useful and should be read thoroughly, or whether only parts of it will be of interest. In the latter case, during the skimming exercise, interesting passages can be marked for further study, whilst others can be skipped altogether. If the ability to assimilate two or more lines vertically has been acquired, this attribute will materially assist in successful skimming.

As with most activities, practice increases efficiency, and a deliberate effort to increase reading efficiency and comprehension will amply repay the work involved. Full expositions on how to improve reading ability will be found in the Pelican publication *Read Better, Read Faster*, by Manya and Eric de Leeuw, and in a companion volume, *Rapid Reading Made Simple*, by Gordon R. Wainwright.

Listening

Everybody hears, but how many listen? Yet listening is a very important part of communication. It may be defined as conscious hearing, and it is this definition that points the defect in most people's capacity to listen—consciousness.

The main cause of faulty listening is, in fact, mind wandering or loss of concentration. Allowing your attention to lapse whilst you are listening results in an incomplete reception of the transmission. So let us look at some of the pitfalls that exist for the unwary in the art of effective listening.

Concentration

It is not easy to maintain concentration when you are listening: there are so many distractions around. In any event, it is difficult to maintain full concentration on a speaker for more than twenty minutes at a time. In the case of a formal lecture or talk, thirty minutes is the maximum time the speaker can expect to hold his audience's undivided attention, even if he is absolutely expert, and even during this period his audience's concentration will wax and wane at something like ten-minute intervals. The skilled speaker will, therefore, intersperse his talk with a small diversion every now and then. In ordinary conversation, or at an interview, the problem does not arise as there is variety in the content of the talking.

A positive attempt, therefore, must be made to maintain concentration when listening.

Interest

This is very much allied to concentration. If we have little interest in the subject we will not listen attentively unless we make a determined effort. In a formal situation it helps to prepare oneself with some fore-knowledge of the topic to be dealt with, so that a mental challenge can be set up as the expected points arise. Equally, the purpose for listening to the speaker must be clearly appreciated, which will increase interest. An accountancy student may not find a lecture on company law intrinsically interesting, but the purpose of attending the lecture, to pass the examinations and become qualified, is a spur to interest.

Barriers to Effective Listening

Emotional Disturbance

You will not listen effectively if you have something on your mind. A quarrel with someone, unpleasant personal news—such things upset the emotional balance and so upset concentration, which in turn leads to ineffective listening. Your mind will be elsewhere, trying to deal with your emotional upset, and not in accord with the speaker. Great efforts must be made to forget the problem temporarily and to listen to what is being said. Even in informal conversations emotional upsets are likely to lead to ineffective listening.

Dislike of the Speaker

If we like a person we are inclined to accept what he says and to evaluate it objectively: we will listen to him sympathetically. However, if we dislike a speaker we are likely to adopt a negative attitude to him and this will colour what we hear. Attitude has, in fact, been discussed in Chapter 2, and it occurs just as much in listening as it does in other activities concerned with communication. Even an accent we do not like can cause us to look on a speaker with disfavour and so distort our listening. The way to overcome this pitfall and listen effectively in such cases is to try to hear the speech and not the speaker.

Distractions

There are many ways in which a listener may be distracted. First it must be recognised that a good listener who has interest and concentration will not be distracted very easily. If extraneous noises or movement, for instance, cause you to be distracted from what is being said, then it is evident that your interest and concentration are not deep enough. The answer is greater effort to listen attentively.

Relaxing Whilst Listening

Listening is a positive activity, and can never be done in a passive manner. Therefore, the good listener does not relax when listening, but is engaged in a purposeful pursuit requiring his positive cooperation. The listener's mind is not a pint pot that can be filled by pouring in speech. The input has to be monitored, analysed and filed by the mind, and these activities cannot be carried out effectively in a relaxed state.

Speech Lag

The average talking speed is 120 words per minute: the average possible hearing speed is nearer 400 words per minute or even faster. This means that the listener's mind has to slow down to keep pace with the speaker. Herein lies a difficulty, particularly to the active mind. What can the listener do about this speech lag which, if not dealt with, may result in mind wandering and loss of concentration? He can use it to question mentally what is being said, to analyse the substance of the speech as it goes along, or to anticipate what the speaker will say next and have a questioning attitude to it. He should not use this speech lag time to think about matters not appertaining to the speech. Neither should he dwell on the points of the speech long passed.

The points made above have been directed to listening to a formal speech, such as a lecture or a public talk. However, the application of many of them would not be without merit in informal situations, including simple conversations.

The path to effective listening is not easy. It needs attention and concerted effort. The unfortunate fact is that we so often do not realise that we are not good listeners and so make no effort to improve. The same could be said about breathing.

Questions

1. What do you understand by *either* 'effective reading' *or* 'effective listening'? Discuss how this skill may be acquired and developed.

(ICSA, Part I)

2. What do you understand by the words 'effective listening'? What are the main features that are needed in a good listener?

(ICSA, Part I)

3. Explain what is meant by the terms 'visual span' and 'speech lag'. How can an understanding of these factors help us to improve our reading and our listening?

4. It is generally felt that good listening is a vital part of good business communication. Comment briefly on the points which you consider important under this heading. (AIA, Foundation Part A)

5. To understand, absorb and interpret the information provided during an interview, the interviewer must listen attentively. Comment upon the factors which contribute to ineffective listening and suggest how listening may be made more effective. (AIA, Foundation Part A)

Appendix

SUGGESTED FURTHER READING

Whilst *Effective Communication Made Simple* is designed to be self-contained, some readers may like to extend their reading, particularly in regard to specific topics. The following list is by no means exhaustive but the titles mentioned can be recommended. In every case it is essential to obtain the very latest edition of a publication, consequently no dates are given in the list below.

General Reading

Chappell, R. T., and Read, W. L., *Business Communications*, Macdonald & Evans, Plymouth.
Deverell, C. S., *Communication*, Gee & Co., London.
Evans, Desmond W., *Communication at Work*, Pitman, London.
Little, P., *Communication in Business*, Longman, Harlow.
Maude, B., *Practical Communication for Managers*, Longman, Harlow.

English, Language and Style

Ashe, G., *The Art of Writing Made Simple*, Heinemann, London.
Waldhorn, A., and Zeiger, A., *English Made Simple*, Heinemann, London.

Mass Communication

Williams, R., *Communications*, Penguin, Harmondsworth.

Reading

De Leeuw, E., and M., *Read better, Read faster*, Penguin, Harmondsworth.
Wainwright, G. R., *Rapid Reading Made Simple*, Heinemann, London.

Selected Chapters

On Export Forms
Deschampsneufs, H., *Export Made Simple*, Heinemann, London.
Whitehead, G., *Commerce Made Simple*, Heinemann, London.

On Speech
Dodding, J., *The Art of Speaking Made Simple*, Heinemann, London

On the Telephone
Whitehead, G., *Office Practice Made Simple*, Heinemann, London.

On Word Processing
Eyre, E. C., *Office Administration Made Simple*, Heinemann, London.

Specialist Publications

British Association for Commercial & Industrial Education, *A Guide to the Overhead Projector. A Guide to the Use of Visual Aids. A Guide to the Use of the Telephone. A Guide to the Writing of Business Letters. Interviewing in Twenty-six Steps. Lecturing to Large Groups. Report Writing. Tips on Talking.*

Institute of Administrative Management, *Form Design.*

Simplification of International Trade Procedures Board (SITPRO), *Systematic Export Documentation.*

Reference Books

Fowler, H. W. and F. G., *The Concise Oxford Dictionary of Current Usage*, Oxford University Press, London.

Roget, P. M., *Thesaurus of English Words and Phrases*, Longman, Harlow; Penguin, London.

The Post Office Guide, The Post Office.

Index